PLATONIC MYTH AND PLATONIC WRITING

Robert Zaslavsky

VERSITY
SS OF
ERICA

LANHAM • NEW YORK • LONDON

Copyright © 1981 by

University Press of America,™ Inc.

4720 Boston Way
Lanham, MD 20706

3 Henrietta Street
London WC2E 8LU England

Library of Congress Cataloging in Publication Data

Zaslavsky, Robert.
    Platonic myth and Platonic writing.

    Bibliography: p.
    Includes indexes.
    1. Plato.   2. Mythology.   I. Title.
B398.M8Z37   184   80-5563
ISBN 0-8191-1381-6 (pbk.)
ISBN 0-8191-1382-4

To my daughter

CORDELIA

"So young my lord, and true."
      --<u>King Lear</u> I.i.106

All yet seems well, and if it end so meet,
The bitter past, more welcome is the sweet.

--All's well that ends well,
V.iii.327-328.

ACKNOWLEDGEMENTS

The person who wrote this book owes far too much to
far too many others ever to repay them properly.
Yet insofar as the acknowledgement of a felt debt
is a repayment in however small a measure, the acknowledgement must be made--

To my parents, Harry and Sally Zaslavsky,
against whose better judgment I decided to study
philosophy, but through whose better instincts I
had the tenacity to do so anyway, for good or for
ill. And still now the living presence of my father
and the memory of my mother are the sources of much
in me, perhaps of much more than I will ever know
with certainty.

To my first teachers at Temple University:
Robert Anderson, now at Washington College, who
taught me that in the reading of philosophical
texts less could be more and the canon of philosophers as circumscribed by philosophy departments
is far too small; Victor Gourevitch, now at Wes-
leyan, who taught me how to read a philosophical
text word by word and who introduced me to the writings of Leo Strauss; William Rossky, still at
Temple, who taught me that a person formally un-
trained in philosophy could still be philosophical.

To my teachers in the graduate department of
English Literature at New York University, who
showed me that academically I belonged--if anywhere
--in philosophy.

To my teachers in the Philosophy Department
of the Graduate Faculty of the New School for
Social Research: Hans Jonas, still at the Graduate
Faculty, whose lecturing showed me the power of
philosophy and whose breadth showed me that philosophy need not be a narrow cell; Aron Gurwitsch,
now deceased, whose lectures and counsel (especially in the year during which I was his teaching
assistant) opened up to me the tradition of modern
rationalism and whose classes were like cathedrals
of clarity; Howard White, now deceased, whose
seminars were exhilarating journeys through the
great texts in political philosophy, from Plato
and Aristotle to Shakespeare, from Jefferson to
Melville, and who taught me that philosophy is
always a journey without an end; Seth Benardete,
still at the Graduate Faculty, whose command of
ancient languages made them seem new and inspired
many to learn them, whose lectures on ancient
texts were models of thoroughness, whose mesmeric
διδασκαλία drew from his students work far beyond
that of which they believed themselves capable,
and whose person demonstrated that brilliance and
scholarly competence could be combined. Anyone who
has studied at the Graduate Faculty realizes what
a privileged place it has been for the study of
philosophy.

To my friend and colleague, Walt Soffer, now
at State University College of New York at Geneseo,
who--with respect to this manuscript at least--is
ἡ ἐμὴ ἀρχὴ ἢ ὡσία, whose steadfast confidence in
my abilities even when my own wavered was the mid-
wife which brought this project to birth.

To my daughter, Cordelia, now nine, who bore
all of the irascibilities which attended the pre-
paration of this manuscript and who forbore
scorning me or it; to her this book is dedicated--
I would that when she reads it however many years
from now, she will not be embarrassed for her
father on account of it.

Robert Zaslavsky

Bryn Mawr, PA

PREFACE

This manuscript is a revised version of a Ph.D. dissertation submitted to the Graduate Faculty. Of those there, I would thank my dissertation adviser, Stewart Umphrey, the chairman of the philosophy department, Reiner Schuermann, and the philosophy department secretary, Gail Mensh, for all their efforts on my behalf and on behalf of the department.

I would also thank the philosophy faculty and students of S.U.C. of N.Y. at Geneseo and the members of the Fullerton Club (Bryn Mawr College) for listening to earlier versions of portions of this manuscript and asking the kind of penetrating questions which showed me where revision was needed.

Finally, I would thank the library staff of Bryn Mawr College, where the manuscript received its final revision, for their generous indulgences.

R.Z.

NOTE

Unless otherwise specified, all translations are mine.

CONTENTS

Having a desire to see those Antients, who were most renowned for Wit and Learning, I set apart one Day on purpose. I proposed that <u>Homer</u> and <u>Aristotle</u> might appear at the Head of all their Commentators; but these were so numerous, that some Hundreds were forced to attend in the Court and outward Rooms of the Palace. I knew and could distinguish those two Heroes at first sight, not only from the Croud, but from each other.......I soon discovered, that both of them were perfect Strangers to the rest of the Company, and had never seen or heard of them before. And I had a whisper from a Ghost, who shall be nameless, that these Commentators always kept in the most distant Quarters from their Principals in the lower World, through a Consciousness of Shame and Guilt, because they had so horribly misrepresented the Meaning of those Authors to Posterity. I introduced <u>Didymus</u> and <u>Eustathius</u> to <u>Homer</u>, and prevailed on him to treat them better than perhaps they deserved; for he soon found they wanted a Genius to enter into the Spirit of a Poet. But <u>Aristotle</u> was out of all Patience with the Account I gave him of <u>Scotus</u> and <u>Ramus</u>, as I presented them to him; and he asked them whether the rest of the Tribe were as great Dunces as themselves.

--Lemuel Gulliver, in
<u>Gulliver's Travels</u>,
Part III, Chapter VIII,
in <u>The Writings of
Jonathan Swift</u>, edd.
Robert A. Greenberg and
William B. Piper (New
York, Norton Critical
Edition, 1973), pp. 168–
169.

INTRODUCTION

If one assumes, as many do,[1] that philosophy is
something which asserts the supremacy of reason
or logos, how is one to explain its use of the
non-rational or mythos? Perhaps it uses the non-
rational as the sweet outercovering of the bitter
pill of rationality, i.e., as a window-dressing
(an allurement, a charm, an incantation) enticing
non-philosophers toward the pursuit and/or acqui-
sition and/or acceptance of the rational (i.e.,
philosophically achieved) truth.[2] There would be
two possible justifications for this usage: (1) the
justification grounded in the notion that although
all humans are capable of achieving philosophical
insight, not all are capable of achieving it philosophically; (2) the justification grounded in
the notion that although not all humans are capable
of achieving philosophical insight, they are all
capable of non-philosophically accepting philosophical insight which has been achieved philosophically by others. There are difficulties which
beset both of these approaches.

To the first justification, one should object that
the only meaningful way in which one is able to
speak of the achieving of philosophical insight is
in terms of its philosophical achievement. For
philosophy is not simply truth achieved but a way
to achieve truth. Even more than this, philosophy
seems to require a <u>way-to</u> the way-to-achieve-truth
(e.g., a qualified acceptance of all human opinions
and sensings, the meta-way for Socratic philosophy,
or a methodical doubt with respect to all human
opinions and sensings and knowledges, the meta-way
for Cartesian philosophy). Hence, it would seem

self-violating and self-contradictory for philosophy to assume that it can bestow the fruits of its labors upon, and that these fruits can be assimilated by, those who are themselves incapable of laboring to produce those fruits. For this would be tantamount to the assumption that the mere eating of an apple makes one a farmer, a patently false assumption. In this way, then, one is forced, it would seem, to fall back upon the second justification, namely that although not all humans are capable of becoming, say, farmers, they are all capable of discerning the quality of apples. The difficulty here, however, is that the promulgation of philosophical insight would depend upon a catering, as it were, to the taste of the non-philosophical multitude based upon the assumption that non-philosophical taste is or can be consonant with philosophical nourishment which—for to non-philosophical taste, simply philosophical nourishment is unpalatable—is non-philosophically prepared. How, then, if such a consonance is possible, can it be achieved? Presumably by the education of non-philosophical taste. But on the level of taste itself, taste is multifarious. How, then, can one guarantee the proper consonance? Presumably either by persuasion or by force, either of which would have to be limitless in its power, as the material on which each works would have to be limitless in its malleability. In either case, one would have to rely on the wisdom of the persuaders or forcers and on their justice, an apparently utopian demand. Besides, even if the proper consonance could be brought about in either of these ways, one would have to ask whether this is the proper means of effecting the already agreed proper end or whether the employment of such a means necessitates paying the price of vitiating the end.[3] In addition, what if the possessors of philosophical insight are by this very insight rendered powerless to effect changes in the non-philosophical multitude? How, then, can that multitude be protected from domination by powerful purveyors of an improper consonance?[4] In any case, if it should turn out that the proper means of effecting the proper consonance is myth (by which here is meant some form of persuasive non-rational speech), then one would have to create a speech which is both rationally composed and non-rationally intelligible to, acceptable to, and capable of compelling assent from all humans, a clearly utopian requirement.

In short, these justifications for the use of myth by the philosopher founder on the respective rocks of self-contradiction and utopianism. And as a set, they assume that although myth is essential to the dissemination of philosophical insight, it is somehow extrinsic to philosophy itself, i.e., to the philosophical practice of philosophy.

Perhaps then myth is, although somehow not intrinsic to philosophy itself, yet somehow not extrinsic to it either. In other words, perhaps the non-rational is the complement to the rational, i.e., perhaps it expresses what is beyond and/or below reason, what reason only divines and hence must articulate oracularly, i.e., mythically.[5] The first difficulty which besets this view of myth is that its own justification cannot be a rational one, for by definition myth is a representation of that which is intractable or inaccessible to and unrepresentable by reason. In addition, this extra-rational realm is the realm of those things without which reason becomes contextless, so that as a result reason becomes dependent for its meaning and value upon things with respect to the validity of which it is criterionless, at least rationalistically criterionless. In other words, the pursuit of philosophical insight is deprived of the legitimacy of its claim to self-validation, to self-reflexiveness, on the very level that is most damaging to itself, namely on the level of its claim, as distinguished from that of the other knowledges, to be able to justify not only the grounds of the other knowledges but the ground of itself.[6] In other words, the relegation of philosophy to the position of handmaiden to an extra-philosophical authority de-philosophizes philosophy to such an extent that it would be virtually impossible for philosophy to retain its identity, but rather philosophy would become, like a slavish dog, little more than a mirror-image of its extra-philosophical master.[7]

In short, then, this justification for the philosopher's use of myth, i.e., the non- or extrarational, founders on the rock of self-dissolution.

Therefore, if the apparent result of philosophy entering into a relationship with what is today called myth is to vitiate in one way or another the philosophical enterprise itself, how is one to explain the use of myth, even the preeminent place of myth, in the work of someone who is acknowledged to be a philosopher, namely Plato? We must, it seems, at least to begin with, entertain the notion that Plato's understanding of myth differs considerably from our own, and the corollary notion that Plato's understanding of logos differs considerably from our own. Or, to put the matter more neutrally, we must, it seems, at least to begin with, ask the question what a mythos is from Plato's point of view.

Before trying to answer this question, let us briefly survey the fundamental terms, 'mythos' and 'logos,' as they were used by the Greeks in general and by Plato in particular.

NOTES

[1]In this introductory discussion, I have not
cited in each instance the specific works which
explicitly or implicitly employ the arguments
which I formulate. Instead, all of the works
which I have consulted I have placed in the bibliography. Since I have formulated the arguments
out of my impressions from the literature on
Greek 'myth' generally and on Platonic 'myth'
specifically, and since I have not wished to
engage in individual polemics, I have let the
arguments stand as impressions. I only hope
that, whether I am correct or incorrect in my
criticism, I have at least fairly stated the
positions which I have criticized. And to give
the reader an opportunity to judge this, in the
bibliography, after each work which pertains to
this discussion, I have placed in brackets the
relevant chapters and/or page references.

[2]This view would be particularly congenial to
the classical modern philosophers. Cf. Leibniz,
Discourse on metaphysics, section 26: "And nothing
could be taught us, of which we do not already
have in the mind the idea which is as the matter
of which this thought forms itself. This Plato
has indeed excellently considered, when he has
put forth his /doctrine of/ recollection which
has much solidity, so long as one grasps it well,
purges it of the error of pre-existence and does
not imagine that the soul ought already to have
known and thought distinctly at another time
what it learns and thinks now. Also he has con-
firmed his feeling by a beautiful experiment,
introducing a little boy whom he insensibly
leads to the very difficult truths of geometry
touching incommensurables, without teaching him
anything, only by asking ordered and relevant
questions. Which shows that our soul knows all
of that virtually and needs only attention in

order to cognize the truths, and, consequently, that it has at least the ideas on which these truths depend. One can even say that it already possesses these truths, when one takes them for the relations of the ideas." (Et rien ne nous saurait être appris, dont nous n'ayons déjà dans l'esprit l'idée qui est comme la matière dont cette pensée se forme. C'est ce que Platon a excellement bien considéré, quand il a mis en avant sa réminiscence qui a beaucoup de solidité, pourvu qu'on la prenne bien, qu'on la purge de l'erreur de la préexistence, et qu'on ne s'imagine point que l'âme doit déjà avoir su et pensé distinctement autrefois ce qu'elle apprend et pense maintenant. Aussi a-t-il confirmé son sentiment par une belle expérience, introduisant un petit garçon qu'il mene insensiblement à des vérités, très difficiles de la géometrie touchant les incommensurables, sans lui rien apprendre, en faisant seulement des demandes par ordre et à propos. Ce qui fait voir que notre âme sait tout cela virtuellement, et n'a besoin que d'animad-version pour connaître les vérités, et, par conséquent, qu'elle a au moins ses idées dont ces vérités dépendent. On peut même dire qu'elle possède déjà ces vérités, quand on les prend pour les rapports des idées. —Leibniz, Discours de métaphysique et correspondance avec Arnaud, intr., texte et comm. par George Le Roy, deuxieme éd. (Paris, 1966), p. 64.)

[3]This problem is treated by--among others-- Plato in The Republic and Hegel in The Philosophy of history.

[4]Cf. Leo Strauss, Natural right and history (Chicago, 1953), p. 141: "The few wise cannot rule the many unwise by force. The unwise multitude must recognize the wise as wise and obey them freely because of their wisdom. But the ability of the wise to persuade the unwise is extremely limited.... Therefore, it is extremely unlikely that the conditions required for the rule of the wise will ever be met. What is more likely to happen

is that an unwise man, appealing to the natural
right of wisdom and catering to the lowest desires
of the many, will persuade the multitude of his
right: the prospects for tyranny are brighter than
those for rule of the wise."

[5]This is a view with which it is difficult to
deal because of its eminent respectability and
even justifiability from the points of view of
both its non-rationalistic adherents and its
rationalistic critics who are sympathetic to its
non-rationalistic adherents, i.e., from the points
of view of both theists and sympathetic non-theists.

[6]Cf. _Charmides_ 166c2-3 et passim.

[7]I should perhaps add that if philosophy tries
to free itself from this subjugation and remem-
bers the 'mythical' attachment which apparently
led to it, it may then abjure altogether what it
regards as myth and restrict itself of its own
volition to a realm which is free from the uncer-
tainty of the mythically represented realm, i.e.,
it may restrict itself to a realm of unitary
structure to which a universal method is to be
applied. In other words, philosophy may autono-
mize itself by scientizing itself and its objects,
an avenue of liberation which yields philosophy
an enormous power, an enormous ability to create.
But here again philosophy becomes a slave, not to
an extra-philosophical authority, but to an intra-
philosophical methodology and its creations. And
when philosophy tries to free itself from this
slavishness, it does not turn back to its origins,
for that is seen as a return to the source of the
enslavement, but instead it turns forward and
away from its current situation, and the result
is that philosophy, having rejected the certainty
to which it has become enslaved, becomes a cosmic
alien, rootless and homeless, atomistic and nihi-
listic. Cf. Leo Strauss, _Liberalism, ancient and
modern_ (New York, 1968), pp. 26-27: "Classical
political philosophy...is today generally rejected as obsolete. The difference between, not to
say the mutual incompatibility of, the two grounds

on which it is rejected corresponds to the difference between the two schools of thought which
predominate in our age, namely positivism and
existentialism. Positivism rejects classical
political philosophy with a view to its mode as
unscientific and with a view to its substance as
undemocratic. There is a tension between these
grounds, for, according to positivism, science is
incapable of validating any value judgment....
But 'the heart has its reasons which reason does
not know,'.... Moreover there is an affinity between present-day positivism and sympathy for a
certain kind of democracy; that affinity is due
to the broad, not merely methodological, context
out of which positivism emerged or to the hidden
premises of positivism which positivism is unable
to articulate because it is constitutionally unable to conceive of itself as a problem. Positivism may be said to be more dogmatic than any
other position of which we have records. Positivism can achieve this triumph because it is able
to present itself as very skeptical.... It is the
latest form and it may very well be the last form
in which modern rationalism appears; it is that
form in which the crisis of modern thought becomes
almost obvious to everyone. Once it becomes obvious to a man, he has already abandoned positivism, and if he adheres to the modern premises,
he has no choice but to turn to existentialism.
    "Existentialism faces the situation with which
positivism is confronted but does not grasp the
fact that reason has become radically problematic.
According to positivism, the first premises are
not evident and necessary, but either purely fac-
tual or else conventional. According to existentialism, they are in a sense necessary, but they
are certainly not evident; all thinking rests on
unevident but nonarbitrary premises. Man is in
the grip of powers which he cannot master or com-
prehend...." Also cf. Hans Jonas, The phenomenon
of life (New York, 1966), p. 234: "The disruption
between man and total reality is at the bottom of
nihilism. The illogicality of the rupture, that
is, of a dualism without metaphysics, makes its
fact no less real, nor its seeming alternative

y more acceptable: the stare at isolated self-
od, to which it condemns man, may wish to ex-
ange itself for a monistic naturalism which,
ong with the rupture, would abolish also the
ea of man as man. Between that Scylla and this
r twin Charybdis, the modern mind hovers. Whe-
er a third road is open to it—one by which
e dualistic rift can be avoided and yet enough
the dualistic insight saved to uphold the huma-
ty of man--philosophy must find out." In addi-
on, cf. Jonas, pp. 213-215, 233.

> This story, my dear young folks,
> seems to be false, but it really
> is true, for my grandfather,
> from whom I have it, used always,
> when relating it, to say: "It
> must be true, my son, or else no
> one could tell it to you."
> —"The hare and the hedgehog,"
> in The Complete Grimm's Fairy
> Tales, tr. Margaret Hunt, rev.
> James Stern (New York, Pantheon,
> 1944), p. 760.

ΛΟΓΟΣ AND ΜΥΘΟΣ

When one surveys the meanings of λόγος and μῦθος
and their derivatives, one is met by an apparently
bewildering variety of shades of meaning, in particular of λόγος. The Liddell-Scott Lexicon (LSJ),
for example, lists altogether fifty-four different but related renderings of λόγος.[1] However,
the two fundamental renderings seem to be 'speech'
and 'account,' initially without any distinction
of true or false, but later with an apparent restriction to 'true account.' One would expect the
case of μῦθος to be radically different, but this
is not so. For out of twelve different but related
renderings, μῦθος too receives the two fundamental
renderings 'speech' and 'account,' initially without any distinction of true or false, but later
with an apparent restriction to 'false account.'
How, then, is one genuinely to distinguish the
meanings of the two terms without artificially
imposing upon them a construction which their origins will not bear? The root of an answer lies, I

believe, in the senses in which each of these is
an account. Λόγος is an account more in the sense
of 'a reckoning,' i.e., it is more closely connected with the here and now, with the domain in
which one is 'called to account' for one's present
actions (hence the renderings 'plea,' 'law,' 'rule
of conduct,' 'command,' 'reputation,' 'worth,'
'enumeration'). Μῦθος, on the other hand, is an
account more in the sense of 'une histoire,' i.e.,
it is more closely connected with the there and
then, with the domain in which one is 'inclined to
recount' one's motives (hence the renderings 'un-
spoken word,' 'design,' 'tale,' 'narrative'). Yet
even this distinction is not hard and fast, for a
μῦθος can be a 'public speech' and a λόγος can be
a 'story.'[2] Indeed, any distinction which one attempts to draw between the two terms is blurred
at some point in their origin and/or in their
later usages. The Greek language preserves this
blurring not only in such words as μυθέομαι ('I
speak,' 'I give an account'), μυθολόγος ('story-
teller,' 'pertaining to storytelling') and its
corresponding denominative μυθολογέω ('I am
μυθολόγος,' 'I tell a story'), παραμυθέομαι ('I
chat someone beside/beyond himself,' 'I console'),[3]
and λογοποιέω ('I make up a story'), but also in
the words λόγος and μῦθος themselves. In other
words, if it is possible to give a 'μύθιος' λόγος
(cf. τὸ λογομύθιον), then the distinction between
λόγος and μῦθος seems to be sufficiently blurred
as to cast a shadow of doubt over any ostensibly
non-ambiguous usage of the terms. Hence, one
should never, even if only in the interest of
pedantic precision, presuppose that an ostensibly
non-ambiguous usage is only that.[4]

What, then, is a myth in Plato? Or, more precisely,
by what criterion are we entitled to call a given
account in Plato's writings a myth? It would seem
that the only safe and unprejudicial operating
criterion is the simple principle that one is entitled to call a myth in Plato's writings only
what is explicitly so called, and that one is not
entitled to call a myth anything which is not explicitly so called. In other words, we must not

allow ourselves to designate as a myth what modern opinions would lead us to take for granted as a myth. As Socrates warns Callicles:

> Indeed hear, /as/ they assert, a very beautiful logos, which you will regard /to be/ a mythos, as I believe, but I a logos.[5]

Nonetheless, our preconceptions run so deep and so silent that in the commentaries on the Gorgias, the account which follows this remark is universally regarded as a myth. Therefore, it is worth emphasizing that even when such a warning is not explicitly stated, we must state it to ourselves, and we must be ready to accept the possibility that an ostensible mythos is actually a logos or that an ostensible logos is actually a mythos.

What, then, are the explicitly designated myths in Plato's writings? Perhaps a list will be helpful:

(1) Phaedrus: Socrates' Lysian speech and his palinode: the genesis of eros and knowledge.

(2) Republic 2.359c6 ff.: Gyges' ancestor and the ring of invisibility: the genesis of justice in the fear of being caught doing injustice.

(3) Republic 2.376d9 ff.: the entire education of the guardians, a myth about the first myths: the genesis of habitual virtue.

(4) Republic 2-7: the genesis of the best regime.[6]

(5) Republic 3.414b8-415d8: the genic falsehood, the political lie: the genesis of the best regime.

(6) Republic 8.565d4-566a5: the genesis of the tyrant.

(7) Republic 8-9: the de-generating regimes/souls.[7]

(8) Republic 9.588b1 ff.: the genesis of the human soul.

(9) Republic 10.613e6-621d3: the myth of Er: the genesis of the kind of lifetime one leads.

(10) Phaedo 60b1-c7: the genesis of pleasure and pain.

(11) Phaedo 110a8 ff.: the genesis of our knowledge of earth/body.

13

(12) <u>Theaetetus</u> 155e3 ff.: all is motion: the genesis of the assertion that episteme is sensing.

(13) <u>Gorgias</u> 492e7-493d4: the soul as a wine jar: the genesis of a name.

(14) <u>Minos</u> 318c4-321b5: the genesis of an impious genetic account.

(15) <u>Laws</u> 1.636b7-e4: the genesis of homosexuality.

(16) <u>Laws</u> 1.644b6-645c3: the account of animals, especially humans, as divine puppets: the genesis of law-abidingness.

(17) <u>Laws</u> 4.711d6-712a7: the genesis of the best regime.

(18) <u>Laws</u> 4.712e9-714b2: the genesis of (less than best) cities.

(19) <u>Laws</u> 4.719a7-720a2: the genesis of poetic irony.[8]

(20) <u>Laws</u> 6.773b4 ff.: the genesis of marriage.

(21) <u>Laws</u> 7.790b8-d2 & ff.: the prenatal gymnastic rearing of the body: the genesis of habits.

(22) <u>Laws</u> 7.809b3-812b1: the rearing and education of the body in children: the genesis of habits.

(23) <u>Laws</u> 9.865d3-866a2 & ff.: involuntary homicide: the genesis of guilt.

(24) <u>Laws</u> 12.943d4-944c4: loss of arms: the genesis of improper blame.

(25) <u>Statesman</u> 268d5 ff.: the cosmic pathos: the genesis of the king.

(26) <u>Timaeus</u> 22b3 ff.: the genesis of periodic destructions by cosmic forces.

(27) <u>Timaeus</u> 27b7-end: the genesis of the cosmos.

(28) <u>Protagoras</u> 320b8-324d1: the account of the apportionment of powers by Prometheus, Epimetheus, and Zeus: the genesis of the universality of justice and modesty and political virtue in general.

Before I try to characterize the myths, let me cite some of the non-mythical Platonic writings, by which I mean writings in which neither the word μῦθος nor any of its derivatives occurs: (1) <u>Symposium</u>, (2) <u>Parmenides</u>, (3) <u>Euthyphro</u>, (4) <u>Meno</u>.[9] The most striking cases here are the

<u>Symposium</u>, which is virtually universally regarded
by commentators as a dialogue filled with myths
but which in fact has none, and the <u>Meno</u>, which
contains an account which is virtually universally
designated as the myth of recollection but is in
fact not a myth at all.

What, then, are the characteristics which the various interlocutors in the Platonic dialogues
attribute to myths?[10] They are epideixeis of true
beings,[11] pleasant and playful,[12] perishable and
salutary,[13] sometimes imprecise,[14] paradigms,[15]
productive of soul growth,[16] persuasive,[17] partially true and partially false.[18] And myth is
variously described as lacking a logos,[19] opposed
to logos,[20] the same as logos,[21] the genus of
which logos is a species.[22] In addition, it is
asserted of myth that the test of its truth is
its translatability into deed,[23] and that it is
the product of the activity of mythologizing.[24]
Finally, and most pervasively, myths are said to
be accounts of beginnings, of origins, of genesis.[25]

Of these characteristics, while all the others
are equally applicable to logoi, what clearly
marks off a mythos from a logos is that a mythos
is first and foremost an account of the genesis
of a phenomenon. This would imply that a λόγος in
the narrow sense is a non-genetic or descriptive
account of a phenomenon. Λόγος, then, would have
two senses, a generic one and a specific one, i.e.,
it would refer at times to speech καθόλου and at
times to non-myth speech, descriptive speech. This
would mean, for example, with respect to the brief
account of recollection in the <u>Meno</u>,[26] which is
not called a myth, but simply something spoken and
heard,[27] that the account is not a genetic account
of the origin of learning but rather a descriptive
account of the experience of learning as experienced.[28]

To this procedure, someone might object that it is
merely a crazy quilt of remarks from the Platonic
writings, and it is surely not what Plato means.

To him we could reply that at the very least such a patchwork procedure provides us with the range of the possible characteristics of myth for the Greeks who populate the cosmos of the Platonic corpus. But the question remains, how does one read off from that range the characteristic or characteristics which Plato himself would delimit? In a simple way, one cannot, unless one brings to the dialogues a preconceived formulation of Plato's doctrine either independent of the testimony of the dialogues themselves or derived from a composite picture of the various interlocutors whom one designates as Plato's thinly disguised spokespersons. Neither of these alternatives is satisfactory: the former, namely the importing of a criterion extrinsic to the Platonic writings, runs the risk of blinding one to their intrinsic criterion or criteria; the latter is, so to speak, a sane quilt of remarks from the Platonic writings which by virtue of its sanity begs the decisive question as to whether and how one is entitled at all to speak of a Platonic spokesman. Clearly the choice boils down to that between the crazy quilt and the sane quilt. And if we consider Plato's own remark that he says nothing in his own voice,[29] together with Socrates' account of philosophy as the highest kind of craziness,[30] we must opt for the crazy quilt,[31] i.e., we must assume that Plato is somehow in all of the interlocutors of the dialogues. But does this make sense? To show that it does, we must briefly consider Platonic writing.

NOTES

[1]Cf. LSJ; W.K.C. Guthrie, History of Greek philosophy (Cambridge, Eng., 1962-), volume 1, pp. 419-424; Heribert Boeder, "Der fruehgriechische Wort gebrauch von Logos und Aletheia," Archiv fuer begriffsgeschichte, vol. 4, 1959, pp. 82-91 and 101-111.

[2]And if one returns to Homer, one finds that the generic verb for speech (which is λέγω in later Attic) is μυθέομαι, and that the noun λόγος appears only twice (Iliad 15.393 and Odyssey 1.56), both times without an article in the dative plural and in contexts where we would uncritically expect μῦθος.

[3]See chapter VIII, "Paramyths."

[4]Cf. Laws 9.872c7-873b1.

[5]Gorgias 523a1-2: "Ακουε δή, φασί, μάλα καλοῦ λόγου, ὃν σὺ μὲν ἡγήσῃ μῦθον, ὡς ἐγὼ οἶμαι, ἐγὼ δὲ λόγον.

[6]Cf. Republic 6.501e2; Timaeus 25d7 ff.

[7]Cf. pp. 153 ff.

[8]Cf. Laws 10.908e2.

[9]Except in a quotation at Meno 95e4-96a4.

[10]For a complete list of occurrences of the word μῦθος and its derivatives in the Platonic corpus, see Appendix I.

[11]Cf. Laws 6.771a5-d1.

[12]Cf. Timaeus 59c5-d3; Phaedo 108d3, 110b3-4; Republic 10.614b1; Hippias major 285d3-286a2, 297e3-298b1; Phaedrus 276e1-7.

[13]Cf. Philebus 13e4-14a9; also Republic 2.380 c1-3, 3.392a8-c5, 398a1-b4.

[14]Cf. Timaeus 22b3-24a2, 29c4-d6.

[15]Cf. Laws 2.663e5-664a1.

[16]Cf. Republic 2.377b11-c5.

[17]Cf. Laws 2.663d2-664e2; also cf. Laws 8.840 b5-c10, 12.941b2-c4. In addition, consider Hippias major 285d3-286a2; Epistles 8.352c8-353a2. But cf. Laws 8.841b5-c8.

[18]Cf. Laws 1.636b7-e4, 644b6-645c3; Republic 1.330d1-e5, 2.377a4-7 (cf. d4-6), 382c10-d3, 7.522 a3-b4.

[19]Cf. Philebus 13e4-14a9.

[20]Cf. Gorgias 523a1-2; Timaeus 22a4-b3.

[21]Cf. Epinomis 979d7-980a6; Laws 3.680c2-d6; also Republic 3.392d1-3. In addition, consider Republic 1.350d9-e10.

[22]Cf. Philebus 13e4-14a9.

[23]Cf. Timaeus 25d7-26e5.

[24]Cf. Laws 6.751d7-752b2.

[25]Cf. Republic 2.382c10-d3, 8.588b1-e2 (cf. Phaedo 60b1-c7); Critias 110a3-7; Laws 2.663e5-664a1, 3.680c2-d6, 682a1-683d5; Epinomis 974d3-975a7; Timaeus 22a4-24a2, 59c5-d3; Sophist 242c4-243a4.

[26]Meno 81a5-e2.

[27]Cf. ἀκήκοα at a5; Τίνα λόγον λεγόντων at a7; οἱ λέγοντες at a9 and 10; λέγει at b1; λέγουσιν at b2; φᾶσι at b3; τῷ...λόγῳ at d5-6.

28And this is described by Socrates as not only a beautiful account, but a true one: Ἀληθῆ...καὶ καλόν (a8).

29Cf. Epistles 2.314c1-3.

30Cf. Phaedrus 243e9-257b6; Sophist 216c8-d2.

31Cf. Moby Dick, ch. 82 beginning: "There are some enterprises in which a careful disorderliness is the true method."

PLATONIC WRITING

When we read Plato, we always have to face the unavoidable--but all too often avoided--fact that when we inquire into any particular question raised in the dialogues, we are driven back necessarily into a consideration of Plato's manner of writing, a consideration of the dialogue form. And if we take Plato seriously as a philosopher, then we must take him seriously as a writer, and we must assume that the dialogue form is philosophically motivated. Hence, we cannot simply dismiss the dialogic character of the Platonic writings as somehow extraneous to the acknowledged philosophical substance which it encapsulates before we consider its possible philosophical importance for Plato. But this 'Plato' to whom we seem constantly forced to make reference appears nowhere in the dialogues,[1] i.e., as we have said, Plato says nothing in his own voice, but rather he speaks through the interlocutors whom he presents to us. Now, what it means for a poet to speak through interlocutors is discussed by Socrates in a very neglected passage of the Republic (3.392c6-394c6). There, in conversation with Adeimantus, Socrates belabors the obvious distinction between narrating and imitating. Of course, whenever Socrates belabors the obvious, we must scrutinize his assertions very carefully. Let us look at his remarks.

> Therefore have you envisioned that up to these verses...the poet himself speaks and does not take it in hand to turn our thinking elsewhere as though the person speaking were someone other than himself; but in the things after

these he speaks as though he is Chryses, and
he attempts as much as possible with respect
to us to make the person speaking seem to be
not Homer but the priest who is old.[2]

If we apply this to Plato's dialogues, in which
there is not one utterance by Plato himself, we
can see that Plato has virtually totally effaced
himself and has spoken through a variety of persons, speaking as much as possible as though each
speaker himself as himself were speaking. And the
more Plato has effaced himself, the more success-
ful is his method of writing. Therefore, what any
of Plato's personages says is not simply, in any
given instance, what Plato says, but what the
speaker says.

> But whenever then /the poet/ speaks some
> uttering as though he is someone other, then
> will we not assert him to make his speaking
> as much as possible similar to each person
> whom he bespeaks beforehand as the utterer?
> We will assert /so/....[3]

The poet, then, when he imitates another person,
assimilates himself to that person. That is, the
poet does not efface himself, but rather he de-
faces himself into another. And the reader must
deassimilate him. In other words, every imitation
is like a force vector which the interpreter must
resolve into its component forces (Π=Plato axis;
Σ=speaker axis):

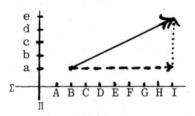

Thus, if $\overrightarrow{(a,B)(e,I)}$ is the utterance of a person
in a dialogue, Plato's view would be $\overrightarrow{ae}$, and the

utterer's utterance would be the sum of $\overrightarrow{ae}$ and
the <u>homo ad hominem</u> $\overrightarrow{BI}$. And one can see from this
how enormously difficult is the task of under-
standing Plato, because one must engage in this
procedure for every remark in a dialogue, however
trivial it may seem. That is, one must deassimilate even a Ναί and an Οὐ γὰρ οὖν, not to mention
an Εἰκός or an Ἀνάγκη or an Ὀρθῶς λέγεις, Καλῶς
λέγεις, and Ἀληθῆ λέγεις.

> And if then the poet should hide himself
> nowhere, both the poeting and narrating
> would have come to be for him without
> imitating.[4]

So, in narrating without imitating, the poet hides
himself nowhere. In other words, even when the
poet indirectly narrates what another speaks and
does, he is peripherally visible as the one determining what is spoken and done for us, the one
selecting and ordering. And by implication, a poet
who should narrate through imitating alone, would
hide himself everywhere, i.e., would be, insofar
as his imitating is perfect, completely invisible.

> Then learn...that the contrary of this
> /i.e., of simple narrating without imita-
> ting/ in turn comes to be whenever anyone,
> taking out the things of the poet between
> the utterings, leaves behind the inter-
> changes.[5]

Socrates' use here of the imperative Μάνθανε,
'learn,'[6] focusses especial attention on what he
says, and surely this is one of the most important passages in the dialogues for understanding
the dialogue form. Socrates says that even in a
purely imitative or dramatic writing, there are
intercalary remarks by the poet, but these intercalary remarks have been rendered, as it were,
invisible. Clearly, then, the task of interpreting involves restoring to visibility, on the
basis of the interchanges that have been left
behind, the utterances which have been taken out,
erased, rendered invisible. In other words, to

23

understand is to recover the poet's own utte-
rances-between on the basis of the utterances
between which his utterances would have been had
they not been removed. Therefore, to write a commentary on a Platonic dialogue is to rewrite the
dialogue in narrative form, and the model for
such an enterprise is provided here by Socrates'
re-rendering of the beginning of the Iliad as
simple narration.[7]

What Plato says, then, is what all of his interlocutors say, not simply, but rather as metamorphosed
Platoes. That is, every interlocutor in a Platonic
dialogue is a monster, composed of the speaker in
front and Plato behind.[8] And one must do with a
Platonic dialogue what Socrates asserts that one
must do when one rationalizes any so-called myth:

> There is a compulsion for him after this to
> correct the look of the Centaurs, and in
> turn the /look/ of the Chimaira, but /then/
> of suchlike Gorgons and Pegasuses and other
> uncontrivable things, a mob and multitudes
> and eccentricities of certain monstrous
> natures flow over him, the which if someone
> distrusting will approach each in accor-
> dance with what is likely, since he uses
> a certain boorish wisdom, he will need much
> leisure.[9]

So, if one is going to penetrate to the core of a
Platonic dialogue, one must provisionally at
least use the crazy quilt or, as we may now call
it, the monster methodology.

And the first tentative product of this methodology for our present inquiry is that myths are
speeches about genesis.[10]

> In fact, genesis is the very soul of any
> myth. To understand the world, the story of
> its genesis has to be told. To understand
> the gods, the story of their genesis has to
> be told. Cosmogony and theogony are the
> primary subjects of any myth. In order

properly to understand any event in human
life or the character of a people or a
city, the event and the character have
always to be related, it seems, to their
mythical origins. To tell the myth of
something means to tell how this something came to be. An enterprise of this
kind does not make much sense unless one
relates everything ultimately to beginnings which make any genesis possible.[11]

And, one might add, the myths in the Platonic dialogues are not chronogenetic, but rather are eido-
genetic or ontogenetic.

NOTES

[1]Plato himself invites us to consider this question through his making no attempt to conceal his authorship and through the only two mentions of himself in the dialogues, the one in the Apology of Socrates (34a1, 38b6), where he is said by Socrates to be present, and the one in the Phaedo (59b10), where he is said by Phaedo to have been absent. Thus he himself indirectly suggests that his presence or absence in the dialogues is a question of some importance.

[2]Republic 3.393a3, 6-b2: Οἶσθ' οὖν ὅτι μέχρι μὲν τούτων τῶν ἐπῶν...λέγει τε αὐτὸς ὁ ποιητῆς καὶ οὐδὲ ἐπιχειρεῖ ἡμῶν τὴν διάνοιαν ἄλλοσε τρέπειν ὡς ἄλλος τις ὁ λέγων ἢ αὐτός· τὰ δὲ μετὰ ταῦτα ὥσπερ αὐτὸς ὢν ὁ Χρύσης λέγει καὶ πειρᾶται ἡμᾶς ὅτι μάλιστα ποιῆσαι μὴ Ὅμηρον δοκεῖν εἶναι τὸν λέγοντα ἀλλὰ τὸν ἱερέα, πρεσβύτην ὄντα.

[3]Republic 3.393c1-4: 'Αλλ' ὅταν γέ τινα λέγῃ ῥῆσιν ὡς τις ἄλλος ὤν, ἆρ' οὐ τότε ὁμοιοῦν αὐτὸν φήσομεν ὅτι μάλιστα τὴν αὐτοῦ λέξιν ἑκάστῳ ὃν ἂν προείπῃ ὡς ἐροῦντα; Φήσομεν....

[4]Republic 3.393c11-d2: Εἰ δέ γε μηδαμοῦ ἑαυτὸν ἀποκρύπτοιτο ὁ ποιητῆς, πᾶσα ἂν αὐτῷ ἄνευ μιμήσεως ἡ ποίησίς τε καὶ διήγησις γεγονυῖα εἴη.

[5]Republic 3.394b3-6: Μάνθανε τοίνυν...ὅτι ταύτης αὖ ἐναντία γίγνεται, ὅταν τις τὰ τοῦ ποιητοῦ τὰ μεταξὺ τῶν ῥήσεων ἐξαιρῶν τὰ ἀμοιβαῖα καταλείπῃ.

[6]In this section as a whole, there is a tremendous density of forms of the verb μανθάνω, 'learn' (see 392c9, d7, 393d2, 394b2, 3, 6, c5; also cf. διδάσκαλος at 392d8). Hence, this section is also a paradigm of teaching and learning.

[7]Republic 3.392e2-393a2, 393d3-394d7. Here one might add that on this basis, one cannot strictly

26

speaking divide the Platonic dialogues into narrated and imitated, but rather they must all--
even those 'narrated' by a Platonic dramatic per-
sona--be classified as purely imitative, since
there is no 'Plato' narrating the so-called narrated dialogues, as there is a Homer narrating
the Iliad and the Odyssey.

8Cf. Iliad 6.180-181: "And the /Chimaira/
then was divine with respect to its race and not
of humans,/ in front a lion, and in back a snake,
and in the middle a she-goat" (ἡ δ' ἄρ' ἔην θεῖον
γένος οὐδ' ἀνθρώπων,/πρόσθε λέων, ὄπιθεν δὲ δράκων,
μέσση δὲ χίμαιρα). Cf. Nietzsche, Beyond good and
evil, tr. Walter Kaufmann (New York, 1966), Part
Five, section 190, p. 103: "He /i.e., Plato/ was
the most audacious of all interpreters and took
the whole Socrates only the way one picks a popu-
lar tune and folk song from the streets in order
to vary it into the infinite and impossible--
namely, into all of his own masks and multiplici-
ties. In a jest, Homeric at that: what is the
Platonic Socrates after all if not prosthe Platon
opithen te Platon messē te Chimaira."

9Phaedrus 229d5-e4: αὐτῷ ἀνάγκη μετὰ τοῦτο τὸ
τῶν Ἱπποκενταύρων εἶδος ἐπανορθοῦσθαι, καὶ αὖθις
τὸ τῆς Χιμαίρας, καὶ ἐπιρρεῖ δὲ ὄχλος τοιούτων
Γοργόνων καὶ Πηγάσων καὶ ἄλλων ἀμηχάνων πλήθη τε
καὶ ἀτοπίαι τερατολόγων τινῶν φύσεων· αἷς εἴ τις
ἀπιστῶν προσβιβᾷ κατὰ τὸ εἰκὸς ἕκαστον, ἅτε
ἀγροίκῳ τινὶ σοφίᾳ χρώμενος, πολλῆς αὐτῷ σχολῆς
δεήσει.

10In the usage of the dialogues, λόγος is used
both as the generic name for any articulated utterance and as the specific name for simple articulated utterances (i.e., descriptive accounts)
which are not μῦθοι. This is parallel to the way
in which, in the discussion of διήγησις, διήγησις
is used as both the generic name for any continuous statement of a sequence of events and/or
thoughts and as the specific name for simple continuous statements which are not imitated or

27

'dramatic.' The fundamental instance (cf. Epinomis 978b7 ff.) of this pervasive characteristic
of human διαίρεσις is the ἡμέρα (i.e., the twenty-
four hour day) which is the genus of the two
species ἡμέρα (i.e., the daylight day) and νύξ
(i.e., the nighttime day). This is one aspect of
what is called the problem of the indeterminate
dyad (δυὰς ἀόριστος) in the Platonic writings. Cf.
Jacob Klein, Greek mathematical thought and the
origin of algebra, tr. Eva Brann (Cambridge, Mass.,
1968), p. 98.

11Jacob Klein, "Aristotle, an introduction," in
Ancients and moderns: essays on the tradition of
political philosophy in honor of Leo Strauss, ed.
Joseph Cropsey (New York, 1964), p. 58. Also consider the following remarks by Leo Strauss, NRH:
"Philosophy is the quest for the 'principles' of
all things, and this means primarily the quest for
the 'beginnings' of all things or for 'the first
things.' In this, philosophy is at one with myth."
(p.82) (It should be noted that here, when Strauss
is speaking generally of philosophy and not specifically of Plato, he uses the term 'myth' rather in its common signification. That he does not
simply regard Platonic myth in this way can be
seen from his analysis of the Protagoras myth, p.
117.) "With a view to the connection between
right and civil society, the question of the origin of right transforms itself into the question
of the origin of civil society or of society in
general. This question leads to the question of
what man's original condition was like" (p.95).
"And the question of the 'essential' origin of
civil society and of right or wrong cannot be
answered without consideration of what is known
about the beginnings or the 'historical' origins."
(p. 96)

THE PLATONIC MYTH

But still is there not anything which Plato himself says about myths? There is and there is not. By that I mean that although Plato never discussed myth in his own voice, he did compose an account which he explicitly calls a myth, and that is the discussion of writings in his seventh epistle. Perhaps if we examine this closely, we will be able to re-discern the Platonic definition of myth.

Let me begin by outlining the passage:[1]

Foreword (341b7-342a6)

    I (341b7-d2): writers and non-writers
    II (341d2-e1): possible purposes of writings
    III (341e1-342a1): the audience
    IV (342a1-6): introduction to the myth (=something true)

The Myth (342a7-344d2)

    I (342a7-e2): genesis of exact-knowledge
      A (342a7-b3): the three/four/five things for each of the beings
      B (342b3-d8): the explanation
      C (342d8-e2): conclusion
    II (342e2-344c1): defects of speeches
      A (342e2-343a4): weakness of speeches
      B (343a4-344c1): the explanation
    III (344c1-d2): conclusion

29

Afterword (344d3-345c3)

I (344d3-9): writers and non-writers
II (344d9-345a1): possible purposes of
writings
III (345a1-c3): the hearers and repeata-
bility

Plato begins (341b7-c4) by classifying past and
future writers who understand nothing about Plato's
business (περὶ τοῦ πράγματος),[2] i.e., who understand nothing about philosophy:

past/future writers

do not claim   claim to envision things
to envision   about which Plato is serious
things about
which Plato   have heard   have heard   have disco-
is serious   them from   them from   vered them
/not expli-   Plato   others   by them-
citly stated,   selves
but implicit/

By restricting his classification to past and future writers, Plato clearly exempts himself as a
present writer. This would suggest that Plato as
a writer is somehow immune to his own charges
against writers. And these charges are directed
only against writers who claim to be cognizant of
Plato's serious concerns, not against writers who
do not claim such cognizance. In addition, Plato
admits that there are things about which he is
serious, although, we recall, this same Plato refers to the childish-playfulness which is the
sibling of seriousness.[3]

And according to Plato (341c4-6), while learning
about the serious things is possible, no writing
down about the serious things is permissible and/
or possible, although other learnings, i.e., learnings about non-serious things, may be spoken or
written. Yet Plato is a writer. But what does he
write and in what way? Perhaps what he condemns

30

is the serious and/or direct writing <u>about</u> the serious things, but not the playful and/or indirect writing <u>of</u> them. Here, then, a tentative definition of Platonic writing is suggested: it is playful writing of the serious things.[4] So, if learnings about non-serious things may be written, and if it is possible by writing about the non-serious things to write of the serious things, then writing of--although not about--the serious things is possible.

But in order to write in this way, one must first learn the serious things. And (341c5-d2) learning the serious things comes from συνουσία (being-together) and συζῆν (living-together), from a togetherness presumably either with the non-serious things, so that one is led to a self-discovery of the serious things, or with those who have learned the serious things, so that one is led by a teacher to the serious things. And this learning the serious things must be the result of a continuous process such as a burning fire undergoes, and it comes as a sudden leap of light. The burning is the συνουσία or συζῆν, the fire is the learning the non-serious things, and the flare is the learning the serious things. But what is the burnable? On the one hand, it is the kindling, and the kindling would seem to represent the non-serious things which in burning (in being learned) are turned into ashes (stripped of non-essentials). On the other hand, it is the coal which becomes the embers, which would seem to represent the soul, for if the fire nurtures itself in the soul, the soul or something in the soul must be burnable. And for the possibility of learning to be ever present to the soul, the soul must at least in principle be pure burnability, inexhaustible.[5] And not only must the soul be pure burnability, but once it catches fire, it must be always burning (which one could call ἡ πρώτη ἐντελέχεια of soul),[6] for the flare of light is the effluence of a fire which has been burning. In addition, the structure (burnability) of the soul and the structure (burnability) of its objects is similar, and hence the requirement that similar be known

31

by similar is satisfied.[7] However, in the soul, as apparently not in its objects·, the persistence of the fire is precarious, because the soul (ἡ ψυχή) is cool (ψυχρά) or a cooling (κατάψυξις).[8]

Plato now (341d2) shifts to the question of the possible purposes of writings, and he does so from the point of view of his own interests. For the Platonic things would best be <u>spoken</u> by Plato (ὑπ' ἐμοῦ), but <u>written</u> badly they would pain Plato (ἐμέ). This is an implicit hierarchy:

    (1) best: spoken by Plato.
    (2) second best: written by Plato (i.e., written well).
    (3) second worst: spoken by someone else.
    (4) worst: written by someone else (i.e., written badly).

Clearly Plato is in a dilemma: even though it is certain that at least some of those to whom Plato speaks will speak and write the Platonic things to others, there is no guarantee that those to whom he speaks will speak and write them properly.[9] And in the repetition of the Platonic things by another whose understanding is incomplete, there is pain for Plato, both the pain of physical abuse (or potential physical abuse) and the pain of seeing the serious things contorted, incorrectly falsified, and dishonored, a pain which seems unsocratic, because Socrates appeared to be indifferent to the career of his speeches as disseminated by others.[10] And it seems that this twofold pain can be eliminated only by writing anonymously and/or correctly of the serious things. Plato's choice of the dialogue form achieves both these goals. On the one hand, since the dialogues present conversations (i.e., <u>ad hominem</u> remarks by a variety of interlocutors, none of which remarks may be attributed simply to Plato), they preserve Plato's anonymity. And on the other hand, if the dialogues falsify the serious things, they do so in a noble, not a shameful, way. In addition, the dialogue form invites repeated συνουσίαι and συζῆν with the dialogues, since one cannot simply read off from them a Platonic teaching.

Then (341d2-e1) Plato indicates why he would write
if he felt compelled to convey his position sufficiently and to convey it to the many, i.e., why he
would write if writing were a beautiful action. He
would write to benefit humans greatly and to bring
nature to light for everyone. Plato phrases his
remark conditionally and interrogatively. And even
though he seems to answer it negatively, there is
the massive fact of the Platonic corpus. That is,
Plato did write. Why? In what follows, Plato denies that one can write to benefit all humans,
because only a few would be benefited. However,
he does not deny that one should write to bring
nature to light for everyone. In addition, it is
implicit that writing should harm no one. On this
basis, then, a second definition of Platonic writing emerges: it is writing for the purpose of
bringing nature to light so as to benefit a few
and harm no one.[11]

In addition, the repetition of the word 'light'
(φῶς: d7) recalls its use a few lines above (d1),
so that perhaps one could further conclude that
the light which flares from the fire, namely
that about which Plato is serious, is nature.
Plato suggests, therefore, that he is a true φυσι-
ολόγος in his writing and that anyone who writes
correctly φυσιολογεῖ.

Next (341e1-342a1), after Plato denies that taking
the serious things in hand is good for all humans,
he classifies humans according to their capacity
with respect to the serious things:
        (1) the few: capable of finding out the seri-
ous things themselves with little ἐπίδειξις
        (2) the many
                (a) some: taking the serious things in
        hand fills them with an incorrect contempt
                (b) others: taking the serious things
        in hand fills them with a lofty and spongy
        hope, based on their assumption that they
        have learned significant things.
Writings, therefore, are not good or beneficial
for the many for two reasons: (α) they breed an
incorrect contempt; (β) they breed the conceit of

33

believing oneself to know when one does not know.
However, writings may be good or beneficial for
the few. Is it, then, possible to write writings
that are beneficial to the few (one's 'friends')
and harmful to no one? That is, is it possible to
write a just writing? What would a just writing
be? For the few, it would seem to serve a twofold
purpose: (α) it would give them the little ἐπίδειξις that they need; (β) it would give them a
paradigm for any writings that they themselves
may take in hand.[12] For the many, it would prevent
them from becoming incorrectly ˷contemptuous, and
it would safeguard them from conceit, i.e., it
would--if it fulfilled both these requirements--
have to be ostensibly both supportive of convention and aporetic or inconclusive. And certainly
the Platonic dialogues satisfy both requirements.[13]

In his conclusion to the foreword (342a1-3), Plato
alludes to another purpose for writing, namely the
clarifying what one has already said and/or written, and its corollary, the clarifying what someone else has said and/or written about what oneself has said and/or written. This is one purpose
of the seventh epistle itself.

Then (342a3-6), Plato refers to a true speech (τις
λόγος ἀληθής) which must be spoken to anyone who
dares to write of the serious things, and that
would include the competent and the others, i.e.,
what follows is written for all writers of the
serious things, and it is written, we must assume,
with the above considerations in mind. That is,
since the true speech is written against writings,
it itself at least must be written in such a way
as to correct for all the defects of writings
which have been and will be mentioned, because "a
precept we cannot suppose to have been consciously
violated by its author in the very /writing/ in
which it occurs."[14] And what is here called "a
certain true speech" is later called "a myth"
(344d3).

Now, we come to the myth itself (342a7-344d2),

which falls into two major parts, the first of
which (342a7-e2) takes up the theme of the genesis of ἐπιστήμη (exact knowledge) and the second
of which (342e2-344c1) takes up again the theme
of the genesis of writings, followed by a brief
conclusion (344c1-d2). And this is written to
clarify what has already been said about writings,
i.e., the discussion of exact knowledge provides
the basis for clarifying Plato's view of writing.
It is not surprising, therefore, that the discussion of exact knowledge is one of the darkest in
the Platonic corpus. This much, however, is clear,
that the discussion of exact knowledge provides
not only an account of exact knowledge in general
but also a methodological paradigm for the exact
knowledge of anything in particular, a paradigm
which is then employed in the account of writings
which follows it. But still we must ask, why does
Plato insert an account of exact knowledge? The
reason seems to be that the writers whom Plato is
accusing are persons who claim that they know the
Platonically serious, i.e., persons who claim
that they know.[15]

Plato begins (342a7-b3) by saying that there are
three things to each being, out of which, by compulsion, exact knowledge arises as the fourth.
The fifth, which must be posited, is the being
itself, and this being itself both is knowable
and truly is. So we have the following five things:
(1) name (ὄνομα), (2) speech (λόγος), (3) look-
alike (εἴδωλον), (4) exact knowledge (ἐπιστήμη),
and (5) the being itself (αὐτὸ...ὄν).[16]

First, it is odd that what we would unthinkingly
call the being itself is here called a look-alike,
and it looks like something of which apparently we
cannot have exact knowledge, although we must posit that it is, presumably as the ground of both
the look of the look-alike and the intellectual
apprehension of what the look-alike looks like,
namely the assumed but indemonstrable being itself.

Second, according to what Plato says, if we have

35

the awareness of the look-alike, its name, and its speech, we have exact knowledge, which apparently is not an independent fourth but rather the unified view of the three. Since in most cases, we have the look-alike and the name, what we lack for exact knowledge primarily and for the most part is the speech, although initially it is not clear precisely what a speech is.

So, Plato's initial statement unleashes more perplexities than it dissolves, as Plato himself seems to recognize when he says (342b3-4) that to learn what he means a paradigmatic case is needed, i.e., we must grasp what Plato says in regard to one thing, and then apply it to all things. And the paradigmatic case here is circle (342b4-d3), a mathematical into which as such simplicity and precision come built.

What new light does the case of the circle shed on the initial perplexities? It specifies, first of all, that a speech is composed of names and verbs,[17] i.e., what is distinctive about a speech is that it contains the actings (the verbs) of that which it bespeaks. And in the case of the circle, whose speech is 'that which holds itself everywhere equal from its extremities to its middle,' its acting is its holding (ἀπέχον). In other words, the circle itself, i.e., the circle which we mean when we draw the circle which we draw, is the inner area, and hence the name 'line' does not appear in the speech of circle.[18] Therefore, the line by which we draw the look-alike circle, the line by which we render the circle visible for ourselves, is merely the visible encapsulation of the invisible inner area of the circle itself. This is why when the name 'circle' is expanded, we find 'rounded and circumferent and circle' but not 'round and circumference and circle.' And as if to give a small example of how what is applicable to circle must be taken as applicable to all things, when the name 'circle' becomes triple, so too does exact knowledge become triple, and true opinion is its rounded and intellectual intuition is its circumferent.

36

nd what is applicable to circle and exact know-
edge must <u>mutatis mutandis</u> be applicable to a
riting. And if we apply it to a writing, we see
hat the speech by which we compose the look-alike
riting, the speech by which we render the writing
tself visible for ourselves, is merely the visi-
le encapsulation of the invisible inner character
·f the writing itself. And if from a defective
.ircle, a circle full of defects (cf. 343a5-7), we
.an achieve exact knowledge of the circle itself,
hen however defective or weak a writing may be,
.e., even if it is thoroughly defective or weak,
·e can still achieve exact knowledge of the wri-
ing itself.

.nd with this in mind, we are now ready to embark
·n--and in a way have been made immune to--Plato's
·iscussion of the defects of writings (342e2-344
·1), or more precisely, the weakness of Λόγοι.

nitially, Plato simply presupposes (342e2-343a1)
·hat Λόγοι are weak. But even so they are not sim-
·ly weak, because they are, it is implied, less
·eak with respect to each thing's ποῖόν τι (cer-
·ain sort) than with respect to each thing's ὄν
·being), and hence a Λόγος must articulate the
·ertain sort with at least as much clarity as the
·eing. In terms of--and in support of--the ear-
·ier discussion of writings, Λόγοι are more capable
·or the non-serious things, the ποῖόν τι, than the
·erious thing, the ὄν, which they look like but
·re not.

·onetheless, Λόγοι are assumed to be weak, and
·heir weakness leads to two consequences for a
·erson with intellect (343a1-4): (1) he will not
·lare to put his intellectual intuitions into Λό-
·οι; and (2) he will not dare to put his intel-
·ectual intuitions into what is untransmovable.
·lato does not say that a person of intellect
·ill not write or speak, but rather only that he
·ill not write or speak his intellectual intui-
·ions. And with respect to writings in particular,
·he fundamental defect is untransmovability. One
·night conjecture, then, that if one could devise

a form of writing which possesses transmovability, a living speech, as it were, one could compose a writing without the usual defects of writings. As Socrates says:

> But I believe you would assert this, namely
> **for it to be** obligatory for every speech to be
> composed as a living thing having its own
> certain body, so as to be neither headless
> nor footless, but to have both middles and
> extremities which have been written /so as
> to be/ proper to each other and to the
> whole.[19]

That is, if a writing could be devised to operate analogously to a living thing by "a certain logographic compulsion,"[20] perhaps a person of intellect would then dare to write.

Then (343a5-343e1) Plato uses the case of the defective look-alike circle[21] to elucidate his meaning. What Plato does not say here is that surely we must know the look-alike circle as defective precisely because we know the non-defective fifth thing, the circle itself.

Next (343a9-b3) Plato turns to the name, and he gives the speech of name (cf. b4). And since names are not stable, since they are arbitrary, the speech of name seems to be that names, i.e., the peculiar sound and letter configurations which have been designated as accepted signifiers of certain objects, are purely conventional. He does not say that the things named by those names are conventional, but only that whether one calls object X a table or a krell is a customarily established practice by which all X's are called, say, table, and although the name krell could have been established, X would still be X, but it would be called krell.[22]

Plato proceeds after name to discuss speech, i.e., he gives the speech of the speech (343b4-6), which is the same as the speech of the name. And he says that if a speech is composed from names and verbs, then the speech of the speech is that the speech is in no way sufficiently stable to be stable. Apparently, then, verbs are so insignificant a part of the speech that the dominant part of speech, namely name, infects the whole speech. And this presupposes that in effect all speeches are purely nominal, i.e., that they are composed of mere rootless names. But this is put conditionally: if speeches are from and of names, then speeches are intrinsically unstable. However, if names were stable,[23] and if speeches were from and of names, then speeches would be stable. Or even if names were intrinsically unstable,[24] then if speeches were not from and of names primarily,[25] speeches might be stable, i.e., perhaps a speech could be composed only from verbs.[26]

In addition, the description of something as unstable is not meant in terms of motion. We recall that one of the defects of a written speech is that it is untransmovable. Perhaps then inanimate, i.e., non-living, writings are both untransmovable and unstable, while one should and could devise a writing which is both transmovable and stable,[27] a writing such as a dialogue.

Plato now (343b6-c5) returns to the distinction between ποιόν τι and the ὄν, and remarks that when there are these two, if the soul seeks the ὄν-- which is the soul's ultimate goal--i.e., if the soul seeks what it ultimately desires to seek, it finds what it is not seeking, and becomes filled with perplexity and indistinctness. It is implicit that in order for the soul to find what it seeks, it must first seek what it does not seek. What is the consequence of this? First, it follows that the ὄν is not directly accessible to humans, and that any attempt to gain direct access to it is destined to be frustrated. Second, it follows that if the ὄν constitutes the core of the serious things,[28] any writing[29] which should be written so as to provide direct access to the serious things will fail precisely by virtue of that to provide access to the serious things. Therefore, if one wants to write so as to provide some access

to the serious things, one must do so by provi-
ding an access mediated through the non-serious
things. In short, as we concluded above, proper
writing would be playful writing of--but not
about--the serious things. More precisely (343c5-
d2), proper writing is directed to those who by
a virtuous nurture are habituated not to seek the
true and to them it presents look-alikes from
which extrapolations may be made. Such writing is
not laughable to one's companions, although it
clearly may be to non-companions, and so, just as
clearly, the laughter of non-companions is not an
important consideration here, even though the
trial and death of Socrates were a consequence of
such laughter.[30]

But what would happen if we should be compelled
to speak about the fifth thing, about the ὅν itself, something which we would do presumably only
under compulsion? This is the question with which
Plato deals next (343d2-e1), as he must, because
he himself is writing the seventh epistle precisely under such a compulsion, a compulsion which
in a way is reflected in the darkness and obscu-
rity and indirection with which he writes. What,
then, would result? Of those persons who are capable of turning things upside down, the person
who wants to turn things upside down overpowers
us. Why? The situation seems to be this. It is
clear that not everyone who is capable of turning
things upside down wants to do so. And surely the
person who answers and clarifies the fifth thing
would be one of those who possess but do not wish
to employ this capability. But those who wish to
and do employ it seem to be interested in victory,
not in being. And they overpower us, it would
seem, not because we are incapable of overpowering
them in turn, if we wished to do so, but because
we do not wish either to turn things upside down
or merely to be victorious. Therefore (343d4-6),
the person who wishes to win by turning things
upside down makes the person giving an exegesis
of the fifth, whether in speeches or in writings
or in answerings, seem to many of the hearers
(readers) to know nothing of things which he takes

it in hand to write or to speak. The overturner,
then, succeeds in making the exegete seem foolish
to the many hearers (readers)but not to all, i.e.,
some do understand what the exegete presents. Finally (343d6-e1), the hearers--presumably the
many of them--sometimes (but not all the time)
fail to recognize two corollary things: (1) that
the speaker's or writer's soul is not refuted;
(2) that the meanly natured nature of each of the
four is refuted. That the many do not recognize
that the soul is not refuted is understandable,
for who can see into another's soul? On the other
hand, if a person could recognize what is refuted,
then the question of soul would be irrelevant. The
hearers, then, take a refutation of what is said
for a refutation of its ground in either the say-
er's soul or being itself. But why does Plato in-
troduce the soul here at all? I would suggest that
just as no direct access to being itself is available to humans, similarly no direct access to the
soul is available. Therefore, with respect to both
the soul and the ὄν, we must extrapolate not only
from the look-alike, but also from the name, the
speech, and the exact knowledge, even though all
of these possess a defective, i.e., a meanly natured, nature. There are two surprises here.
First, there is the somewhat unexpected assertion
of the defectiveness of exact knowledge. I say
somewhat, because earlier (342c4-5, d1-3), when
exact knowledge was expanded by the addition of
intellect and true opinion, intellect was said to
be the nearest of the three to the fifth thing,
while exact knowledge and true opinion were said
to be farther, apparently equally far. That is,
the suggestion there was that exact knowledge and
true opinion are identical, an apparent demotion
of exact knowledge which could perhaps be explained perspectivally by the appearance of intellect, i.e., perhaps from the vantage point of
ignorance exact knowledge seems very high while
from the vantage point of intellect it seems quite
low. The second surprise is that now name and
speech are regarded as natures. But perhaps this
too can be explained perspectivally. Perhaps from
the vantage point of the ὄν itself they seem con-

41

ventional, while from the vantage point of the
upside down world of the overturner they seem to
be natures.[31]

Plato widens the discussion of the natures of the
four by adding a discussion of the natures of human knowers (343e1-344b1). First, there is the
person of good nature, in whom exact knowledge of
that which is good natured is brought to birth
with difficulty, even if he is led repeatedly to
and through it. So, even if the conditions for
the birth of exact knowledge are good, still it
is produced with difficulty, and there is no guarantee of success. In addition, we see that each
of the four, which had just been described as
meanly natured, is susceptible of being well natured too.

Next, there is the person of bad nature, the person whose soul's attitude or aptitude (ἕξις) has
the same nature as the many's soul attitude or
aptitude with regard to learning and what are
called habits. And when habits are corrupted, as
they are in the many, the incapacity with regard
to knowing is incorrigible. Apparently, then,
learning ability and habituatability are in humans
as sight is, and the keen-sighted (Lynceus) may
try to make the dull-sighted humans see what he
sees by pointing and talking, but clearly the
condition of the many cannot be ameliorated. Then
to make this clear, Plato classifies humans according as they are or are not cogeneric of the
just and beautiful things, i..e., of the truth of
virtue and badness:
    (1) the non-cogeneric (regardless of learn-
ing ability): ineducable
    (2) the cogeneric
        (a) learning-resistant and unmemoried:
ineducable
        (b) facile-at-learning and memoried:
educable.
Again, the emphasis is on the educability of only
the few, namely those of good nature who are cogeneric of the just and beautiful things and who
are good learners with good memories. If any one

of these characteristics is missing in a person, that person is ineducable in the ὄν itself.

Now (344b1-c1), Plato returns to the theme of learning with which he started (cf. 341c4-d2), but with a significant shift of emphasis. What was initially called the serious things is now specified as the whole of beingness (τῆς ὅλης οὐσίας). And where initially he discussed the burning allure of learning by συνουσία and συζῆν, now the emphasis is on the effort involved in igniting the fire of learning, the diligence (b2, τριβῆς, literally 'rubbing;' cf. b4, τριβόμενα).[32] And there is a revision of the four things, for although name and speech remain, the look-alike has been replaced by seeings and sensings, a moving back to the by which, as in the case of learning, and exact knowledge and true opinion have been replaced by prudence, a moving back from the more inflexible to the more flexible, as befits a backward deepening of the genetic movement.

And now (344c1-d2) we come to the conclusion of what in the next line after this Plato will call a myth.

Because of all that has been said, every person who is serious about serious things needs a great deal before he writes anything down and publishes it amidst the envy and perplexity of humans. So, the lesson is not that one should not write, but rather that before one risks writing, one should be as non-needy as possible, i.e., as wise as possible,[33] i.e., as free as possible from the envy and perplexity which characterize the human condition.

Finally, if someone sees anyone's writings, whether a legislator's laws or anything else, then if the writer himself is serious, he regards his writings in one or the other of two ways. On the one hand, he may regard these as non-serious things, in which case his serious things are in his most beautiful spot, presumably his intellect. On the other hand, he may regard them as genuinely

43

serious, in which case mortals have destroyed his
senses.

Why are the laws and the legislator singled out?
Apparently Plato wants to single out either laws
as non-serious or legislators as senseless,[34]
perhaps because laws and legislators make humans,
and humans are filled with envy and perplexity as
a result, and so long as they are--which means
always--the position of philosophy or philosophers
is extremely precarious. For the nature which the
philosopher brings to light may be a threat to the
prevailing νόμος. And this is why a philosopher
would be out of his senses if he seriously presented the serious things, for from the vantage point
of philosophy, there will be no cessation of evils
for humans until philosophers become rulers and
Socrates is the only human who is truly capable
with respect to the political things.[35] In addition, the truth is subversive of the city and
dangerous to the truth teller, as Antenor found
in the Trojan assembly.[36]

Nonetheless, a serious person may be a writer, so
long as his writings are non-serious, i.e., as we
have seen before, if a serious person writes, he
writes playfully.

This is the myth, which is also called a wandering,
i.e., a digression. And what does it teach us, according to Plato? In the afterword (344d3-345c3),
he tells us its three lessons.

First, if anyone, e.g., Dionysius or his inferior
or his superior, wrote any of the highest and
first things about nature, then he did not hear
or learn anything healthy about them from anyone,
e.g., Plato or his inferior or his superior. On
the other hand, if anyone did not write unharmoniously and improperly any of the highest and
first things about nature, i.e., if anyone did
not simply throw his writings together and out,
but rather had the reverence for them that Plato
does, then he did hear or learn something healthy
about them from someone. In other words, the pos-

44

sibility is left open that there may be a healthy knower about the highest and first things about nature who writes or speaks about the lowest and nth things about nature, either for the purpose of simply presenting them in themselves or for the purpose of revealing through them indirectly the highest and first things. One may, then, be a Platonic dialogue writer or a Socratic speaker.

In addition, someone who has learned or heard something healthy about the highest and first things will not simply write and throw his writings to the many, and he will not write unharmoniously and improperly. If he did write, then, how would he write? First, he would carefully consider his audience and not simply exile (ἐκ-βάλλω) his writings among them without regard to the exile (the writings) and without regard to the strangers among whom the exile finds itself (an audience for the most part incapable of discerning and/or understanding the highest and first things which the exile adumbrates). And the writing is a stranger or an exile in its own land. That is, in a way, the suggested paradigm for a writing is Odysseus returned to Ithaca in disguise.[37] In other words, the writings must be disguised not as a god,[38] i.e., not as the highest and first things, but rather as a beggar.[39] So, if one writes, one must write, on the one hand, writings which are impoverished, i.e., which are, in philosophic terms, aporetic. On the other hand, just as Odysseus, the writings must be many-minded and many-mannered and wandering. They must have an exoteric surface which is unthreatening to conventional opinion and an esoteric philosophic core. And they must wander or be transmovable (cf. 343a3), i.e., they must be living speech, i.e., they must be truly conversational, truly dialogic. Yet the truly dialogic writing, insofar as it is the product of a self-consciously poly-dianoetic and polytropic writer, must be an artfully dialogic writing, i.e., chance must be eliminated so that the presented conversation, although mimetic of ordinary conversation, is constructed in such a way that the careful, persistent, and suitably natured reader may see through to the golden core which its surface hides.[40]

The second lesson of the myth (344d9-345a1) is concerned with the possible purposes of writings, of which there are two, as reminders (344d9-e2) and from ambition (344e2-345a1).

The composing of writings as reminders is an acceptable purpose for writing when forgetting presents a real problem, but in the case of the highest and first things, forgetting is no problem, because once the soul grasps them, they can be recalled among the briefest things of all. So, once consciousness has memorialized the highest and first things, then even if they recede into forgetfulness, they can virtually instantaneously be brought back again, and hence for the knower, for the wise man, writings as reminders are superfluous. But what about the potential knower? For him, speeches, whether spoken or written, are means of leading him to knowledge of the highest and first things.[41] Even Plato made an attempt to lead Dionysius through to them, to narrate them to Dionysius. Clearly, then, there is a place for speeches, and for speeches which can be repeated more than once, a requirement which can be met by the physical presence of a knower (e.g., Plato) verbally repeating his lessons or by a properly constructed writing which can be read and re-read until the teaching becomes assimilated, at which point --and only at which point--the speeches become superfluous.

The second purpose which a writer may have for writing is his own glorification, i.e., the writings are reminders not of the highest and first things but of the writer himself. In this case, the writer writes from shameful φιλοτιμία (ambition, love of honor) in two senses: (1) he may claim that the teaching is his own; (2) he may claim that he has partaken of an education in the highest and first things and that he consequently understands them. Therefore, someone who does write, must write out of the opposite of shameful φιλοτιμία.[42] He must write without desire for self-glory: he must write so as to preserve his own anonymity as much as possible. This criterion is certainly satisfied by the form of the Platonic dialogue, in which Plato is an invisible and virtually anonymous presence. Whether this kind of absent presence would classify as noble φιλοτιμία is unclear, but it depends upon whether any writing as such involves φιλοτιμία, and whether in writing, nobility and anonymity are directly proportional to each other,[43] and whether φιλοσοφία is consonant even with noble φιλοτιμία. In addition, the claim that the teaching is one's own would seem to be base or shameful, because this teaching can be no one's own.

And (345a1-4) for partaking of an education in the highest and first things, one συνουσία or narration is insufficient. How it could be sufficient, "Zeus /alone/ kens."[44] This applies, of course, only to someone who needs to be educated by another, not to someone who is capable of finding out by himself. And the reference to the Phaedo points to the evidence for the insufficiency of only one συνουσία or narration: Socrates' attempt to free Phaedo and his friends from the fear of death is a complete failure, and when Socrates is dying, they behave as disgracefully as the women at the beginning of the dialogue.[45]

Of course (345a4-7), the teacher must know who it is that is concerned to find out about the highest and first things, in order to determine the need for repeating the education. It is possible, then, that the person who is concerned to find out could envision sufficiently after only one or no hearings, but the person who is not genuinely concerned to find out is immune even to many hearings. There is an unmentioned intermediate person, namely a person who is potentially capable of finding out by himself but who needs a repeated narration of them to activate his power.

47

Finally (345a7-c3), even if someone believes that
he knows the highest and first things sufficiently,
for whatever reason, his dishonoring the leader
and authority in these things is inexplicable.
This, by the way, indicates one of the problems of
φιλοτιμία, or at least of shameful φιλοτιμία: the
seeking of honor for oneself necessarily involves
the dishonoring of someone else. Hence, by honoring
himself, Dionysius de-honored Plato. But then Plato
must de-honor Dionysius and re-honor himself. So,
in order to defend the honor of the highest and
first things, Plato too must practice φιλοτιμία.
But is this noble φιλοτιμία? That is, if the assertion of the false prophet to be a true prophet
is base φιλοτιμία, is the discrediting of that
claim, the assertion of the true prophet to be
the true prophet,--is that noble φιλοτιμία? If it
is, still how is the audience to distinguish the
two competing claims of true prophethood?[46]

This, then, is the Platonic myth. And what is a
Platonic myth? It is a speech, and as such it
must be read the way any speech in a Platonic
dialogue is read. And what kind of speech is it?
It is a speech about a genesis, in this case the
genesis of exact knowledge and of writing.

NOTES

¹For a literal translation of the passage, see Appendix II.

²Cf. Apol. Socr. 20c5; Phaedo 61c8; Theaetetus 168a8.

³Cf. Epistles 6.323d2; also cf. Epinomis 992 b3, Phaedrus 234d8.

⁴Cf. Friedrich Nietzsche, Beyond good and evil, Part Four, section 94, p. 83: "A man's maturity—consists in having found again the seriousness one had as a child, at play."

⁵Cf. Aristotle, De anima B.4.416a15-16: "For the fire's increasing is unto the unlimited, so long as there be something burnable" (ἡ μὲν γὰρ τοῦ πυρὸς αὔξησις εἰς ἄπειρον, ἕως ἂν ᾖ τὸ καυστόν).

⁶Cf. Aristotle De anima B.1.412a27-28 & context.

⁷Cf. Aristotle De anima A.2.404b16-18; Plato Timaeus 45b2 ff.

⁸Cf. Aristotle De anima A.2.405b23-29.

⁹That is, the case of Socrates, who produces such a bewildering variety of reporters (including persons such as Apollodorus, Phaedo, Plato, Euclides and Terpsion, and so on), is repeated in the case of Plato, who produces Dionysius, Aristotle, and so on.

¹⁰Cf. Symposium 173b4-8.

¹¹Cf. Republic 1.335d11-336a10.

¹²And perhaps it would fill them with a correct contempt and a solid hope without conceit.

13Cf. Crito, on the one hand, and Meno, on the other.

14Plato, The Phaedrus of Plato, ed. W.H. Thompson (New York, 1973), p. xiv.

15One might add that the Platonically serious has so far been called nature (341d7-e1) and is about to be called being itself (342a8-b1). Being, then, is nature and nature is being, according to Plato, a formulation which is echoed in the Republic, where the Platonic looks (εἴδη) are called natures by Socrates. (See Republic 10.597b5-e5, where the couch is said to be in nature; cf. also 6.501b2, where reference is made to the just and beautiful as by nature. Also cf. Aristotle Metaphysics A.9.991b7 ff., M.5.1080a5 ff.; cf. Plato Epistles 7.342c6.)

16Cf. Laws 10.895d1-9 & ff.; Epistles 2.312d5-e6.

17Cf. Sophist 261e4 ff.

18The same definition appears as the definition of 'rounded' in the Parmenides 137e1-3: "And the rounded then somehow is this whose extremities everywhere hold themselves equal from the middle" (Στρογγύλον γέ πού ἐστι τοῦτο οὗ ἂν τὰ ἔσχατα πανταχῇ ἀπὸ τοῦ μέσου ἴσον ἀπέχῃ: cf. 145a8-b3). Also cf. Timaeus 33b1-7, 36d8-e5. The Euclidean definitions of circle (Book 1, def. 15 & 16), which do contain the word "line," have the same import: "A circle is the plane shaped-surface which is embraced by one line which is called the circumference, in regard to which all the straight /lines/ falling on the circumference of the circle from one point of those lying within the shaped-surface --and the point is called the center of the circle --are equal to each other" (ιε'. Κύκλος ἐστὶ σχῆμα ἐπίπεδον ὑπὸ μιᾶς γραμμῆς περιεχόμενον ἣ καλεῖται περιφέρεια, πρὸς ἣν ἀφ' ἑνὸς σημείου τῶν ἐντὸς τοῦ σχήματος κειμένων πᾶσαι αἱ προσπίπτουσαι εὐθεῖαι πρὸς τὴν τοῦ κύκλου περιφέρειαν ἴσαι ἀλλήλαις εἰσίν. ις'. Κέντρον δὲ τοῦ κύκλου τὸ σημεῖον καλεῖται): Euclidis, Elementa, text of I.L. Heiberg, ed. E.S. Stamatis (Leipzig, Teubner, 1969), vol. 1, liber 1, def. 15 & 16, p. 2. I have kept the full manuscript reading and not the text as emended by Heath /Euclidis, The thirteen books of Euclid's Elements, tr. with intro. and commentary by Sir Thomas L. Heath, 2nd ed. rev. (New York, 1956), vol. 1, pp. 153-154, 183-185/, and in my rendering I have inserted definition 16 into definition 15 at the proper explanatory place. As to my interpretation of both the Platonic and Euclidean definitions, cf. Heath's unapproving summary (p.184) of an-Nairizī's commentary: "an-Nairizī points to this as the explanation of Euclid's definition of a circle as a plane figure, meaning the whole surface bounded by the circumference, and not the circumference itself."

19Phaedrus 264c2-5: 'Αλλὰ τόδε γε οἶμαί σε φάναι ἄν, δεῖν πάντα λόγον ὥσπερ ζῷον συνεστάναι σῶμά τι ἔχοντα αὐτὸν αὑτοῦ, ὥστε μήτε ἀκέφαλον εἶναι μήτε ἄπουν, ἀλλὰ μέσα τε ἔχειν καὶ ἄκρα, πρέποντα ἀλλήλοις καὶ τῷ ὅλῳ γεγραμμένα. Cf. Philebus 64b6-8, Statesman 277b7-c1, Parmenides 145a5-b1.

20Phaedrus 264b7: τινὰ ἀνάγκην λογογραφικήν.

21See pp. 36-37.

22Cf. Cratylus 433d7-e8 and context.

23Cf. Parmenides 147d1-6, Laches 194c3-6, Timaeus 49e7-50a2.

24Cf. Timaeus 49d3-50a4.

25Cf. Cratylus 438e2-3: "Then, o Cratylus, as is likely, it is possible to have learned the beings without names" ("Εστιν ἄρα, ὡς ἔοικεν, ὦ Κρατύλε, δυνατὸν μαθεῖν ἄνευ ὀνομάτων τὰ ὄντα).

26Cf. Cratylus 421a7-b1: "Socrates. Then 'name' is like a name which is wrought from a speech

which bespeaks that this is a being of which what
is sought chances to be. And you would recognize
it more in that by which we bespeak the namable;
for herein it distinctly bespeaks this /i.e., the
namable/ to be the being for which a search is"
(ΣΩ. "Ἔοικε τοίνυν ἐκ λόγου ὀνόματι συγκεκροτημένῳ,
λέγοντος ὅτι τοῦτ' ἔστιν ὄν, οὗ τυγχάνει ζήτημα
ὄν, τὸ ὄνομα. μᾶλλον δὲ ἂν αὐτὸ γνοίης ἐν ᾧ λέγομεν τὸ ὀνομαστόν· ἐνταῦθα γὰρ σαφῶς λέγει τοῦτο
εἶναι ὂν οὗ μάσμα ἐστίν). I.e., τὸ ὂν οὗ μάσμα
becomes τὸ ὀνομαστόν.

27See pp. 37-38.

28See p. 37.

29Although the instance here is about speaking,
it seems justified to extrapolate it to writings
in accordance with the principle that what is applicable to one is applicable to all (see pp. 36-37).

30Cf. Apol. Socr. 18c8-d2, 19c2-5; Euthyphro
3b9-e3; Republic 7.516e8-517a7, 517d4-e3; Theaetetus 173c6-175d7; Phaedo 64a10-b1.

31Cf. Aristotle Generation of animals A.23.731
a33-b4: "For /the animals/ have sensing, and sensing is a certain knowing. And there is much difference between one who considers its honorable-
ness and dishonorableness in regard to prudence
and one who considers it in regard to the class
of the unsouled things. For in regard to being
prudent, communing with only touch and tasting
seems to be as nothing, but in regard to a plant
or a stone /it seems to be/ wondrous; for /from
the point of view of a plant or a stone/ the
having chanced even upon this knowing /i.e., upon
touch and tasting/ would seem to be cherishable,
but lying-dead and not-being would not." (αἴσθησιν
γὰρ ἔχουσιν, ἡ δ' αἴσθησις γνῶσίς τις. ταύτης δὲ
τὸ τίμιον καὶ ἄτιμον πολὺ διαφέρει σκοποῦσι πρὸς
φρόνησιν καὶ πρὸς τὸ τῶν ἀψύχων γένος. πρὸς μὲν
γὰρ τὸ φρονεῖν ὥσπερ οὐδὲν εἶναι δοκεῖ τὸ κοινω-
νεῖν ἀφῆς καὶ γεύσεως μόνον, πρὸς δὲ φυτὸν ἢ
λίθον θαυμάσιον· ἀγαπητὸν γὰρ ἂν δόξειε καὶ ταύτης

52

τυχεῖν τῆς γνώσεως ἀλλὰ μὴ κεῖσθαι τεθνεὸς καὶ μὴ ὄν.)

32This method is applied by Socrates at Republic 4.434e4-435a4.

33Cf. Symposium 200a5-201c5, 203d8-204b5.

34Cf. Laws 6.769a1-3 & ff.; Statesman 294a6-d2; Gorgias passim.

35Cf. Republic 5.473c11-e2; Gorgias 521d6-8.

36See Iliad 7.348-364 and context.

37Cf. Xenophon Memorabilia IV.6.1 & 13-15.

38Cf. Sophist beginning.

39Cf. Symposium 203c5 ff., the description of eros.

40Cf. Symposium 216d2-217a2, Socrates as Silenus.

41Cf. Phaedo 99c9-d1, Socrates' δεύτερος πλοῦς or second sailing, and context.

42Whether all φιλοτιμία is shameful is unclear.

43Cf. Phaedrus 257c7.

44Cf. Phaedo 62a8.

45Phaedo 117c3-4; cf. 59e8-60b1.

46See p. 3.

THE SOCRATIC MYTH

We must next turn to the <u>Phaedrus</u>, because its
mythical content is closest to the mythical content of the seventh epistle, and because it is
the most originally mythical of the purely Socratic dialogues.[1]

Perceval Frutiger has stressed the originally mythical character of the <u>Phaedrus</u> in his survey of
the sources of what he considered myths in the
Platonic dialogues, and he singles out the fable
of the cicadas and the story of Theuth as the
only two entirely original myths in Plato's works.[2]
Although Frutiger is correct to stress the originality of the <u>Phaedrus</u>, he does so for the wrong
reasons, because the brief account of the cicadas
(258e6-259d9; cf. 230c2-3) and the account of
Theuth (274c5-275b2) are not myths, i.e., they
are not explicitly called myths by either Socrates or Phaedrus. To demonstrate the originality
of the accounts in the <u>Phaedrus</u>, one does not
need to select any specified accounts, but only
to cite Phaedrus' remark to Socrates:

> O Socrates, you easily make speeches /which
> are/ Egyptian and of whatever country, if
> you are willing.[3]

In addition, approximately half the dialogue is
either mythic or a myth, as the following brief
summary will show.
    (227a1-230e5) The setting is mythic insofar
as it is pervaded by the μυθολόγημα (229c5) of
Boreas and Oreithyia, an account of the genesis

55

in eros of the overcoming of death.

(230e6-234c5) Lysias' speech is neither mythic nor a myth. It is described exclusively as a λόγος,[4] i.e., it is regarded as a set of prescriptions for behavior rooted in utility and a low desire for gratification.[5]

(234c6-237a6) This interlude culminates in a reemphasis on the setting of the dialogue.

(237a7-242a1) Socrates' Lysian speech is explicitly called a myth,[6] i.e., it describes the genesis in certain low natural compulsions[7] of the perspective which Lysias adopted in his speech. In other words, the ground of Lysias' speech is the shameful assumption that ἔρως is the vigorous unspeakable natural desire to prey upon beautiful bodies.[8]

(242a1-243e8) In this interlude Socrates expresses his awareness that he needs to compose a purificatory palinode in the manner of Stesichorus.

(243e9-257b6) Socrates' Stesichorean palinode is a purification of Socrates' shameful Lysian account of nature, i.e., it rhetorically elaborates the genesis of erotic ἔργα in the nature of the whole and the nature of the soul, in the latter case by integrating the low natural desires (the hybristic horse) into a more complete psychic schema, by giving them their due without giving short shrift to the high natural desires (the tractable horse and the reins holder). The palinode is referred to as a myth[9] and as "some mythic hymn,"[10] and as such it is the ἐρωτικὸς μῦθος which has as its counterpart the ἐρωτικοὶ λόγοι of the Symposium.[11] In other words, the palinode is the μῦθος περὶ φιλοσοφίας which has as its counterpart the λόγοι περὶ φιλοσοφίας of the Symposium.[12]

(257b7-278b6) This is a lengthy discussion of the characteristics which good writing must have, and it seems to form a long gloss on the dense and elliptical discussion of writing in the seventh epistle. This is not a myth, i.e., it is a non-genetic account.

(278b7-279c8) This is the dialogue's conclusion, and it culminates in a prayer to Pan.

Clearly, then, in accordance with the principle
enunciated earlier,[13] those sections of the Phaedrus which are routinely called myths in the literature are not myths, whereas sections of the
dialogue which are not ever characterized as
myths are indeed myths.

In addition, the connection of the Phaedrus with
the seventh epistle and the setting of the dialogue suggest that the explicit content of the
Phaedrus is to an unusually large extent for a
Platonic dialogue the teaching of Plato himself.[14]
In particular, when Socrates and Phaedrus decide
to talk in the shade of a plane tree, ἡ πλάτανος,[15]
the pun on Plato's name (ὁ Πλάτων)--which is not
surprising in a dialogue full of playful punning--
makes the suggestion very strong that the entire
discussion of the Phaedrus is carried on ὑπὸ τῇ
τοῦ Πλάτωνος σκιᾷ.

Let us begin our discussion of the Phaedrus itself[16] with the interlude following Socrates'
palinode, an interlude which has justly been
called "le pivot du Phèdre."[17]

Phaedrus' first remark (257b7-c7) after Socrates
completes his grand palinode is somewhat puzzling.
For after little more than a perfunctory response
to the palinode and a brief hierarchical ranking
of the three preceding speeches in terms of beauty
(the most beautiful being Socrates' palinode, the
next in beauty being Socrates' Lysian speech, and
the ugliest being Lysias' own speech), he fears
that Lysias' reputation would be diminished if he
should try to compete with Socrates' palinode.[18]
And the puzzling aspects of Phaedrus' remark are,
on the one hand, his apparent immunity to the
power and beauty of Socrates' palinode in any
affective way, so that his wonder leads to nothing
more than a low concern for Lysias' honor, and on
the other hand, his apparent assumption that
speechwriting is fundamentally an activity of the
political arena, an assumption which is puzzling
coming as it does after such a clearly transpoli-

tical paean to erotic craziness as Socrates' mythic hymn is. The political emphasis here is revealing in several ways. First, it suggests that
even though Phaedrus goes outside the city in his
valetudinarian quest for bodily health and vigor,[19]
psychically he is in and of the city in some decisive sense. Socrates, on the contrary, virtually
never goes bodily outside the city,[20] and yet in
some decisive sense, of all humans he is the least
in and of the city,[21] which means that he is the
most erotic.[22] Phaedrus, then, is fundamentally
non-erotic by nature, which explains why Lysias'
speech extolling the non-lover appeals so strongly
to him.

Second, it gives an important clue to understanding Lysias' speech, because it suggests that one
must read the erotic argument also as a political
argument. Indeed, the 'historical' Lysias was
first and foremost a writer of δικανικοὶ λόγοι
δημόσιοι.[23] And although he was capable of writing a λόγος ἁπλῶς ἐπιδεικτικός, and although the
private setting in which the speech was delivered
suggests such a composition, Phaedrus' concern
suggests that what we have here is an ἐπιδεικτικὸς
λόγος τε καὶ δικανικός[24] or, in other terms, an
ἐρωτικὸς λόγος τε καὶ πολιτικός. Socrates himself
had intimated as much even before he heard the
speech itself:

> Phaedrus. For /Lysias/ speaks how one must
> gratify a non-lover rather than a lover.
> Socrates. What noblesse oblige! Would that
> he would write how it is useful /to grati-
> fy/ the poor rather than the rich, and the
> older than the younger, and as many other
> things as there are /which apply/ both to
> me and to the many of us; for then his
> speeches would be urbane and beneficial to
> the populace.[25]

Therefore, any analysis of Lysias' speech which
does not take into account its political dimension
in addition to its erotic dimension will be incom-

plete.

Phaedrus' concern then expands into a fear that speechwriting as such is disgraceful or shameful. This, of course, cannot be a blanket indictment of speeches as such, because Phaedrus himself is a prodigious devotee and generator of speeches,[26] and for him to indict speeches as such would be the same as for him to indict himself as their cause (258c9-10). Phaedrus' indictment of speeches, then, is an indictment of <u>written</u> speeches which he adopts from the political men (257c5), and which he has implicitly embodied from the beginning of the dialogue when he hid the scroll of Lysias' speech under his clothing. Socrates, of course, is ὁ τῶν λόγων ἐραστής,[27] and, even more, he is diseased with the capacity for hearing about speeches,[28] and hence he rallies to the defense of speeches by pointing out that whatever the political men may say in their abuse of speechwriting, the very fact that they themselves write speeches (e.g., laws, resolutions) indicates that their indictment is not a blanket indictment of written speeches as such,[29] but of shameful and bad written speeches:[30]

> <u>Socrates</u>. Then this is clear to all, that the <u>writing</u> speeches itself then is not shameful.
> <u>Phaedrus</u>. What then?
> <u>Socrates</u>. But <u>now</u> I believe this to be shameful, /namely/ the speaking and writing not beautifully but shamefully and badly.[31]

And Socrates' defense clearly is a defense of speaking as well as of writing, i.e., it is a defense of Λόγος.[32] But every Socratic-Platonic defense is a defense against justifiable accusations, a defense which does justice to the accusations insofar as they are justifiable but which simultaneously does justice to the accused insofar as it is justifiable.[33]

And even before he denies that writing in itself is shameful, Socrates adumbrates the double-edged nature of the discussion which will follow:

> Whenever an orator or a king becomes suffi-
> cient, so that he having gotten the power of
> Lycurgus or Solon or Darius becomes an immor-
> tal speechwriter in a city, then does not he
> himself regard himself while still living to
> be the equal to a god, and do not the persons
> who come to be afterwards, when they behold
> his writings, customarily believe these same
> things about him?[34]

The use of Λόγος, then, has three consequences.
First, it enables one to become immortal, i.e.,
it has a power even beyond the political or ora-
torical power alone of Lycurgus or Solon or Dari-
us, and this power is implicitly more a power of
written speeches over and above spoken speeches
and political deeds. And although the specific
examples here suggest self-glorifying writings,
one must also consider writings which glorify
and/or immortalize others. For example, how well
would we know Socratic philosophizing without the
writings of Aristophanes, Xenophon, and Plato?
And in the case of Plato at least, the glorifying
and immortalizing of Socrates[35] is an indirect
immortalizing of Plato himself.[36] In other words,
although the explicit case here[37] is of one who
makes writings which praise himself and praise
his praisers, one can conceive of a writing which
is made as a praise of someone else, although
here too there would seem to have to be an ele-
ment, however indirect, of self-praise.[38]

Second, it results in a deification of the speech-
writer by his audience to such an extent that he
comes to regard himself as the equal of a god.[39]
This is one of the dangers of speech, that the
power which it gives one over others, whether to
rule or to enchant, is reflected back from the
others onto the writer himself, so as to evoke in
him an excessive self-regard. And the height of
conceit or hybris is to regard oneself as equal
to a god while living, something which is fitting
for no human.[40]

Third, future readers of writings also will regard the speechwriter as an immortal equal to a
god. Indeed, it will be customary (νομίζουσι) for
them to do so. Can there be a sober understanding
of this apparently hyperbolic claim? I believe
that there can, if one takes seriously the demand
that is placed on writings in the Phaedrus,[41]
namely that every writing must be composed as a
ζῷον according to a logographic compulsion. Or as
Socrates puts it elsewhere:

> For the speech now appears to me to be worked
> forth as some non-bodily cosmos for the pur-
> pose of ruling an ensouled body.[42]

If the making of a speech (whether spoken or written) is properly done only if one makes the speech
as a ζῷον or a κόσμος, and if the making a ζῷον or
a κόσμος is a work for a god or one who is similar
to a god,[43] then the maker of a speech is in a
sense ἰσόθεος[44] and must be regarded so if through
time he is regarded as a writer who writes in a
beautiful way.

Finally, the explicit question for the remaining
discussion is asked:

> Socrates. Therefore what is the manner of
> writing both beautifully and not /beautifully7?[45]

The discussion will apply to all writers, future
as well as past, and it will make no difference
whether their writings are political or private
(ἰδιωτικόν), whether they are in meter as a poet's
are or are without meter as a prosewriter's (ἰδιώτης) are (258e8-11). In short, from Socrates'
point of view at least, the discussion of writing
in the Phaedrus is applicable to any writing
whatsoever which, so to speak, deserves the name
of writing.

But before the general question about writing is
faced, Socrates deflects Phaedrus' attention and
ours toward the cicadas. Why? Let us examine

Socrates' remarks and see.

At first, there were humans, but no Muses. Then
the Muses came to be and by their coming to be
(οὕτως) songs somehow appeared. What does this
signify? The Muses are the daughters of Zeus and
Mnemosyne, i.e., of philosophy and memory.[46] In
other words, the Muses are philosophical reminders.[47] But what is the manner of this reminding?
It is indicated when Socrates first mentions the
cicadas (258e7–259a1): it is διαλέγεσθαι (conversing), and conversation is treated here as identical to singing.[48] In other words, when the
cicadas are διαλεγόμενοι ἀλλήλοις, the sound of
their conversation is what we regard as their
singing (ᾄδοντες). In the same way, I suggest,
the appearance of songs with the Muses is equivalent to the appearance among humans of διαλεκτική,
both in the ordinary sense and in the service of
philosophical inquiry.[49] Before the Muses came to
be, then, speech must have been atomic or totally
idiosyncratic or a chaotic manifold of noises. In
other words, for speech to become a genuine means
of interanthropic communication, memory had to
arise, and the Muses as the progeny of memory
(Mnemosyne) are the expression of that. So we may
restate the first stage in the account of the
cicadas thus: at first, there were humans, but
their speech was a chaotic manifold of noise, because they had neither memory nor διαλεκτική.
This is very reminiscent of the movement of the
soul which Socrates describes in the Republic:

> Then only the skillfully conversational method
> proceeds in this way, taking out the hypothe-
> ses, to the beginning itself, so that it will
> become steadfast, and it gently drags the
> soul's seeing thing which has been sunk down
> beingly in some barbaric bog and leads it up
> upward, using the arts which we narrated as
> /being its/ co-laborers and co-leaders-around.[50]

The songs which arise, then, signify the dialectical method and the arts which it uses to reach

an unhypothetical beginning of something.[51] This may explain why in the account of the discussion between Theuth and Thamus (274e1-4), all the arts except writing are omitted, namely because in the cicada interlude and the discussion which follows, their function has at least been adumbrated.

Once conversational skill (i.e., singing) comes to be among humans, some humans are smitten by the pleasure (ὑφ' ἡδονῆς) which they derive from it:

> They are gratified hearing humans being exa-
> mined, and many times they themselves imitate
> me, and then they take it in hand to examine
> others.....................................
> For it is not unpleasant.[52]

Those who are overcome by the pleasure of dialectic become unconcerned about food and drink. The most massive example of this in the Platonic corpus is the Republic, in which the interlocutors never partake of the dinner promised by Polemarchus.[53] And the explicit connection between this attitude and philosophy is made by Socrates in the Phaedo:

> "Does it appear to you to be /proper/ for
> a philosopher, who is a man, to have been
> serious in respect to suchlike so-called
> pleasures, such as about foods and drinks?"
> "Least so, o Socrates," Simmias asserted.
> "And what of the /pleasures/ of sexual
> activities?"
> "In no way."[54]

Although in the Phaedrus interlude, there is no explicit mention of τὰ ἀφροδίσια, they too are meant, as one can see if one considers that Aristophanes asserts in his λόγος at the banquet that before Zeus moved humans' genitals to the front of their bodies, humans "used to generate and bring forth not into each other but into the earth, as cicadas do."[55] But whereas for Aristophanes, distinctly human sexuality is the compul-

63

sory tragic way for approaching without ever
achieving our originary bodily unity, which as
such is all that we desire, for Socrates, human
progress is toward a freedom from the tyranny of
distinctly human sexuality (which is not an absti-
nence) toward a psychic sexuality, the full extent
of which he sketches in his great mythic palinode.

The singing humans, then, become unconcerned about
sex,[56] food, and drink, and they sing (converse)
until they come to their end without even noticing
it and then metamorphose into cicadas. But how
could they experience death without noticing it?
Clearly, their transformation into cicadas was
instantaneous,[57] so that their singing (conversing) was uninterrupted, for since they were aware
of it and it alone, only if it were interrupted
would they have noticed a change. Διαλεκτική, then,
is a means to a sort of immortality, although
clearly not to any individual immortality.

And for the humans who were consumed, as it were,
by the pleasure of singing (conversing), their
being themselves means their singing εὐθὺς...ἕως
ἂν τελευτήσῃ (259c4-5), i.e., conversing from
birth until death, and their knowing themselves
means their becoming themselves only insofar as
they are capable of continuously exhibiting their
nature as singer-conversationalists. And the continuous exhibiting of their nature means the
abandonment of a human body for the body of a cicada, so that they are cicadas in body but still
distinctly human in their νοῦς. In other words,
each is a monster, a monstrous nature, and although each may be "an animal both gentler and
simpler /than Typhon/, /an animal/ partaking of
a certain divine and non-fuming portion by nature,"[58] still each is one member of "a mob...of
certain monstrous natures."[59] And the example of
the cicadas suggests that to recognize (γνῶναι)
oneself, κατὰ τὸ Δελφικὸν γράμμα (229e5-6), is to
recognize in oneself the look, τὸ εἶδος (cf. 229
d5-6), of a monster, i.e., the tasks of knowing
oneself and σοφίζεσθαι τὰ μυθολογήματα (cf. 229c7)
are not different, but rather to do one is to do

the other.[60]

Furthermore, although the cicadas die, τὸ τεττίγων γένος (259c2) persists. The race, then, must perpetuate itself. But how? As we have seen, they generate into the earth. As R.G. Bury asserts: "the female lays her eggs in the sand, where the young are hatched out by the sun's heat."[61] It is now noon (ἐν μεσημβρίᾳ, 259a2), i.e., the sun's heat is perfect for the propagation of the cicadas. But there is no laying of eggs. What form, then, does their propagation take here? I.e., what do they bestow in order to perpetuate themselves? On humans who converse, i.e., on humans who act as the cicadas did when they were humans, the cicadas bestow the gift which they have from the gods, the Muses,[62] and that gift is the not needing nurture (e.g., food and drink) in any way. So, ἄνθρωποι διαλεκτικοί are the recipients of a lack of concern for nurture, and this unconcern will result in the metamorphosis of new humans into new cicadas. Therefore, the perpetuation of the race of cicadas depends on the perpetuation of διαλεκτική among some humans at least,[63] a perpetuation which is difficult to achieve because most humans doze on account of the idleness[64] of their thinking. That is, most humans behave like slaves, which is to say like sheep or like "a horse /which is/ more sluggish and needs to be wakened."[65] However, some humans doze under the very influence of the cicadas conversing, and these are beguiled by the cicadas themselves,[66] which means, I believe, that if διαλεκτική is used as an empty method, it does not produce knowledge, but rather produces a destructive skepticism and the conceit of believing oneself to know when one in fact does not know.[67] In other words, whatever positive function it may serve, διαλεκτική can beguile humans into thoughtlessness and it can lure them by its siren song to destruction.[68]

How is one to prevent this? Presumably by energizing, i.e., putting to work, one's διάνοια.[69] And indeed the discussion which follows the interlude

is a discussion of the requirements for knowledge[70] in a speaker or writer, and it culminates
in a description of how "it is obligatory to
think through about any nature whatever."[71] And
insofar as the speaking about this of Socrates
and Phaedrus is a conversing which prevents the
laughable dozing of their διάνοια, they are
enacting the very method about which they are
conversing (cf. 259d7-9). And only those who are
capable of doing this should be called skilled
conversationalists or dialecticians.[72] We will
return to this method, but first let us consider
the deities which preside over διάνοια κατὰ ἐνέρ-
γειαν, or τὸ διαλέγεσθαι, or ἡ φιλοσοφία. These
deities are the Muses, or rather some of the Muses.
When Socrates lists the Muses to whom the dead
cicadas report, i.e., the Muses to whom disembodied conversing reports, he lists only four (Terpsichore, Erato, Kalliope, and Ourania) and apparently singles out two (Kalliope, Ourania) as the
Muses of philosophy. Yet the context would suggest that all of the Muses mentioned would have
something to do with philosophy (διαλεκτική). Why
else would Socrates mention them? I mean, since
he does not list all nine Muses, and since he is
distinguishing humans who converse from humans
who do not, i.e., humans who are dialectical from
humans who are not, the suggestion is very strong
that all the Muses whom he explicitly mentions
are the Muses of philosophy.[73] Why, then, does it
seem that persons passing time in philosophy[74]
are announced to the Kalliope-Ourania pair of
yoke-Muses? It seems so because the precise way
in which Socrates phrases his remark here is over-
looked. Socrates has said that the cicadas announce to the Muses "who of those here honor
which of them."[75] He adds that the announcement is
"in accordance with the look of each honor."[76] In
other words, the determining factor is what one
honors, not what one does. And when Socrates
speaks of those who are announced to Kalliope and
Ourania, he speaks of them as honoring the music
of Kalliope and Ourania.[77] Clearly, simply with
respect to being announced to these two Muses,
this latter criterion alone would seem to be suf-

ficient. But Socrates says that those are announced who <u>both</u> engage in philosophy <u>and</u> honor
their music.[78] Why? I would suggest that the
double requirement indicates that the Muses for
those who simply engage in philosophy are Terpsichore and Erato. Is there any other evidence to
support this? There is. First, I believe that
Terpsichore, whose name means 'delight in choral
activities,' and whose honorers are the honorers
of choruses,[79] is intended as the Muse of ἡ διαλεκτική, i.e., τὸ διαλέγεσθαι. This function is
suggested by the following considerations. When
Socrates makes his Lysian speech, he begins with
an invocation to shrill Muses.[80] And the only
other group of beings in the dialogue who are described by shrillness are the cicadas, whose song
is said to produce a shrill echo.[81] In addition,
later (263d3-4) the cicadas are called those who
talk for the Muses. There is, then, an extremely
close connection between the cicadas and the
Muses, and in particular between the cicadas and
Terpsichore, because the cicadas in their singing-
conversing are called a chorus.[82] In other words,
τὸ διαλέγεσθαι is a choral activity and as such it
falls within the province of Terpsichore, the dialectic Muse, who represents one aspect of engaging
in philosophy. And insofar as Terpsichore presides
over cicadian immortal dialectic and insofar as
the way of the cicadas is in a sense a dying and
being dead, i.e., insofar as the proto-cicadian
humans and the post-human cicadas represent the
practice of dying and being dead in the service of
the immortality of speech, the <u>Phaedo</u> is an elaboration of the Terpsichorean aspect of philosophy
(cf. <u>Phaedo</u> 63e8 ff., 89b9-c1, 88e2).

Second, Erato, whose name means 'lovable' or
'lovely,' and whose honorers are the honorers of
the erotic things,[83] is intended as the Muse of ἡ
φιλοσοφία as the erotic striving to be with the
beings themselves, to see the beings in their nature.[84] The identification between philosophy and
erotics is a strong one in Plato, especially in
the person of Socrates. Socrates goes so far as to
claim that he knows nothing but the erotic things[8]

and that he can recognize a lover or a beloved.[86]
Further, he recognizes himself as a lover, a lover of speeches and of young men.[87] And not only
is the philosopher an ἐραστής and ἐρωτικός, but
philosophy too is an ἔρως and ἐρωτική, and this
is its Eratonic aspect. For example, in the Symposium, the speeches spoken at the banquet are
first called "erotic speeches"[88] and then "speeches about philosophy,"[89] thus suggesting that in
a sense at least philosophy is identical to the
erotic.[90] In addition, Diotima explicitly demon-
strates that Ἔρως is a philosopher:

> "For it holds thus. None of the gods philo-
> sophizes or desires to become wise--for /each/
> is /wise/--nor if any other is wise, does he
> philosophize or desire to become wise...."
>
> "Therefore, who, o Diotima," I asserted,
> "are the philosophizers, if they are neither
> the wise nor the unlearned?"
>
> "Indeed this then is clear," she asserted,
> "already even to a child, that they are the
> persons between both, among whom also Eros
> would be. For indeed wisdom is among the most
> beautiful things, and Eros is eros in respect
> to the beautiful, so that it is compulsory
> for Eros to be a philosopher, and /for Eros/
> being a philosopher to be between wise and
> unlearned."[91]

The Symposium, then, is an elaboration of the Eratonic aspect of philosophy.

But if Terpsichore and Erato are the Muses of philosophy, of what are Kalliope and Ourania the
Muses? They are not simply, as there is a tendency
to assume,[92] concerned with the divine and the
human heaven and divine and human speeches,[93] for
all the Muses are concerned with these to some degree, although Kalliope and Ourania are especially
concerned with them.[94] So, their concern with divine and human heaven and speeches does not as
such distinguish them by kind from the other Muses
but only by degree. Nor does their music,[95] i.e.,
that they throw off the most beautiful sound,[96]

distinguish them by kind from the other Muses but only by degree. Kalliope and Ourania, then, are the superlative Muses, superlative in their concern and in the beauty of their sound and in age (cf. 259d3-4). Since the other two Muses represent ἡ φιλοσοφία, what is the superlative, as it were, of philosophy? I would suggest that it is ἡ σοφία, and that Kalliope and Ourania are the Muses of wisdom. And while philosophy may be the greatest music,[97] still "the most beautiful and greatest of the consonances would most justly be spoken to be the greatest wisdom."[98] And if "the true Muse /is/ the one /which is/ together with both speeches and philosophy,"[99] then the truest Muse is the one which is together with wisdom. But what is wisdom? On the one hand, it is beholding or contemplating, and this is presided over by Kalliope, as her name suggests. For although the usual derivation of Kalliope is from beautiful voice (ὄψ), one could also derive it from beautiful eye (ὄψ).[100] And certainly the derivation 'beautiful eye' would be more consistent with the imagery of Socrates' mythic palinode, in which there is, it seems to me, a greater density of vision terms than in any other Socratic utterance: as Socrates says, "the beingness which beingly is, is a spectacle,"[101] and this spectacle is also a sight, an ὄψις,[102] i.e., an ὄψ, namely--to use the word in both its subjective and objective meanings (cf. 250d3 to 250b6-7)--the seeing a sight. And it sees two things, both represented by Ourania, the divine heaven and the human heaven.[103] In other words, it sees the οὐρανὸς ὁρατός (τόπος ὁρατός[104] or οὐράνιος τόπος) and it sees the οὐρανὸς νοητός (τόπος νοητός[105] or ὑπερουράνιος τόπος[106]).[107] Thus, ἡ Οὐρανία represents τὰ οὐράνια, the heavenly things,[108] of which the beholding or contemplating constitutes wisdom,[109] and toward which the erotic striving and conversing constitute philosophy.

The final aspect of the Muses of wisdom is their especial concern with divine and human speeches. What is meant by this? To answer this question, we must look to the Phaedo, where the same two

types of speeches are distinguished by Simmias, a
superlative Phaedrus[110] (italics mine):

> for /it seems to me/ to be obligatory to acti-
> vate some one then of these things, either to
> learn /from someone else/ in what way it holds
> or to find /it for oneself/ or, if these things
> are impossible, /it seems to be obligatory/ for
> a person who has grasped the best and hardest
> to refute of human speeches, being carried on
> this as on a float-raft to sail through his
> lifetime running a risk, unless someone should
> be capable of proceeding through /his life-
> time/ more unfalteringly and in a less risky
> way on a more steadfast carriage, a certain
> divine speech.[111]

Clearly, the best way, the first sailing, as it
were, is the way of the divine speech, while the
second best way, the second sailing (cf. διαπλεῦσαι
at Phaedo 85d2 to τὸν δεύτερον πλοῦν at 99c9-d1),
is the way of human speeches. But what is the difference between divine speech and human speech,
between a divine λόγος and a human λόγος? The answer to this is suggested in Socrates' philosophical autobiography, in the contrast which he draws
between his first and second sailings, which could
be referred to as his searches first for divine
and then for human λόγοι. If this is so, then divine speeches would be speeches which concern the
final causes of phenomena, the causes of their
being better in the way that they are.[112] Ultimately, this means that the λόγος θεῖος is the
μῦθος λέγων τὸ ἀγαθὸν αὐτό, the myth which bespeaks the good itself.[113] Perhaps such a μῦθος
is utopian:

> "But, o blessed ones, what ever is the good
> itself let us let go for the now being--for
> it appears to me more than in accordance with
> our present impulse to hit what seems so to
> me for the things now--but what appears to me
> to be a progeny of the good and most similar
> to it I am willing to speak, if it is also
> friendly to you, but if not to let it go."

70

> "But speak," /Glaucon/ said, "for you will
> pay off the narrating of the father at another
> time."
> "I would wish," I spoke, "for me to_be capa-
> ble of giving_it /i.e., the narrating/ forth
> and for you /to be capable/ of receiving it
> itself, but not, as now, only the interest.
> And therefore indeed receive this interest
> and progeny of the good itself."[114]

The promise of a future narrating of the good itself seems to be an unfulfilled promise for the
Platonic corpus, and that makes the suggestion
that such a μῦθος is utopian very strong indeed.[115]

And in the Phaedrus, it is suggested that the μῦθος
of the soul is as utopian as the μῦθος of the good
itself seems to be, and that the divine μῦθος of
soul must be abandoned in favor of the human μῦθος:

> Of what sort it is, is for a narrating which is
> everywhere in every way divine and long, but_to
> what it is like /is for a narrating which is/
> both human and lesser; therefore in this way
> /i.e., in the human and lesser way/ let us
> speak.[116]

On the other hand, the μῦθος of the superheavenly
place is suggested to be a divine μῦθος:

> But not any poet of those here yet hymned or
> ever will hymn the superheavenly place in
> accordance with its worth. But it holds thus
> --for one must dare to speak the true thing
> then, both otherwise and for a person speak-
> ing about truth....[117]

Socrates' mythic palinode, then, is a combination
of a human and a divine Λόγος ἢ μῦθος, and hence
it especially does honor to Kalliope and Ourania.
In addition, insofar as it is Stesichorean (cf.
244a2), i.e., insofar as it is for the purpose of
setting up choruses or choral activities,[118] it
does honor to Terpsichore,[119] and insofar as it
is concerned with erotic things, it does honor to

Erato. It is not surprising, therefore, that when
it is completed, the conversing of the cicadas is
heard, presumably announcing to these Muses that
they have been honored. And it is to the speech
by which they have been honored, the mythic palinode, that we must now turn.[120]

The occasion for the palinode is Socrates' reali-
zation that his Lysian myth speech was shameful
and wrong, and that he, the progenitor of the
speech, needs to purify himself so as to forestall
the punishment of blindness which is meted out to
those who lie in published speech, whether the lie
be about something divine (e.g., Eros or nature)
or about something human (e.g., Helen). That blindness as a punishment is severe in the extreme becomes clear later in the myth, as we will see. The
two liars to whom Socrates refers in this connection are Homer and Stesichorus, the former of whom
failed to recant his lie and hence remained blind
and the latter of whom "having made all the so-
called Palinode on the spot gazed again."[121] Since
for us, as also undoubtedly for the Hellenes, the
Homeric lie prevailed over the Stesichorean recantation, and since Socrates surely knew this, one
must wonder whether the Socratic Lysian myth error,
all recantation notwithstanding, will prevail over
the Socratic Stesichorean myth correction of that
error, i.e., whether the view of eros and nature
as animated by a low predatoriness and desire for
success will prevail over the view of eros and
nature as animated and nourished by a lofty eidetic vision and banquet.[122]

The introduction to the palinode is in two parts,
a genealogy and a classification.[123]

The genealogy re-stresses the contrast between the
Lysian perspective and the Socratic perspective.
The progeneration of Socrates' Lysian speech (and
by extension, insofar as Socrates' Lysian speech
reveals the genesis of the perspective of Lysias'
own epideictic speech, the progeneration of Lysias' enscrolled speech) is attributed to the desire

of a man (ἀνδρός) for the radiantly beautiful
(Φαίδρου) body of another man, and its inspiration is Apollonian (τοῦ Πυθοκλέους), i.e., its
inspiration is the traditional muses,[124] the muses of Homer,[125] who, it is suggested, are amusical by contrast to the truly musical Stesichorean
muses.[126] And the Apollonian muses, who are identical to the Homeric muses, are concerned with
the power of song and low erotic success (both
heterosexual and homosexual),[127] and they are
concerned with fame.[128] In addition, Apollo became identified with sobriety (μηδὲν ἄγαν) after
leading a life of excess.[129] In short, Apollo is
an appropriate god for a lover whose desire is a
compulsion[130] in a world characterized by compulsion, a lover who uses sobriety in the service of
excess,[131] namely a coldly calculating lover of
the type which Lysias and Socrates pretend to be
in their combined speeches. On the other hand,
the progeneration of Socrates' Socratic speech is
grounded in the establishment of choral activities (Στησιχόρου), which means grounded in dialectic,[132] and it contains no blasphemy (τοῦ
Εὐφήμου).[133] In addition, it is Himeraian ('Ιμε-
ραίου), i.e., it expresses the gentle (ἥμερος)
longing (ἵμερος)[134] for day (ἡμέρα) to come out
of darkness,[135] i.e., for knowledge to dissipate
ignorance.

In short, then, the Lysian perspective of savage
sobriety will be replaced by the Socratic perspective of gentle craziness, but with the implicit suggestion that these two perspectives, the
low and the high, are not simply unrelated, but
rather that the high is a purified[136] version of
the low.

Now Socrates turns to his classification of the
kinds of craziness,[137] and he begins by denying
that it is obligatory for the non-lover to be
gratified because he is sober or moderate (σωφρο-
νεῖ) while the lover is crazy (μαίνεται). And to
assert such a thing is to assert what is both not
beautiful and not true, the not beautiful being
the assertion that craziness is simply bad[138] and

the not true being the assertion that one should
gratify a non-lover. The truth of the simple
goodness or badness of craziness is not explicitly decided, but it is clear that even if craziness
is not simply bad, it does not follow therefrom
that it is simply good. Indeed the craziness which
generates the biggest goods is the craziness which
is given by a divine gift, which suggests that
there is a human craziness[139] which at the least
generates lesser goods and at most generates
bads.[140]

The διαίρεσις of craziness into human and divine
then yields to a further διαίρεσις of divine craziness alone[141] into three: (1) 244a8-d5, divination (μαντική); (2) 244d5-245a1, solvent (λύσις);
(3) 245a1-8, poetizing (ποίησις). Then (245b1-c4)
in what appears to be a conclusion from the other
three, Socrates adds what then appears to be a
fourth, love (ἔρως).[142]

Several things should be observed about this classification. First, an implicit bisection runs
through it, so as to suggest the following two
sets of categories:

$$\text{craziness}$$

(1)	divine (or by divine portion/ gift)	human[143]
(2)	τὸ κεκινῆσθαι	moderation[144]
(3)	beautiful	ugly[145]
(4)	complete	incomplete[146]
(5)	inspiration and τέχνη together	τέχνη alone[147]
(6)	correct	in error[148]
(7)	ancient	new[149]

Presumably, then, such a division could be made of
each of the four types of craziness.[150]

In addition, the four kinds look very much like
Apollo's four powers,[151] with the exception that

ἔρως replaces τοξική.[152] Is there, then, some
connection between erotic activity and archery?
Perhaps there is, if one considers the analogy
between them which could be based on the arrow's
trajectory, an ascent followed by a descent much
like the course of the soul as described in the
palinode or the journey of the released prisoner
in the image of the cave. The difference, however,
would be that for eros, the target would be at the
peak of the curve rather than at the end of its
descent where the arrow becomes fixed and untransmovable, and for eros, the target and the arrow
together would keep moving. And the difference in
the placing of the targets roughly corresponds to
the difference between the Apollonian-Lysian perspective (target low) and the Stesichorean-Socra-
tic perspective (target high). And the difference
between the way of ἔρως and the way of ἡ τοῦ
Ἀπόλλωνος τοξική is the difference between the
way of knowledge and the way of opinion,[153] as
Socrates suggests (italics mine):

> Socrates. "Opinion" indeed has been so
> nicknamed either by the chasing with respect
> to which the soul proceeds chasing the en-
> visioning in whatever way things hold, or
> by the throwing from the bow. And it is more
> like this latter.[154]

The way of the bow, of Apollo, of the arrow fixed
in the target, is the way of δόξα.

Finally, although the kinds are presented as four,
the equivocal way in which ἔρως appears suggests
that it is the fundamental kind, that erotic craziness is the root of the other three.

Divine craziness, then, is that through which the
biggest goods and beautifuls come to us (244a6-8)
and bads are loosed from us (244d5-245a1), that
through which the soul is awakened and intoxicated
(245a3-4), and that through which the greatest
good luck comes to us (245b7-c1). In addition, it
is that which corrects us (244b4-5),[155] educates
us (245a4-5), and benefits us (245b4-6). And al-

though this is not explicitly stated here, divine craziness is a craziness of the soul, and hence in order to understand it, it is necessary to see its πάθη and ἔργα (245c3-4) and to intellectually intuit the truth about the nature of divine and human soul.[156] This intellective seeing and intuition will be a showing forth.[157] And the beginning of this ἀπόδειξις is the conclusion that "all soul is deathless,"[158] and what follows is a dense and elliptical triad of arguments (argument 1 at 245c5-8, argument 2 at 245c8-e2, argument 3 at 245e2-6) followed by a concluding statement (245e6-246a3).

Argument 1 is the most elliptical of the three:

> Conclusion: all soul is deathless.
> (1) the always movable is deathless.
> (2)(a) the other moving and moved is not always moving.
> (2)(b) the not moving is the not living.
> (3) the self-moving is always itself.

What is missing here is a series of steps which involve the double character of soul κατὰ φύσιν as cause of life and cause of motion, i.e., a series of steps based on Socrates' analysis of the name 'soul':

> /Socrates./ I believe the persons who named the soul intellectually intuited something suchlike, how then this, when it be present to the body, is the cause for it of living, furnishing it the power of breathing in and recooling /i.e., reviving/ it, and simultaneously when the recooling is left out of it the body both is destroyed and comes to an end; whence indeed they seem to me to have called it 'soul.'
> ....
> What seems to you both to hold and to carry the nature of all the body, so as for it both to live and to go around, other than soul?
> Hermogenes. None other.

76

Socrates. And what /of this/? Do you not also
trust Anaxagoras /who asserted/ intellect and
soul to be that which thoroughly orders and holds
the nature of all other things?

Hermogenes. I at any rate do.

Socrates. Then this name would hold beautifully /for/ nicknaming this power which carries
and holds nature, 'nature-holder.' And it is
permissible also for a person who is refined to
speak /this to be/ 'soul.'

Hermogenes. Therefore altogether so, and this
seems to me at any rate to be more artful than
that / i.e., onomatogenesis 1/.

Socrates. For also it is; yet how it, being
named so truly, was posited appears laughable.[159]

So, soul as a nature has a double character, although both the Phaedrus and the Cratylus agree
that of life and motion, motion is the more fundamental. On this basis, then, the first Phaedrus
argument would have to be completed thus (additions in brackets):

(1) the always movable is deathless.

(2)(a) the other moving and moved is not
(always) moving.

(b) the not moving is not living.

/(c) the other moving and moved is not
(always) living./

/(d) the other moving and moved (sometimes) dies./

/(e) the other moving and moved is not
deathless./

(3)(a) the self-moving is always itself.

/(b) the always movable is always moving./

/(c) the moving is the living./

/(d) the always movable is always living./

/(e) the self-moving always itself is the
self-movable always itself./

/(f) the self-movable always itself is
always movable./[160]

/(g) the self-movable always itself is
always living./

/(h) the self-movable always itself never
dies./

77

/‾(i) the self-movable always itself is deathless._/
    /‾(j) soul is the self-movable always itself./
    /‾(k) soul is deathless._/

The problem with the argument is that it does not prove that soul is deathless, because such a conclusion depends upon the undemonstrated step (3)(j), that soul is the self-movable always itself. One therefore expects the second argument to provide a demonstration of this, but that expectation is unfulfilled, although argument three returns to it with the tentative but still apparently undemonstrated assertion (245e2-3) that "the thing which is moved by itself has appeared to be deathless," and that soul's beingness and speech is self-moving, an assertion which is made in such a way as to suggest that it has been demonstrated. With this in mind, then, let us turn to the second argument.

The second argument is composed of an introductory statement (245c8-9) followed by three parts, one part (245d1-6) which positively elaborates the double character of the ἀρχή of moving (ungeneratable, d1-3; uncorruptable, d3-6), a second part (245d6-8) which positively returns to the self-moving always itself, and a third part (245d8-e2) which apparently negatively establishes what has already been positively established. And the second argument is full by comparison to the bareness of the first argument, a fullness which may derive from its tautological generality. This argument is the following (additions in brackets):

    Introductory statement: the moving self-movable always itself is the ἀρχή and fountain[161] of the moving of the other movable.
    (1)(a) the ἀρχή of moving is ungeneratable.
        (a₁) everything which becomes, becomes from an ἀρχή.
        (a₂) the ἀρχή itself becomes from nothing.
        (a₃) if an ἀρχή became from anything, it could not have become from an ἀρχή.[162]

(b) the ἀρχή of moving is uncorruptable.

(b₁) the ungeneratable is uncorruptable.

(b₂) if (1)(a₁), then if the ἀρχή is destroyed, i.e., totally corrupted, the ἀρχή itself will not become again and none of the things which would have become from it will become from it.

(2) the self-moving always itself is the ἀρχή of moving.

(a) the ἀρχή of moving is indestructible and unbecomable.

/̄(b) the self-moving always itself is indestructible and unbecomable./̄

/̄(c) the indestructible and unbecomable is deathless./̄

/̄(d) the self-moving always itself is deathless (cf. argument 1, (3)(g)-(i))./̄

/̄(e) soul is the self-moving always itself (cf. argument 1, (3)(e) and (j))./̄

/̄(f) soul is deathless./̄

(3) /̄reductio ad absurdum/̄

(a) the self-moving always itself (=the ἀρχή of moving) would be destroyed or would become.

/̄(b) moving would be destroyed./̄

(c) all heaven and all genesis would fall together and stand still.¹⁶³

(d) the still-standing all will have nothing from which to ever come to be moving again.

/̄(e) the self-moving always itself is always moving (cf. argument 1, (3)(a), (b), and (e))./̄

/̄(f) the ἀρχή of moving can neither be destroyed nor become./̄

/̄(g) the indestructible and unbecomable is deathless (cf. this argument, (2)(c))./̄

/̄(h) the ἀρχή of moving is deathless./̄

/̄(i) soul is the ἀρχή of moving./̄

/̄(j) soul is deathless./̄

The second argument, then, generalizes the showing of soul's deathlessness in such a way as to suggest that the deathlessness of every (distributive 'all') soul is derived from the deathless-

ness of all (collective 'all') soul, that all soul
is the cosmic soul, and that the cosmos is a living thing.[164]

The third and final argument consists not of syl-
logistic reasoning but rather of two sets of
assertions (self-moving at 245e2-4, other moving
at 245e4-6) thus:

(1) self-moving
    (a) the self-moving has appeared to be
deathless.
    (b) self-moving is the beingness and
speech of soul.
(2) other moving
    (a) all[165] body which is moved only
from outside is unsouled.
    (b) all[165] body which is moved from
inside is ensouled.
    (c) moving from inside is the nature
of soul.

This argument adds a new dimension to the discussion of soul by asserting what has been implicit
all along, that in addition to its double natural
character, soul has a non-natural character. In
other words, soul may be regarded as a nature, on
the one hand, and as an οὐσία and λόγος,[166] on
the other, and these two aspects of soul roughly
correspond to soul insofar as it is partitive and
embodied (nature), on the one hand, and soul insofar as it is simple unembodied intellectual intuition (οὐσία and λόγος), on the other.[167] This is
the problem of the soul in its being in the world
and the soul as the knower of its own being in
the world, of the soul as other moving and the
soul as self-moving. And broadly speaking, the
Timaeus treats the soul in its genesis as a nature (and hence is a physiological myth)[168]
whereas the rest of Socrates' palinode treats the
soul in its genesis as a beingness and speech
(and hence is an ousiological myth). Whether
these two aspects of soul can ever be satisfacto-
rily put together is a problem which in our present context we must leave open,[169] as Socrates

does implicitly by concluding (245e6-246a2: italics mine):

> And <u>if</u> this holds thus, /<u>namely</u>/ <u>if the same</u>
> <u>thing moving itself is</u> nothing other than
> <u>soul</u>, from compulsion soul would be both
> ungenerated and deathless.[170]

I believe that he means that if soul is <u>only</u> self-
moving, then it is deathless, but since it is not,
its deathlessness in any literal sense at least is
problematic at best.

And this may explain why[171] when the gods and
their followers ascend to the subheavenly loop
(τὴν ὑπουράνιον ἁψῖδα, 247a8-b1) on their way to
the divine meal and feast[172] in the superheavenly
place (Τὸν...ὑπερουράνιον τόπον, 247c3) where
intellectual intuition may feed on the beingly
being[173] and the true (cf. τἀληθῆ, 247d4),[174]--
this may explain why "Hestia remains alone in the
house of the gods."[175] But to flesh out the explanation, we must again turn to the <u>Cratylus</u>[176]:

> Socrates. Therefore are we not to begin from
> Hestia, in accordance with law?
> Hermogenes. Therefore it is just at any rate.
> Socrates. Therefore what would someone assert
> the person who has named Hestia to have thought
> through to name /her/?
> Hermogenes. By Zeus, I believe not even this
> to be easy.
> Socrates. Therefore then, o good Hermogenes,
> the first name positers run the risk of being
> not mean but speakers about things in midair
> and idle chatterers.
> Hermogenes. Indeed what?
> Socrates. The positing of names appears to
> me /to be the work/ of certain such humans,
> and if anyone reconsiders foreign names, none-
> theless he will refind what each /name/ wishes
> /to be/. There are those who call such as also
> in this which we call 'beingness' 'beness,' and
> /there are those/ who in turn /call it/ 'pushi-
> ness.' Therefore first in accordance with the

other name of these, the beingness of things
has a speech for being called 'Hestia,' and
in that then in turn we assert the thing
partaking of beingness /to be/ 'is,' also in
accordance with this Hestia would be called
so correctly; for we too are likely to call
beingness the ancient 'beness.' And in addition also in accordance with sacrifices,
anyone who has internally intellectually
intuited would regard the positers to intellectually intuit these things thus; for the
sacrificing to Hestia first before all gods
is likely for those persons who nicknamed
the beingness of all things 'beness.' And in
turn as many persons as /nicknamed it/
'pushiness,' these persons in turn almost
somehow, in accordance with Herakleitos,
would regard all the beings to go and none
to remain; therefore /they would regard/
the cause and leading-ruling-beginning of
them to be the thing pushing, whence indeed
/they would regard/ its having been named
'pushiness' to hold beautifully. And indeed
let these things be spoken in this way as
though by persons having envisioned next
to nothing....[177]

In other words, Hestia represents the two apparently irreconcilable but equally compelling aspects of soul, the ousiological as represented
by the 'is' (the ἔστιν) and the physiological as
represented by the 'pushiness' (the ὠσία). And to
these two aspects of soul, there correspond two
apparently irreconcilable but equally compelling
accounts of the whole,[178] the Parmenidean and the
Herakleitean. And the conjunction of these two
aspects in Hestia finds its living embodiment in
Socrates:

/Euthyphro./ for he /i.e., Meletus/, by
taking it in hand to do injustice to you
/i.e., to Socrates/, absolutely seems to me
to begin to work something bad for the city
/by beginning/ from its Hestia /i.e., from
Socrates/.[179]

82

Socrates, then, mediates, and by mediating somehow unifies, the Parmenidean and Herakleitean
perspectives, and one example of this mediation is
his conversation with Cratylus and Hermogenes,[180]
the former of whom begins with an onomatic crypto-
Parmenideanism and ends with an onomatic Heraklei-
teanism, and the latter of whom undergoes the re-
verse movement: and it is Socrates who effects the
change, and only Socrates can be, as it were, in
both places at the same time, whereas Cratylus and
Hermogenes can be in only one or the other. And
the being in two places at the same time seems to
be the essential characteristic of eros, which is
simultaneously a lack and a fullness,[181] a poverty
and a resource,[182] the first born and the youngest,[183] a capability and a willingness,[184] a
reins-holder and two good and beautiful horses
(cf. 246a6-8).

And in the likeness of the soul which Socrates
constructs, if the reins-holder is νοῦς, then the
good horse would be purified ἔρως, and the bad
horse would be unpurified ἔρως (thymoeidetic epithymia).[185] And the divine soul--the soul to
which the philosopher is near (cf. 249c5-6, d1)--
is a soul which consists of νοῦς and purified ἔρως
moving together toward a vision[186] of the beingly
being beingness,[187] a vision which eventuates in
the energizing (inspiring) of the philosopher's
διάνοια by memory or re-remembering[188] of the di-
vinely serious things, by comparison to which the
humanly serious things are moving askew, so that
the non-philosophical many, who do not notice the
truth of the situation and who are chained[189] to
the humanly serious, sees the philosopher as
moving askew and tries to set him straight.[190]

And since no soul is humanly embodied without a
prior vision of the beings, every presently living
human is, by nature and simply in accordance with
being human, the possessor of that vision, and the
difference in strict anamnetic ability among humans derives from the relative length or brevity
of the vision, according to which one is more or
less blinded by immersion in injustice, i.e., un-

purified ἔρως. And why must humans have the prior vision? Socrates offers the following explanation:

> for the /soul/ then which has never seen the truth will not come unto this shaped-surface /i.e., the human one/. For it is obligatory for a human to be cognizant in accordance with a bespoken look, going from many sensings unto one thing which is taken together by reckoning; and this is re-remembering those things which our soul once saw when it proceeded with and supersaw the things which we now assert to be, and when it lifted its head unto the beingly being.[191]

The process that is described here has the following steps: (1) the soul sees (=supersees) the truth (=the beingly being); (2) the soul is humanly embodied; (3) the human senses many sensings; (4) the human reckons (speaks out) the many to be one (=the human re-remembers the truth/the beingly being); (5) the human is cognizant that the one which is spoken (reckoned) is in accordance with a look. Therefore, speech presupposes an already existing eidetic organization which is formulated by the speech. In other words, to speak at all bespeaks an eidetic unity which is stretched through all things about which speaking is, and a speech is a taking together into one of an aisthetic many which is visible as the kind of many which it is. And this speech is the product of ἡ διαλεκτική, the energized speaking through, which corresponds to ἡ διάνοια, the energized thinking through, to both of which the εἶδος (look) radiantly shines through its εἴδωλον (look-alike). And hence insofar as every human by nature speaks, every human is more or less cognizant of the eidetic unity in things, the difference between the philosopher and the many being that the many is only operatively cognizant of it while the philosopher is thematically cognizant ot it.[192] And the person who engages in this thematizing activity is the skilled conversationalist, the dialectical person, the lover of dividings and leadings-together.

Let us now turn outside the mythic palinode to the discussion of dialectic which follows it,[193] a discussion in which Socrates descends from the divine childishly playful craziness of eros to the humanly sober method of art.[194]

Socrates begins by recapitulating his fourfold classification of divine craziness, although as with every Socratic recapitulation there are refinements:

> Socrates. And then of craziness /there are/ two looks, the one /coming to be/ by human diseases, and the one coming to be by a divine release from the accustomed lawful things.
> Phaedrus. Altogether so then.
> Socrates. And of the divine we having divided four parts of four gods, having posited divinative inspiration of Apollo, and initiatory /inspiration/ of Dionysus, and in turn poetic /inspiration/ of the Muses, and a fourth /inspiration/ of Aphrodite and Eros, /having done this/ we asserted erotic craziness to be best....[195]

The refinement which is introduced here is that the value of craziness lies in its ability to release us from the fetters of our habits, customs, and laws, and this is no less characteristic of poetry, for example, than it is of philosophy.[196] And the instrument of release, as Socrates is about to explain before identifying it explicitly, is ἡ διαλεκτική,[197] whose two looks are συναγωγή and διαίρεσις,[198] which he discusses in that order and all too briefly.[199]

First, and most briefly,[200] he outlines συναγωγή, leading-together or collecting:

> And /the one look is/ for the person who sees together to lead the things which have been dispersed in many ways into one look so that the person delimiting it makes clear each thing about which he is always willing to teach. As in the things /spoken/ just now

> about eros, which is the thing which has been
> delimited, whether it was spoken well or badly,
> because of these things the speech had there-
> fore then /this/ to speak, that which is dis-
> tinct and the same thing agreeing with itself.[201]

This partially repeats and partially amplifies the
earlier statement regarding collection. It specifies that the person who practices this method
must be synoptic.[202] Further, the unifying of a
manifold is a delimiting, i.e., a horizoning, and
the εἶδος of a manifold, its whither, is its
horizonal schema.[203] And the context of bringing
together a manifold into a unity is pedagogical.
In addition, the method is productive of distinct-
ness and internal consistency, although the price
that it pays for achieving this twofold gain is
that it may lose the particular phenomena which
are being gathered together, i.e., it may not see
the mountains for the range. Clearly, then, συναγωγή alone is not sufficient, and another method
supplementing it is required.

And it is to this other method, διαίρεσις, that
Socrates now turns:

> The reverse is the being capable in accordance
> with looks of cutting through in accordance
> with joints where they are by nature, and not
> taking it in hand to break down any part using
> the manner of a bad butcher; but as the /two/
> speeches just now grasped the senselessness of
> thinking to be some one look in common, and as
> of a body from one thing there are by nature
> two homonymous things, the ones having been
> called left, and the ones right, so also the
> /two/ speeches, having regarded the look of
> dementedness as though it were by nature in
> us, the one cutting a part on the left, /then/
> cutting this again, did not leave off until
> it having found in them that which is named a
> certain left eros reviled it very much in
> justice, and the one having led us unto the
> things of craziness on the right and it in
> turn having found a certain divine eros

86

/which was/ homonymous to that one and having
stretched it forth praised it as cause of the
biggest goods for us.204

The first striking thing about Socrates' description here is the assertion of what the two methods
have in common: they are both in accordance with
looks.205 And the looks are the natural articulations of beings, and in the case of a good butcher
of being, the cutting of being is only at these
points. In addition, if the method is used badly--
in contradistinction to synoptic delimiting or
collecting--it clearly makes a difference, although precisely what is the difference is not so
clear. That the butcher is called κακός cannot
mean, as Hackforth renders it, "clumsy,"206 but
rather it must mean either not knowing the εἴδη
in accordance with which one must cut or disregar-
ding them. In the case of the bad butcher, capability is not in question but doing is, as the
language itself strongly suggests.207 I mean, the
same butcher of being could cut a leg of being and
make ground being, but in the first case he would
be cutting κατ' ἄρθρα ᾗ πέφυκεν, while in the second he would not, although in neither case would
he be clumsy. Socrates next gives two examples,
which--however different they may seem--are presented as identical in import: both are introduced
by a ὥσπερ (265e3, 4), and the double ὥσπερ is
answered by the οὕτω (266a2) which signifies the
consequent of the two together. In other words,
Socrates gives a two which he suggests is a one,
and from which as a one he draws a conclusion.
And the example of the two speeches--and this
seems rather curious--adumbrates their embodiment
of the method of συναγωγή, in which the manifold
"senselessness of thinking" is collected into one
common look, a method which Socrates himself ex-
emplifies in his explanation by using three names
for the single phenomenon of craziness208 and by
suggesting that the two examples be fused together as one. The example of the body, on the
other hand, adumbrates the method of διαίρεσις,
in which in the case of the body, a natural one
presents itself as a natural two. The example of

87

the body is an interesting one. The body is symmetrical, at least from the front and back,[209]
having symmetrically corresponding similarly
named pairs of parts, for example, right leg and
left leg, right ear and left ear, and so on. But
this must not simply be taken for granted, especially if indeed "the navel /is/ the memorial of
the ancient /human/ affection"[210] or if we reflect
upon the placement of male and female genitals in
the way that Aristophanes suggests in his λόγος,[211]
for the human sphere body would not be symmetrical
--if indeed one can speak of any sphere as symme-
trical--in the way in which the present human
trunk is symmetrical. And this indicates an insufficiency in the method of διαίρεσις, a sterility,
as it were, in that διαίρεσις can reveal εἶδος
only as γένος but not as γένεσις. Indeed the Aristophanean account of the result of bodily τμῆσις
can be taken as a caricature of the consequences
of the employment of διαίρεσις alone:

> Therefore when the nature was cut in two, each
> yearning for the /other/ half of itself used to
> go with /it/, and throwing their arms around
> and being interwoven with each other, desiring
> to co-nature, they died by hunger and other
> idleness because of their being willing to do
> nothing separate from each other.[212]

In other words, the splitting fails to provide a
natural fulfillment, a natural τροφή and ἔργον,
for the yearning which that same splitting acti-
vates. And this, by the way, is the failure of
Aristophanes' own account as well.[213] And one of
the purposes of both Diotima's account in the
Symposium and Socrates' mythic palinode in the
Phaedrus is to adumbrate the natural τροφή and
ἐνέργεια of humans.

Διαίρεσις, then, is purely or abstractly descriptive, i.e., it is a λόγος in the narrow sense,[214]
but it is not and cannot be a μῦθος, a genetic
account. And this is why in the Statesman, the
Elean Stranger must supplement his διαίρεσις (258
a7-267c4) with a μῦθος (267c5-277a2), a μῦθος

which he introduces (268e8 ff.) as a συναγωγή of
a previously cut many (including the strife between Atreus and Thyestes with the concomitant
change in the rising and the setting of the heavenly bodies, Kronos' kingdom, and the earth-born):

> Stranger. Then these things all together are
> from the same affection, and in addition to these
> things ten thousand others even still more won-
> drous than these, but through the multitude of
> time the ones of them have extinguished, and the
> ones having been thoroughly dispersed have been
> spoken each severally separate from each other.
> But the affection which is the cause of all
> these things no one has spoken, but now indeed
> it must be spoken....[215]

The Statesman myth, then, which perfects the preceding διαίρεσις,[216] is an implicit συναγωγή. And
in like manner, then, Socrates' Aesopic myth about
the pleasant and the painful is a small paradigm
designed to illustrate that a μῦθος is a genetic
συναγωγή:

> And Socrates sitting up on the bed both bent
> his leg and rubbed /it/ by his hand, and simul-
> taneously as /he was/ rubbing he asserted, "How
> eccentric, o men, is likely to be this something
> which humans call pleasant; how wonderfully it
> is naturally related to the thing seeming to be
> its contrary, the painful, so as for them not to
> be willing to come to be present to a human
> simultaneously, and /yet/ if anyone chases and
> catches one of the two, /he seems/ in some way
> almost to be compelled always to catch also the
> other of the two, as though the two are fas-
> tened from one head. And it seems to me," he
> asserted, "if Aesop had intellectually intuited
> these things, he would have composed a myth how
> the god wishing to release them from warring,
> since he was not capable /of doing so/, fastened
> their heads together for them into the same
> thing, and because of these things, if the one
> of the two comes to be present to anyone, also
> the other of the two follows later.[217]

89

The Socratic Aesopic myth[218] here, then, is an
attempt to account for the genesis of the concomitance without coincidence of the pleasant and the
painful, and its method is synagogic, i.e., it
adumbrates their unitary source which depends on
an underlying natural relatedness which their
manifest contrariety belies. But who is the god?
As we will see from the <u>Phaedrus</u>--although perhaps
it can be suggested here--the synagogic god is ὁ
διαλεκτικός, who is also the diairetic god (cf.
<u>Sophist</u> 216a1-c4).

So, neither διαίρεσις nor συναγωγή alone is sufficient, but rather what is required is a combination of διαίρεσις and συναγωγή,[219] of respectively
λόγος in the narrow sense of classificatory description and μῦθος in its sense of genetic account. In some dialogues, the one or the other
method predominates, e.g., in the <u>Republic</u> συναγωγή[220] or in the <u>Sophist</u> διαίρεσις.[221] In other
dialogues, e.g., the <u>Statesman</u>, the two methods
are used side by side as mutual supplements. And
in the rare case, they interpenetrate, as they
seem to do in the <u>Phaedrus</u>, as Socrates suggests
when he says:

> Indeed I at any rate am a lover, o Phaedrus, of
> these dividings and leadings-together, so that
> I am able both to speak and to think; and if we
> regard anyone else /to be/ capable of seeing
> that which is by nature into one and over many,
> I will chase this person behind after his track
> as though he were a god. And yet also therefore
> up to now I call persons who are capable of do-
> ing it, whether I proclaim them correctly or not
> god knows, dialectical persons.[222]

Here Socrates in his usual allusive and elliptical
way indicates the importance of διαιρέσεις and
συναγωγαί, for without them no speech or thinking
would be possible, i.e., clearly διαίρεσις/συνα-
γωγή and λέγειν/φρονεῖν are coeval:

> Somehow we assert the one and the many which
> came to be the same by speeches to run around

90

in every way in accordance with each of the
things which are spoken, /and we assert them
to do so/ always, both anciently and now. And
this neither ever ceases nor now began, but
the suchlike is, as it appears to me, a certain deathless and old-ageless affection in
us of speeches themselves.[223]

Therefore, διαίρεσις and συναγωγή are an affection
of λόγος itself. In addition, Socrates' divine
erotic craziness, his ἔρως, is no less of dividings and leadings-together than it is of speaking
and thinking. And this ἔρως eventuates in seeing
the natural ones which are over natural manies,
and such seeing is a seeing of monsters, as Socrates indicates in the Philebus:

> Someone, having divided by speech both the
> limbs and parts of each thing, having agreed
> all these things to be that one thing, may
> refute /himself/, laughing in that he has
> been compelled to assert monsters, /such
> monsters as that/ there is a way in which
> the one is many and unlimited, and a way
> in which the many is only one.[224]

Socrates, then, constantly employs the very monster methodology, synagogic diairesis, which he
disclaims early in the Phaedrus, and his ἔργον in
this respect simply reflects the essential character of λόγος itself. And any person whose ἐνέργεια
this is, any person for whom this is his πρᾶγμα,
is the equal of a god. Therefore, the god (or
demigod, if one prefers) who knows whether Socrates' proclaiming is correct or not is none
other than ὁ διαλεκτικός, namely Socrates himself.[225] And in chasing the tracks of such a god,
Socrates is chasing himself, i.e., the synagogic
diairesis of which dialectic consists is nothing
other than the trail of self-knowledge, and self-
knowledge is the knowledge of the good[226] and of
the beingness of the nature of the soul,[227] the
knowledge which the serious and perfect rhetorical
artist[228] must possess[229] in order to convey it to

another soul[230] or to persuade[231] or teach[232]
another soul in speeches or in writings.[233]

The <u>Phaedrus</u> concludes with an elaboration of
what perfect writing is, of what appropriate or
beautiful[234] writing is, an elaboration which is
consonant with the view of writing suggested by
Plato himself in his own myth in the seventh
epistle (see ch. IV), except that what there was
presented in terms of its genesis in the form of
a μῦθος is here presented in terms of classificatory description or λόγος in the narrow sense.

What, then, is perfect writing? In the first
place, it is a τέχνη[235] which is by nature[236] and
about nature.[237] But, and in this it differs from
most writing, it shows nature[238] through like-
nesses for which the ground is truth and beingness:

> everywhere the person who has envisioned the
> truth knows how to find /the similarities/.
> So that...if anyone does not enumerate the
> natures of the persons who hear, and if he be
> not capable of both dividing the beings in
> accordance with looks and embracing with one
> look in accordance with each one, he will
> never be skilled in art about speeches in
> accordance with as much as is possible for a
> human.[239]

So, in addition to διαίρεσις and συναγωγή, perfect
writing prerequires a vision of the truth such as
Socrates described in his palinode, a vision which
leads to knowledge of the similes for truth,[240]
and a classification of human soul types and speeches which leads to knowledge of how to adapt
one's utterance to those types. In short, it prerequires a complete knowledge of soul:

> <u>Socrates</u>. Then it is clear that..whoever...
> seriously gives the rhetorical art, first will
> both write /soul/ with all precision and will
> make /others/ see soul, whether it is by nature
> one and similar or multilooked in accordance
> with /i.e., as is/ the shape of the body; for

92

we assert this to be to show nature.

Phaedrus. Therefore all in all so.

Socrates. And second then, what it is its nature to do to what and to be affected by what.

Phaedrus. What then?

Socrates. And indeed third, /the writer/ who has thoroughly ordered for himself the classes of both speeches and soul and the affections of these will go through all causes, in addition harmonizing each to each and teaching which sort of being /soul/ by which sorts of speeches because of which cause is the one person persuaded and the one unpersuaded.[241]

Knowledge of soul is needed, then, because writing or speaking is soul-leading, ψυχαγωγία,[242] through speeches,[243] whether in public or in private.[244] It is significant that the only two occurrences of the word ψυχαγωγία in Plato are in the Phaedrus,[245] although the process is described in the Republic.[246] In other words, the way of leading the soul is by speech, in particular by writing. But not all souls can be led (i.e., persuaded) and not all souls which can be led can be led in the same way. Therefore, a perfect writing must be constructed in such a way as to simultaneously lead different souls in different ways, i.e., in such a way as to simultaneously speak different things to different persons, and at the same time to leave unled or unpersuaded those souls which cannot be led or persuaded. "And yet," as Phaedrus remarks with marvellous understatement, "it does not appear to be then a small work."[247] And the ultimate audience for whose gratification such a writing is composed is an audience of gods, of "masters who are both good themselves and from good /progenitors/."[248] But whether by "gods" Socrates means those of the traditional Hellenic pantheon or whether he means perfectly dialectical humans is at least an open question.[249]

The account[250] of Theuth and Ammon which Socrates presents next could almost be taken as a dialogue between the Socratic ἔργον (Ammon) and the Plato-

nic ἔργον (Theuth) on the basis of an implicit
identity between the Socratic Λόγος and the
Platonic Λόγος. And the account is rather, as its
prologue in the Philebus (18b6-d2) indicates, a
λόγος in the narrow sense than a μῦθος. In the
Philebus, Theuth is credited with having invented
written equivalents of spoken sounds by intellectually intuiting that an unlimited aisthetic (i.e.,
acoustic) multiplicity could not be reduced to a
noetic oneness, but rather that it could only be
rendered intelligible by reducing it to a limited
noetic manyness. That is, faced with the choice
between a Herakleitean aisthetic heterogeneity and
a Parmenidean eidetic homogeneity, Theuth decided
that there was a mediation possible by means of a
finite eidetic heterogeneity. Then Theuth saw what
his discovery meant:

> and /Theuth/ seeing how none of us would learn
> /any/ one itself in accordance with itself with-
> out all of them, he in turn having reckoned this
> bond as being one and somehow making all these
> things one, he in addition having spoken, uttered
> over them one art as being grammar.[251]

This contains a strong warning for everyone who
reads Plato, in that it suggests that not one of
the εἴδη can be learned without all the others,
i.e., no partial whole can be discerned without
the whole whole of which it is a part, just as no
single Platonic dialogue can be discerned without
discerning all the others.

Presumably it was after making his decision about
the letters as symbols of the eidetic structure
of the unlimited continuum of articulate sound
that Theuth presented himself before Ammon, and
between them they confront one of the key questions about written things, the question of harm
and benefit,[252] and on this basis Ammon rejects
written things as harmful to memory and productive
of an incorrect or harsh contempt.[253] All we see
is the presentation of the problem without any
solution within the story itself, although the
sequel draws one. For written things may have been

94

superfluous, even dangerous, when humans were
filled with naivete,[254] i.e., when humans lis-
tened to an oak and a rock,[255] but since Socrates
as a representative human is not "from an oak or
from a rock"[256] and since regimes do not come to
be from an oak or from a rock,[257] writing may be
desirable, even salutary.

But what is the character of such writing? In
what follows, Socrates answers that question, partially by repetition of what he has already said,
partially by amplification. Most writing (as painting) has speeches which one would think could
speak and teach, but they cannot,[258] and if you
try to engage them in conversation, they say only
the same one thing, and they say it in the same
way indiscriminately both to those who can understand it and to those for whom it is not fitting
to hear such a thing (cf. 275d4-e2). In short,
most writing "does not know to whom then it is
obligatory to speak and not /to speak/."[259] But
there is a kind of speech which does know this,
namely "the one which is written with knowledge
in the soul of the learner."[260] And as to whether
writing should be a playful and festive planting
in the soul such as farmers do in window boxes
for a festival or whether it should be serious,
Socrates asserts that it is a childishly playful
reminder both for himself and for everyone who
follows him (cf. 276b1-c4). Therefore, when the
truly dialectical person writes with ink on paper,
he will write playfully an imitation of what he
'writes' seriously in the soul of someone with
whom he converses directly (cf. 276c3-277a5). Perfect writing, then, is a playful μίμησις of the
serious activity of the skilled conversationalist,
the dialectician.[261] The relationship, then, between serious spoken conversations and playful
written conversations, if the playful written conversations are written perfectly, is the relationship between a father and his legitimate progeny (cf. 277a6-279b4). In other words, the relationship between Socrates in Athens and the Platonic dialogues is analogous to the relationship
between the good and the sun.

It is appropriate, then, that Socrates should conclude his only thorough discussion of writing with a prayer to Pan,[262] who "is either speech or the sibling of speech,"[263] and whose double nature[264] is reflected in the doubleness of Socratic speech and Platonic writing.

Therefore, there is nothing wondrous in the tradition which has arisen which regards the <u>Phaedrus</u> as the first Platonic dialogue.[265]

Before we turn to other myths in the Platonic corpus, let us briefly summarize the classification, however incomplete, of the kinds of accounts which we have found in the Platonic dialogues. The broadest category is Λόγος in the broad sense, which is used to designate any articulated verbal utterance, whether audible or not, i.e., whether spoken to another or to oneself in the soul. Within the genus Λόγος, there have emerged three species: (1) λόγος in the narrow sense, which is used to designate a classificatory descriptive account, a διαίρεσις; (2) μῦθος, which is used to designate a synoptic genetic account, a συναγωγή; (3) ἀκοή, which straddles the distinction between λόγος and μῦθος, and which is used to designate what we might loosely call a story, although it may be further distinguished with regard to whether it is a λόγος or a μῦθος.[266] And in none of these cases does the designation depend upon the truth or falsity of the account. In other words, if one were to formulate a false λόγος or a hypothetical λόγος, one could formulate a corresponding false μῦθος or hypothetical μῦθος, and the accounts-- whatever their 'truth value'--would still be the kinds of accounts that they are.[267]

Now that we have, however tentatively, developed our classification, we must rub it on the touchstone of other Platonic dialogic accounts to see if the Platonic dialogic usage is as consistent as it seems.

NOTES

¹A purely Socratic dialogue is a dialogue in
which Socrates is the primary speaker. The remaining dialogues are either mixed dialogues, i.e.,
dialogues in which Socrates is present but not the
primary speaker (Sophist, Statesman, Parmenides,
Symposium, Timaeus, Critias), or purely non-
Socratic dialogues, i.e., dialogues in which Socrates is totally absent (Laws, Epinomis). For discussions of other legitimate divisions of the dialogues, see Leo Strauss, City and man (Chicago,
1964), pp. 55-58, and Diogenes Laertius III. 49-
51, 56-62.

²Perceval Frutiger, Les mythes de Platon; étude
philosophique et littéraire (Paris, 1930), p. 233.

³Phaedrus 275b3-4: ῏Ω Σώκρατες, ῥᾳδίως σὺ Αἰ-
γυπτίους καὶ ὁποδαποὺς ἂν ἐθέλῃς λόγους ποιεῖς.

⁴See Phaedrus 227b6, c4, d2, 228a7, b4-5, 6,
c1, d7, 230d8, 234c6, d3, e5-6, 235b2, e6, 236e2.

⁵Cf. χρή...ἀστεῖοι καὶ δημωφελεῖς at 227c9-d2,
συμφέρειν at 230e7, ὑπολογίζεσθαι at 231b4 (cf.
Thompson, note ad 231b), περὶ πλείονος ποιήσονται
at 231c5, ὠφελεῖσθαι at 232d7, ὠφελίαν at 233c1
and 234c3; also cf. χάριν at 231b1, 233d8, e4, 7,
χάριτος at 234c1, χαριεῖσθαι at 231b7, χαρίζεσθαι
at 231c4, 233d5, e6, 234b7.

⁶Cf. τοῦ μύθου at 237a9, ὁ μῦθος at 241e8; also
cf. μυθολογίαν at 243a4.

⁷Cf. ἔμφυτος at 237d7-8, φύσει at 239a6, and ἡ
φύσις at 240b2. Also cf. ἀναγκάζει at 237a9, ἀναγ-
κάζεται at 241b5, ἀνάγκη at 237c2, 238e3, 239a5,
7, b5, 240a4, ἀνάγκης at 240d1, e1, 241b4, 7,
ἀναγκαῖον at 240c4, 241c2. In addition, consider
οἴστρου at 240d1, and the conclusion that ὡς λύκοι
ἄρνας ἀγαπῶσιν, ὡς παῖδα φιλοῦσιν ἐρασταί at 241d1.

97

8Cf. 238b7-c4, 236e7-8, 241d1; for the shame attached to it, see 237a4-5, 243b4-7, d3.

9253c7: τοῦδε τοῦ μύθου.

10265c1: μυθικόν τινα ὕμνον; cf. 247c3-4.

11Cf. Symposium 172b2.

12Cf. Symposium 173c3.

13See pp. 12-13.

14For a full account of what follows, see my article, "A hitherto unremarked pun in the Phaedrus," Apeiron, vol. 15, no. 2, 1981.

15Of the five occurrences of πλάτανος in Plato's works, four are in the Phaedrus (229a8, 230 b1-2, 6, 236e1). The fifth is at Laws 4.705c4, where it is listed as absent from the site of the colony which is being founded by the interlocutors there.

16The most penetrating analysis of the whole Phaedrus is in John Sallis, Being and Logos: the way of Platonic dialogue (Pittsburgh, 1975), ch. III, which consistently takes into account the arguments as dramatic elements of the dialogue. (This work will hereafter be cited as Sallis.) An incisive analysis of sections of the Phaedrus may be found in Jacob Klein, A commentary on Plato's Meno (Chapel Hill, 1965), pp. 10-16, 20-22, 151-152, 169-171. (This work will hereafter be cited as Klein, Meno.) Also helpful is Herman L. Sinaiko, Love, knowledge and discourse in Plato (Chicago, 1965), ch. 2. One should also consult the following works: Plato, Plato's Phaedrus, tr. with intro. and comm. by R. Hackforth (Indianapolis, 1952) /cited hereafter as Hackforth/; Plato, Oeuvres complètes (Paris, 1920-1964), tome IV, part 3, Phèdre, tr. L. Robin /Robin's introduction to this edition will hereafter be cited as Robin, "Notice"/; G.J. de Vries, Commentary on the Phaedrus of Plato (Amsterdam, 1969) /cited hereafter as Vries/; M.J. Verdenius, "Notes on Plato's Phaedrus," Mnemosyne, ser. 4, vol. 8, 1955; Eric Voegelin, Order and History, vol. 3, Plato and Aristotle (Baton Rouge, 1957); R.S. Bluck, "The second Platonic epistle, Phronesis, vol. 5, 1960, pp. 140-151; Plato, Phaedrus and the Seventh and Eighth Letters, tr. Walter Hamilton (Penguin Classics); Plato, Plato's Epistles, tr. with critical essays and notes by Glenn R. Morrow (Indianapolis, 1962); Josef Pieper, Enthusiasm and divine madness, tr. Richard and Clara Winston (New York, 1964).

17Robin, "Notice," p. xxxvii.

18Consider on this Klein, p. 14: "Phaedrus, who before the Palinode was quite certain (243d8-e1) that he could prevail upon Lysias to write another speech competing with the one Socrates was about to deliver, is very doubtful now (257c) whether Lysias would consent to join the contest. Has he not already been abusively called a mere 'speech-writer'?" What should be added here is that Phaedrus has been aware of the 'abuse' hurled at Lysias for some time but it had not shaken his confidence in Lysias even through Socrates' first speech. Clearly the Socratic palinode has shaken that confidence, but whether the root of the change is a burgeoning conversion to philosophy on Phaedrus' part (cf. Klein, Meno, p. 14, n. 34; Hackforth, pp. 13, 111-112, 169) or something else is here unclear.

19Cf. Phaedrus 227a4-b1, and Robin's description of Phaedrus, cited by Hackforth, p. 13.

20Cf. Phaedrus 230c5-e4.

21The Aristophanean portrait of Socrates hanging from the sky in a basket is the most graphic representation of this.

22Cf. Symposium 177d7-8; also see Sallis,

p. 111. There seems to be a fundamental tension between νόμος and ἔρως.

23Cf. Lysias, Selected speeches, ed. C.D. Adams (Norman, Okla., 1970), intro., p. 24.

24Cf. Socrates' use of ἐπιδεικνύμενος at 258a7, and Vries, note ad loc.; also cf. Hackforth, p. 115.

25Phaedrus 227c7-d2: /ΦΑΙ./ λέγει γὰρ ὡς χαριστέον μὴ ἐρῶντι μᾶλλον ἢ ἐρῶντι. ΣΩ. Ὦ γενναῖος. εἴθε γράψειεν ὡς χρὴ πένητι μᾶλλον ἢ πλουσίῳ, καὶ πρεσβυτέρῳ ἢ νεωτέρῳ, καὶ ὅσα ἄλλα ἐμοί τε πρόσεστι καὶ τοῖς πολλοῖς ἡμῶν· ἦ γὰρ ἂν ἀστεῖοι καὶ δημωφελεῖς εἶεν οἱ λόγοι. Hackforth's rendering of the last phrase ("What an attractive democratic theory that would be!") suggests the political reference but makes the mistake of prejudging that the reference is to democracy rather than, say, oligarchy or something else. Cf. Stanley Rosen, "The non-lover in Plato's Phaedrus," Man and world, vol. 2, no. 3, August 1969, pp. 434-435.

26Cf. Phaedrus 242a7-b5; Symposium 177d2-5, esp. d5.

27Cf. Phaedrus 228c1-2.

28Phaedrus 228b6-7: τῷ νοσοῦντι περὶ λόγων ἀκοήν.

29It should be noted here that what is presented externally here as a confrontation between the anti-writing people and the pro-writing people must be considered internally with regard to any discussion of writing in the Platonic corpus. In particular, the explicit assertions of the anti-writing people are belied by their very practice of writing, even if they write against writing. And certainly in accordance with the generalization of the discussion, Plato would be an example of an ostensible anti-writing person who explicitly in deed and implicitly in speech is pro-writing. Cf. Sallis, p. 162.

³⁰Of course, they may define a beautiful
speech as one which glorifies themselves and
their deeds and a shameful speech as one which
denigrates them, but that does not affect the
point which Socrates makes.

³¹<u>Phaedrus</u> 258d1-5: ΣΩ. Τοῦτο μὲν ἄρα παντὶ
δῆλον, ὅτι οὐκ αἰσχρὸν αὐτό γε τὸ γράφειν λόγους.
ΦΑΙ. Τί γάρ; ΣΩ. Ἀλλ' ἐκεῖνο οἶμαι αἰσχρὸν ἤδη,
τὸ μὴ καλῶς λέγειν τε καὶ γράφειν ἀλλ' αἰσχρῶς τε
καὶ κακῶς.

³²The generality of the defense is also sug-
gested at 258b1-5 when Socrates alludes briefly
to the poet in the theater. Cf. Vries, note ad
258b2-3. Also cf. 272a8-b2: "/Socrates./ But if
anyone speaking or teaching or writing leaves out
any of them, and /still/ asserts himself to speak
by art, the person who is not persuaded /by his
assertion that he speaks by art/ is the master of
the situation." (ἀλλ' ὅτι ἂν αὐτῶν τις ἐλλείπῃ
λέγων ἢ διδάσκων ἢ γράφων, φῇ δὲ τέχνῃ λέγειν,
ὁ μὴ πειθόμενος κρατεῖ.) Also cf. 277b6, λέγει ἢ
γράφει, and context, and 278b7 ff. In addition,
compare 259e1-2 to 258d7. Finally, especially consider 258a6-b1: /Socrates./ indeed after this next
the writer speaks showing off his own wisdom to
his praisers, sometimes making an altogether long
writing; or does the suchlike appear to you to be
anything other than a /spoken/ speech which has
been written down? <u>Phaedrus</u>. To me at any rate it
does not." (/ΣΩ./ ὁ συγγραφεύς--ἔπειτα λέγει δὴ
μετὰ τοῦτο, ἐπιδεικνύμενος τοῖς ἐπαινέταις τὴν
ἑαυτοῦ σοφίαν, ἐνίοτε πάνυ μακρὸν ποιησάμενος
σύγγραμμα· ἤ σοι ἄλλο τι φαίνεται τὸ τοιοῦτον ἢ
λόγος συγγεγραμμένος; ΦΑΙ. Οὐκ ἔμοιγε.)

³³The same applies to Socratic-Platonic accusa-
tions, namely that they always (even if only as an
undertone of the surface argument) contain a defense of the accused insofar as it can be defend-
ed. This is certainly the case with the ostensibly
scathing attacks against democracy in <u>Republic</u> 8
and against poetry in <u>Republic</u> 10. And the <u>Apology</u>

of Socrates is no exception to this: cf. George
Anastaplo, "Human being and citizen; a beginning
to the study of Plato's Apology of Socrates," in
Ancients and Moderns, p. 23 et passim.

34Phaedrus 258b10-c5: /ΣΩ./ ὅταν ἱκανὸς γένηται
ῥήτωρ ἢ βασιλεύς, ὥστε λαβὼν τὴν Λυκούργου ἢ Σόλω-
νος ἢ Δαρείου δύναμιν ἀθάνατος γενέσθαι λογογράφος
ἐν πόλει, ἆρ' οὐκ ἰσόθεον ἡγεῖται αὐτός τε αὐτὸν
ἔτι ζῶν, καὶ οἱ ἔπειτα γιγνόμενοι ταὐτὰ ταῦτα περὶ
αὐτοῦ νομίζουσι, θεώμενοι αὐτοῦ τὰ συγγράμματα;

35Cf. Epistles 2.314c4.

36The Socratic philosophy could have remained
an oral teaching--as did the Pythagorean and Or-
phic traditions--although there would have been
an ultimate writing by someone, to the inexorabi-
lity of which hints in the dialogues abound (as
in the external settings of the Theaetetus, Symposium, and so on). Better for it to be done,
then, by a knower in the proper way.

37Cf. Phaedrus 257e4-258a2.

38This problem came up in connection with
φιλοτιμία in the seventh epistle. One could also
point to each speech delivered in the Symposium
as an example of the compulsion when praising
another (e.g., Eros) to praise oneself (cf. Philebus 28b1-2). Another way in which this is suggested by Plato is that if all of the so-called
Platonic dialogues are actually the writings
Σωκράτους καλοῦ καὶ νέου γεγονότος (cf. Epistles
2.314c4 and context), then the bulk of the so-
called Platonic corpus is a praise of a Socrates
by a Socrates, and hence as writing it is in
principle no different in this respect from the
writings of the political men. Perhaps it should
be re-emphasized here that when one considers any
passage of the Platonic corpus which is concerned
with writing, one must always hold before one the
Platonic practice of writing.

[39]That this is simply humorous or sarcastic, as Hackforth (p. 116) supposes, is debatable, to say the least.

[40]Cf. Phaedrus 278d3-6. Of course, there is an equality to a god which is possible for humans, but this is not treated until after Socrates' palinode.

[41]Phaedrus 264c2-5, cited p. 38.

[42]Philebus 64b6-8: ἐμοὶ μὲν γὰρ καθαπερεὶ κόσμος τις ἀσώματος ἄρξων καλῶς ἐμψύχου σώματος ὁ νῦν λόγος ἀπειργάσθαι φαίνεται.

[43]Cf. Republic 10.596a5-597e5; Timaeus 41a3-d3 et passim.

[44]Cf. William Faulkner's remark: "I created a cosmos of my own. I can move these people around like God, not only in space but in time too." (Writers at work: the Paris Review interviews, ed. Malcolm Cowley (New York, 1959), p. 141.) Also cf. Phaedrus 253a7-b1.

[45]Phaedrus 258d7: ΣΩ. Τίς οὖν ὁ τρόπος τοῦ καλῶς τε καὶ μὴ γράφειν;

[46]See Hesiod Theogony 915-917. Cf. Phaedrus 252e1-3.

[47]Cf. H.J. Rose, Handbook of Greek mythology (New York, 1959), p. 174.

[48]Cf. Republic 7.532d6-e3 (Glaucon speaking, italics mine): "indeed let us go toward the song itself and narrate in this way as we narrated the proemium. Therefore speak what is the manner of the power of conversing, and indeed in accordance with what sorts of looks it has been separated, and what in turn are its ways; for these now, as is likely, would be the ones leading toward it, /i.e., toward/ where it would be for a person coming /to it/ as a resting-up from the way and

an end of the journey." (ἐπ' αὐτὸν δὴ τὸν νόμον
ἴωμεν, καὶ διέλθωμεν οὕτως ὥσπερ τὸ προοίμιον
διήλθομεν. λέγε οὖν τίς ὁ τρόπος τῆς τοῦ διαλέγεσθαι δυνάμεως, καὶ κατὰ ποῖα δὴ εἴδη διέστηκεν,
καὶ τίνες αὖ ὁδοί· αὗται γὰρ ἂν ἤδη, ὡς ἔοικεν,
αἱ πρὸς αὐτὸ ἄγουσαι εἶεν, οἷ ἀφικομένῳ ὥσπερ
ὁδοῦ ἀνάπαυλα ἂν εἴη καὶ τέλος τῆς πορείας.) This
remark could almost be taken as a capsule summary
of the setting and contents of the <u>Phaedrus</u>.

[49]For the identification of τὸ διαλέγεσθαι and
ἡ φιλοσοφία, cf. <u>Parmenides</u> 135b5-c7 (italics
mine): "'But yet,' Parmenides spoke, 'indeed, o
Socrates, then if anyone in turn will not allow
looks of the beings to be, he having gazed off
unto all the things /<u>spoken</u>/ just now and other
suchlike things, and /<u>if</u>/ he does not delimit
some look of each one thing, he will not even
have /any place/ whither he will turn his thinking, he having disallowed the same look of each
of the beings always to be, and thus <u>he all in all
corrupts the power of conversing</u>. Therefore you,
and very much so, seem to me to sense the suchlike.' 'You speak truly,' /Pythodorus asserted
Socrates/ to assert. 'Therefore <u>what will you do
about philosophy</u>? Where will you turn when these
things are unrecognized?' 'I altogether do not
seem to myself to see /where/ in the present at
any rate.'" ('Αλλὰ μέντοι, εἶπεν ὁ Παρμενίδης, εἰ
γέ τις δή, ὦ Σώκρατες, αὖ μὴ ἐάσει εἴδη τῶν ὄντων
εἶναι, εἰς πάντα τὰ νυνδὴ καὶ ἄλλα τοιαῦτα ἀπο-
βλέψας, μηδέ τι ὁριεῖται εἶδος ἑνὸς ἑκάστου, οὐδὲ
ὅποι τρέψει τὴν διάνοιαν ἕξει, μὴ ἐῶν ἰδέαν τῶν
ὄντων ἑκάστου τὴν αὐτὴν ἀεὶ εἶναι, καὶ οὕτως τὴν
τοῦ διαλέγεσθαι δύναμιν παντάπασι διαφθερεῖ. τοῦ
τοιούτου μὲν οὖν μοι δοκεῖς καὶ μᾶλλον ᾐσθῆσθαι.
'Αληθῆ λέγεις, φάναι. Τί οὖν ποιήσεις φιλοσοφίας
πέρι; πῇ τρέψῃ ἀγνοουμένων τούτων; Οὐ πάνυ μοι
δοκῶ καθορᾶν ἔν γε τῷ παρόντι.)

[50]<u>Republic</u> 7.533c7-d4: Οὐκοῦν, ἦν δ' ἐγώ, ἡ
διαλεκτικὴ μέθοδος μόνη ταύτῃ πορεύεται, τὰς ὑποθέσεις ἀναιροῦσα, ἐπ' αὐτὴν τὴν ἀρχὴν ἵνα βεβαιώ-
σηται, καὶ τῷ ὄντι ἐν βορβόρῳ βαρβαρικῷ τινι τὸ
τῆς ὄμμα κατορωρυγμένον ἠρέμα ἕλκει καὶ ἀνάγει

ἄνω, συνερίθοις καὶ συμπεριαγωγοῖς χρωμένη αἷς διήλθομεν τέχναις. Cf. Phaedo 69c5-7.

[51]Cf. Phaedrus 264e7-266c8; Republic 6.511b3-d5.

[52]Apology of Socrates 23c4-5, 33c4: χαίρουσιν ἀκούοντες ἐξεταζομένων τῶν ἀνθρώπων, καὶ αὐτοὶ πολλάκις ἐμὲ μιμοῦνται, εἶτα ἐπιχειροῦσιν ἄλλους ἐξετάζειν........ἔστι γὰρ οὐκ ἀηδές. Cf. 33b9-c3.

[53]Cf. Republic 1.328a7-8; cf. 1.352b3-6 et passim.

[54]Phaedo 64d2-7: φαίνεταί σοι φιλοσόφου ἀνδρὸς εἶναι ἐσπουδακέναι περὶ τὰς ἡδονὰς καλουμένας τὰς τοιάσδε, οἷον σιτίων τε καὶ ποτῶν; Ἥκιστα, ὦ Σώκρατες, ἔφη ὁ Σιμμίας. Τί δὲ τὰς τῶν ἀφροδισίων; Οὐδαμῶς. Also cf. 116e1-6 and Socrates' reply.

[55]Symposium 191b7-c2: ἐγέννων καὶ ἔτικτον οὐκ εἰς ἀλλήλους ἀλλ᾽ εἰς γῆν, ὥσπερ οἱ τέττιγες.

[56]If humans are indifferent to distinctly human sexual pleasure, then they are indifferent to whether or not they have a distinctly human body. If thinking or singing/conversing is one's be all and end all, then it certainly can be carried on in any body, if psychic migration from one body to another, even of another sort, is assumed possible. Cf. Odyssey 10.237-243, esp. 240.

[57]Cf. Franz Kafka, "The metamorphosis," in The Penal Colony, tr. Willa and Edwin Muir (New York, 1961), p. 67: "As Gregor Samsa awoke one morning from uneasy dreams he found himself transformed in his bed into a gigantic insect." Also consider the account of Gregor's death, p. 127.

[58]Phaedrus 230a5-6: εἴτε ἡμερώτερόν τε καὶ ἁπλούστερον ζῷον, θείας τινὸς καὶ ἀτύφου μοίρας φύσει μετέχον.

[59]Phaedrus 229d7, e1-2: ὄχλος...τερατολόγων τινῶν φύσεων.

[60]The image of were-cicadas is no more monstrous than the image of the were-gadfly which
Socrates is (Apol. Socr. 30e1-6).

[61]Plato, The Symposium of Plato, ed. with intro.
and commentary by R.G. Bury, 2d ed. (Cambridge,
Eng., 1973), note ad 191c. He also says: "This is
not merely a piece of natural history; it contains
also an allusion to the cicada /i.e., the cicada
hair clasp/ as the symbol of Athenian autochthony...."

[62]Cf. Phaedrus 259b1 to c3-4; also see Ion 533
e3-535a5.

[63]Cf. Symposium 210d3-6: "but he, having turned
toward the great open sea of the beautiful and beholding it, brings forth many beautiful and magni-
ficent speeches and thoughts in abundant philosophy (ἀλλ' ἐπὶ τὸ πολὺ πέλαγος τετραμμένος τοῦ
καλοῦ καὶ θεωρῶν πολλοὺς καὶ καλοὺς λόγους καὶ
μεγαλοπρεπεῖς τίκτη καὶ διανοήματα ἐν φιλοσοφίᾳ
ἀφθόνῳ).

[64]Phaedrus 259a3: ἀργίαν.

[65]Apol. Socr. 30e4-5: ἵππῳ...νωθεστέρῳ καὶ δεο-
μένῳ ἐγείρεσθαι.

[66]Phaedrus 259a3: κηλουμένους ὑφ' αὐτῶν.

[67]Cf. Republic 7.538c4-539d2.

[68]This is one of the lessons of Aristophanes'
Clouds.

[69]Cf. Republic 7.523a10 ff.

[70]Phaedrus 259e5: τὴν...διάνοιαν εἰδυῖαν.

[71]Phaedrus 270c10-d1: δεῖ διανοεῖσθαι περὶ
ὁτουοῦν φύσεως.

[72]Phaedrus 266b7-c1: καὶ τοὺς δυναμένους αὐτὸ
δρᾶν...καλῶ...διαλεκτικούς.

[73] I believe that one could go further and say that for Socrates' palinode at least, the four Muses whom Socrates mentions are all the Muses. For the connection between the Muses and philosophy, cf. Cratylus 406a3-5: "/Socrates./ And this name /i.e., 'Muses'/ nicknamed both the Muses and music wholly from searching, as is likely, and seeking and philosophy" (τὰς δὲ Μούσας τε καὶ ὅλως τὴν μουσικὴν ἀπὸ τοῦ μῶσθαι, ὥς ἔοικεν, καὶ τῆς ζητήσεως τε καὶ φιλοσοφίας τὸ ὄνομα τοῦτο ἐπωνόμασεν).

[74] Phaedrus 259d4: τοὺς ἐν φιλοσοφίᾳ διάγοντας.

[75] 259c6: τίς τίνα αὐτῶν τιμᾷ τῶν ἐνθάδε.

[76] 259d2-3: κατὰ τὸ εἶδος ἑκάστης τιμῆς.

[77] 259d4-5: τιμῶντας τὴν ἐκείνων μουσικήν.

[78] Phaedrus 259d4-5. The structure of the clause is: τοὺς...διάγοντάς τε καὶ τιμῶντας. The use of only one article to govern both participles and the emphatic τε καὶ connective between the participles demand that the clause be rendered by an emphatic "both...and." Vries, note ad loc., takes the τε καὶ as self-evidently explanatory, although this is not the most typical use of the connective. Its most typical use is rather to connect clauses which are not identical but are either similar or contrary, and this use could be called amplificatory. Cf. J.D. Denniston, The Greek particles (Oxford, 1970), pp. 512, 514, 515, 516.

[79] 259c7: τοὺς ἐν τοῖς χοροῖς τετιμηκότας αὐτήν.

[80] 237a7: ὦ Μοῦσαι...λίγειαι.

[81] 230c1-3. So far as I know, the word λιγύς and its derivatives appear in no other Platonic writing than the Phaedrus.

[82] 230c2-3: τῷ τῶν τεττίγων χορῷ.

[83] Phaedrus 259d1-2: τοὺς ἐν τοῖς ἐρωτικοῖς.

[84]Cf. Symposium 210e4-212a7, esp. 210e5, 211 b1-2, c7-8, c8-d1, d3, d8, e1, e3.

[85]Symposium 177d7-8: "I...who assert myself to know nothing other than the erotic things" (ἐγὼ... ὃς οὐδέν φημι ἄλλο ἐπίστασθαι ἢ τὰ ἐρωτικά). Also consider Theages 128b3-6: "/Socrates./ I chance to know, so as to speak a word, nothing except a certain small learning, /namely the learning/ of the erotic things. Yet with respect to this learning I make the claim that I am formidable above and beyond anyone whomsoever of both the humans who have been born before /me/ and those now." (ἐγὼ τυγχάνω ὡς ἔπος εἰπεῖν οὐδὲν ἐπιστάμενος πλήν γε σμικροῦ τινος μαθήματος, τῶν ἐρωτικῶν. τοῦτο μέντοι τὸ μάθημα παρ' ὁντινοῦν ποιοῦμαι δεινὸς εἶναι καὶ τῶν προγεγονότων ἀνθρώπων καὶ τῶν νῦν.) Cf. Symposium 198d1-2, Lysis 205a1-2.

[86]Lysis 204b8-c2: "/Socrates./ And I am mean and useless with respect to the other things, but this somehow has been given to me from a god, /namely/ being of such a sort as quickly to recognize both a lover and a beloved." (εἰμὶ δ' ἐγὼ τὰ ἄλλα φαῦλος καὶ ἄχρηστος, τοῦτο δέ μοί πως ἐκ θεοῦ δέδοται, ταχὺ οἵῳ τ' εἶναι γνῶναι ἐρῶντά τε καὶ ἐρώμενον.)

[87]Cf. Phaedrus 228c1-2 (τοῦ τῶν λόγων ἐραστοῦ); Charmides 154b8 ff., esp. 155d3-4 ("and I saw the things inside his cloak and became inflamed and no longer was I inside myself": εἶδον τε τὰ ἐντὸς τοῦ ἱματίου καὶ ἐφλεγόμην καὶ οὐκέτ' ἐν ἐμαυτοῦ ἦν). Also cf. Rival-lovers 133a3-5; Alcibiades I 103a1-2, 104e4-6; Symposium 213c6 ff., 216d2-4. Also cf. Sallis, pp. 111-113.

[88]Symposium 172b2: τῶν ἐρωτικῶν λόγων.

[89]Symposium 173c3: περὶ φιλοσοφίας λόγους.

[90]Later, Diotima's speech, which is initially called a speech about Eros (τὸν...λόγον τὸν περὶ τοῦ Ἔρωτος, 201d1-2), clearly turns out to be a

λόγος περὶ τῆς φιλοσοφίας. Cf. 209e5.

91Symposium 204a1-4, 8-b5: ἔχει γὰρ ὧδε. θεῶν
οὐδεὶς φιλοσοφεῖ οὐδ' ἐπιθυμεῖ σοφὸς γενέσθαι--
ἔστι γάρ--οὐδ' εἴ τις ἄλλος σοφός, οὐ φιλοσοφεῖ.
οὐδ' αὖ οἱ ἀμαθεῖς φιλοσοφοῦσιν οὐδ' ἐπιθυμοῦσι
σοφοὶ γενέσθαι......Τίνες οὖν, ἔφην ἐγώ, ὦ Διοτίμα,
οἱ φιλοσοφοῦντες, εἰ μήτε οἱ σοφοὶ μήτε οἱ ἀμαθεῖς;
Δῆλον δή, ἔφη, τοῦτό γε ἤδη καὶ παιδί, ὅτι οἱ
μεταξὺ τούτων ἀμφοτέρων, ὧν ἂν εἴη καὶ ὁ Ἔρως.
ἔστιν γὰρ δὴ τῶν καλλίστων ἡ σοφία, Ἔρως δ' ἐστιν
ἔρως περὶ τὸ καλόν, ὥστε ἀναγκαῖον Ἔρωτα φιλόσοφον
εἶναι, φιλόσοφον δὲ ὄντα μεταξὺ εἶναι σοφοῦ καὶ
ἀμαθοῦς.

92See Vries, note ad 259d6-7; Hackforth, p. 118;
Sallis, p. 165; Robin, "Notice," p. xxxvi.

93I am baffled at the absolute unanimity among
translators and commentators in assuming that the
phrase τε οὐρανὸν καὶ λόγους...θείους τε καὶ ἀν-
θρωπίνους (259d6) is to be rendered as though the
adjective 'divine' is to be construed with 'heaven' and the adjective 'human' with 'speeches.'
The construction clearly means for both adjectives
to be taken with both nouns, as the emphatic τε
καί connective and the plural θείους demand. See
note 78 above.

94Phaedrus 259d5: μάλιστα.

95259d4-5: τὴν ἐκείνων μουσικήν.

96259d7: ἴασιν καλλίστην φωνήν.

97Phaedo 61a3-4: φιλοσοφίας...οὔσης μεγίστης
μουσικῆς.

98Laws 3.689d6-7: ἡ καλλίστη καὶ μεγίστη τῶν
συμφωνιῶν μεγίστη δικαιότατ' ἂν λέγοιτο σοφία.

99Republic 8.548b8-c1: τῆς ἀληθινῆς Μούσης τῆς
μετὰ λόγων τε καὶ φιλοσοφίας.

100See LSJ; ὄψ, voice, is a poetic form unto itself, while ὄψ, eye or face, is a variant of the word ὄψις. Consider also Phaedrus 250c8 ff., esp. d3 ff.

101247c7: οὐσία ὄντως οὖσα...θεατή. Cf. especially ὄψιν τε καὶ θέαν at 250b6-7. Also cf. ἰδοῦσα at 247d3, καθορᾷ at 247d5-6 (thrice), τῆς ...θέας at 248b4, ἰδεῖν at 248b6, κατίδῃ at 248c3, ἴδῃ at 248c6, ἰδοῦσα at 249b6, εἶδεν at 249c2 (with which cf. εἶδει at 249b1 and εἶδος at b7), ὑπεριδοῦσα at 249c3, βλέπων at 249d7, τεθέαται at 249e5, εἶδον at 250a2 and 4, ἴδωσιν at 250a6, θεῶνται and ἰδεῖν at 250b5, εἶδον at 250b8, ἐποπτεύοντες at 250c4, and so on.

102See 250b6-7 and preceding two notes.

103Cf. Republic 7.532a2-3, b1-2.

104Cf. Republic 7.516c1: τῷ ὁρωμένῳ τόπῳ.

105Cf. Republic 7.517b5: τὸν νοητὸν τόπον.

106Cf. Phaedrus 247c3.

107Cf. Republic 6.509d1-4: "'Then,' I said, 'intellectually intuit, as we speak, these two to be, and the one to be king of the intellectible class and place, and the one in turn of the seeable, so that I having spoken "of the heaven" /instead of "of the seeable_7 will not seem to you to be a wise guy in respect to the name.'" (Νόησον τοίνυν, ἦν δ' ἐγώ, ὥσπερ λέγομεν, δύο αὐτὼ εἶναι, καὶ βασιλεύειν τὸ μὲν νοητοῦ γένους τε καὶ τόπου, τὸ δ' αὖ ὁρατοῦ, ἵνα μὴ οὐρανοῦ εἰπὼν δόξω σοι σοφίζεσθαι περὶ τὸ ὄνομα.)

108The connection between Kalliope (ὄψις, sight) and Ourania (τὰ οὐράνια, the heavenly things) is suggested by the onomatology of Οὐρανός at Cratylus 396b7-c3: "/Socrates.7 And he /i.e., Kronos/ is the son of Ouranos, as the speech /speaks_7; and in turn the seeing toward that which is upward has to be beautifully called this name,

110

'ourania,' the seeing those things which are upward, whence indeed also, o Hermogenes, the speakers about things in midair assert the pure intellect to become present, and /whence they assert/
the name for the heaven to be laid down correctly"
(ἔστι δὲ οὗτος Οὐρανοῦ υός, ὡς λόγος· ἡ δὲ αὖ ἐς
τὸ ἄνω ὄψις καλῶς ἔχει τοῦτο τὸ ὄνομα καλεῖσθαι,
"οὐρανία," ὁρῶσα τὰ ἄνω, ὅθεν δὴ καί φασιν, ὦ
Ἑρμόγενες, τὸν καθαρὸν νοῦν παραγίγνεσθαι οἱ
μετεωρολόγοι, καὶ τῷ οὐρανῷ ὀρθῶς τὸ ὄνομα κεῖσθαι). One might add here that onomatogenetically
at least there is a close connection between τὰ
οὐράνια and οἱ ἄνθρωποι, as suggested at Cratylus
399c1-6: "/Socrates./ This name 'human' signifies
that none of the things which the other beasts
see do they consider or reckon up or look up at,
but the human simultaneously has seen--and this
is the 'he had seen'--and looks up at and reckons
this which he has seen. Indeed thence the human
alone of the beasts was named 'human' correctly,
he looking up at the things which he has seen"
(σημαίνει τοῦτο τὸ ὄνομα ὁ "ἄνθρωπος" ὅτι τὰ μὲν
ἄλλα θηρία ὦν ὁρᾷ οὐδὲν ἐπισκοπεῖ οὐδὲ ἀναλογίζε-
ται οὐδὲ ἀναθρεῖ, ὁ δὲ ἄνθρωπος ἅμα ἑώρακεν--
τοῦτο δ' ἐστὶ τὸ "ὄπωπε"--καὶ ἀναθρεῖ καὶ λογίζε-
ται τοῦτο ὃ ὄπωπεν. ἐντεῦθεν δὴ μόνον τῶν θηρίων
ὀρθῶς ὁ ἄνθρωπος "ἄνθρωπος" ὠνομάσθη, ἀναθρῶν ἃ
ὄπωπε).

109Cf. Republic 7.516a8-c3.

110See Phaedrus 242a7-b4: "Socrates. O Phaedrus, you are divine in respect to speeches at
any rate and absolutely wondrous. For of the
speeches which have come to be in your lifetime,
I believe no one to have made more come to be
than you, either speaking yourself or compelling
in addition others by some one manner then--I
take out of the speech Simmias the Theban; but
you altogether much overpower the others /i.e.,
all others but Simmias/" (ΣΩ. θεῖος γ' εἶ περὶ
τοὺς λόγους, ὦ Φαῖδρε, καὶ ἀτεχνῶς θαυμάσιος.
οἶμαι γὰρ ἐγὼ τῶν ἐπὶ τοῦ σοῦ βίου γεγονότων
λόγων μηδένα πλείους ἢ σὲ πεποιηκέναι γεγενῆσθαι
ἤτοι αὐτὸν λέγοντα ἢ ἄλλους ἐνί γέ τῳ τρόπῳ

111

προσαναγκάζοντα--Σιμμίαν Θηβαῖον ἐξαιρῶ λόγου·
τῶν δὲ ἄλλων πάμπολυ κρατεῖς).

111Phaedo 85c7-d4: δεῖν γὰρ...ἕν γέ τι τούτων
διαπράξασθαι, ἢ μαθεῖν ὅπῃ ἔχει ἢ εὑρεῖν ἤ, εἰ
ταῦτα ἀδύνατον, τὸν γοῦν βέλτιστον τῶν ἀνθρωπίνων
λόγων λαβόντα καὶ δυσεξελεγκτότατον, ἐπὶ τούτου
ὀχούμενον ὥσπερ ἐπὶ σχεδίας κινδυνεύοντα διαπλεῦσαι τὸν βίον, εἰ μή τις δύναιτο ἀσφαλέστερον καὶ
ἀκινδυνότερον ἐπὶ βεβαιοτέρου ὀχήματος, λόγου
θείου τινός, διαπορευθῆναι. (I accept, with Burnet,
note ad Phaedo 85d3, Heindorf's seclension of ἤ.)

112Cf. βέλτιστα at 97c6, βέλτιστον at 97c8; τὸ
ἄριστον καὶ τὸ βέλτιστον at 97d3; τὸ χεῖρον at 97
d4; τὸ ἄμεινον at 97e2 (twice), e4, 98a5; βέλτιστον at 98a8, b2; τὸ βέλτιστον at 98b5-6; τὸ χεῖρον
at 98b6; βέλτιον at 98e2, 3; τοῦ βελτίστου at 99
a2, b1; βέλτιστα at 99c1. Also cf. δικαιότερον at
98e4, 99a2.

113Cf. τὸ κοινόν...ἀγαθόν at 98b2-3; τὸ ἀγαθόν
at 99c5. Also cf. Republic 7.516b5-6.

114Republic 6.506d8-507a4: ἀλλ', ὦ μακάριοι,
αὐτὸ μὲν τί ποτ' ἐστὶ τἀγαθὸν ἐάσωμεν τὸ νῦν εἶναι
--πλέον γάρ μοι φαίνεται ἢ κατὰ τὴν παροῦσαν ὁρμὴν
ἐφικέσθαι τοῦ γε δοκοῦντος ἐμοὶ τὰ νῦν--ὃς δὲ ἔκ-
γονός τε τοῦ ἀγαθοῦ φαίνεται καὶ ὁμοιότατος ἐκείνῳ,
λέγειν ἐθέλω, εἰ καὶ ὑμῖν φίλον, εἰ δὲ μή, ἐᾶν.
'Αλλ', ἔφη, λέγε· εἰς αὖθις γὰρ τοῦ πατρὸς ἀποτεί-
σεις τὴν διήγησιν. Βουλοίμην ἄν, εἶπον, ἐμέ τε
δύνασθαι αὐτὴν ἀποδοῦναι καὶ ὑμᾶς κομίσασθαι, ἀλλὰ
μὴ ὥσπερ νῦν τοὺς τόκους μόνον. τοῦτον δὲ δὴ οὖν
τὸν τόκον τε καὶ ἔκγονον αὐτοῦ τοῦ ἀγαθοῦ κομί-
σασθε.

115Cf. Adam, note ad Rep. 6.506e: "The emphasis
on τὸ νῦν εἶναι and τὰ νῦν seems to hint that a
description of the ἀγαθόν, as it is in itself, may
be expected on some future occasion. But there is
no dialogue in which the Idea of the Good is so
clearly described as in the Republic, and it is
not without reason that every historian of Philosophy regards this passage as the locus classicus

on the subject." Also cf. Plato, _Plato's Phaedo_,
tr. with intro. and comm. by R. Hackforth (Cambridge, Eng., 1972), p. 132.

116_Phaedrus_ 246a4-6: οἷον μέν ἐστι, πάντῃ πάν-
τως θείας εἶναι καὶ μακρᾶς διηγήσεως, ᾧ δὲ ἔοικεν,
ἀνθρωπίνης τε καὶ ἐλάττονος· ταύτῃ οὖν λέγωμεν.
Cf. 245c2-3.

117_Phaedrus_ 247c3-6: Τὸν δὲ ὑπερουράνιον τόπον
οὔτε τις ὕμνησέ πω τῶν τῇδε ποιητὴς οὔτε ποτὲ ὑμ-
νήσει κατ' ἀξίαν. ἔχει δὲ ὧδε--τολμητέον γὰρ οὖν
τό γε ἀληθὲς εἰπεῖν, ἄλλως τε καὶ περὶ ἀληθείας
λέγοντα....

118For the meaning of the names in the palinode's introduction, see above pp. 72-73.

119The dialogic character of the speech is
another aspect of this.

120The palinode may be subdivided in the following way:
   I. 243e9-245c4: introduction
        A. 243e9-244a3: genealogy
        B. 244a3-245c4: kinds of craziness
   II. 245c5-256e2: the myth (cf. 253c7), ἀπόδειξις of the soul
        A. 245c5-246e4: soul
             1. 245c5-246a3: soul's deathless-
        ness
             2. 246a3-e4: soul's ἰδέα
        B. 246e4-247e6: heaven
             1. 246e4-247c2: the subheavenly
        loop
             2. 247c3-e6: the superheavenly
        place
        C. 248a1-249d3: human soul types
             1. 248a1-249b6: the seeing human
        souls
             2. 249b6-d3: the superseeing human
        soul, the philosopher
        D. 249d4-252b1: longing
             1. 249d4-250c8: memory

113

121Phaedrus 243b2-3: ποιήσας...πᾶσαν τὴν κα-
λουμένην Παλινῳδίαν παραχρῆμα ἀνέβλεψεν

122The development of modern philosophy, at
least of modern political philosophy, from its in-
ception in Machiavelli, Bacon, and Hobbes, seems
to suggest that the former prevailed. And in like
manner, in the terms of the Symposium, in modern
philosophy, the penultimate level of Diotima's
narration, namely the desire for immortality
through fame and glory (208b7-209e4), prevailed
over the ultimate level, namely the desire for
immortality through the love and beholding of the
beautiful itself (209e5-212c3). And in like manner in turn, in the terms of the Phaedo, in
modern philosophy, the fear of death is in principle eradicated in a physico-political way
rather than in the psychico-transpolitical way
suggested by Socrates' incantations. For a lucid
account of the modern development in relation to
the ancient position, cf. Leo Strauss, NRH, pp.
161-162, and the chapter "Modern natural right,"
pp. 165-251, esp. pp. 165-202 and 249-251. In
some sense, this theme in all its variations is
the theme of Leo Strauss' corpus as a whole.

123This is roughly also the structure of Diotima's great speech in the penultimate section of
the Symposium, except that there one finds a genealogy of Eros followed by a classification of
eros. And of course, the genealogy there is as
little meant literally as the genealogy here. And
this is not only a recurring intradialogic structural feature, but it is also a recurring inter-
dialogic structural feature. For example, within
the sequence of eight dialogues surrounding Socrates' trial and death (Theaetetus, Euthyphro,

114

Cratylus, Sophist, Statesman, Apology of Socrates, Crito, and Phaedo, in that chronological
order: compare Theaetetus 210d1-4 to Euthyphro
2a1-6; also consider Cratylus 396d4-8; κατὰ τὴν
χθὲς ὁμολογίαν at Sophist 216a1; and Cratylus
396e3-397a1)--within that sequence, the Cratylus
as a genealogy (of names) is followed by the
classification of the projected Sophist-Statesman-
Philosopher trilogy (the last of which is either
not extant or was never written, either because
its purpose was achieved in the two which were
written or because it could not be written or
because of some other circumstance, to speculate
upon which alternatives goes beyond the scope of
this work). Or, in analogous manner, in the dramatic
sequence of the Republic, the Timaeus, the incomplete Critias, and the projected (but non-existent)
Hermocrates, the Republic and Timaeus are genetic
accounts of the city and the cosmos respectively,
while the Critias is a descriptive account of the
city and the Hermocrates, if the parallel were to
hold, would have been a descriptive account of the
cosmos (although its absence in the sequence after
it has been explicitly projected may have been
Plato's way of obliquely suggesting that such an
account is impossible). We will return to this in
Chapter VI.

124Cf. Iliad 1.603-604. For the close connection between Apollo and the traditional muses,
see Pindar Pythian 1, ll.1-2, Hesiod Theogony,
ll. 94-95. Also cf. Cratylus 404d8 ff.; Hymn to
Apollo, ll. 189-193, 516-519. And compare Iliad
1.603-604 to Hymn to Apollo, ll. 130 ff. Also cf.
Pythian 5, l. 65.

125For the close connection between Homer and
Apollo, see The contest of Homer and Hesiod (in
the LCL volume, Hesiod, the Homeric Hymns and Homerica, Cambridge, Mass., 1936), 324, Homer's in-
scription to Apollo: "Lord Phoebus, I, Homer,
gave then a beautiful gift to you for the thoughts
/which you gave to me/; and would that you would
make fame follow me always" (Φοῖβε ἄναξ, δῶρόν τοι
Ὄμηρος καλὸν ἔδωκα/ σῇσιν ἐπιφροσύναις· σὺ δέ μοι

κλέος αἰὲν ὀπάζοις). The <u>Contest</u> is contemporary
with Plato, and that he knew it is suggested by
the occurrence later in the <u>Phaedrus</u> (264d3-6) of
a series of verses which precede the Homeric in-
scription in the same work. Also cf. Vries, note
ad 264d3 ff.

126This is why Socrates preceded his palinode
with this remark (243a2-7): "Therefore there is a
compulsion for me, o friend, to purify myself;
and there is for those who err in respect to myth-
speaking an originary purification, which Homer
failed to perceive, but /which/ Stesichorus /per-
ceived/. For he /i.e., Stesichorus/ having been
deprived of his eyes because of his badmouthing
of Helen did not fail to recognize /the cause/,
as Homer /failed to do/, but since he /i.e., Ste-
sichorus/ was musical, he recognized the cause"
(ἐμοὶ μὲν οὖν, ὦ φίλε, καθήρασθαι ἀνάγκη· ἔστιν
δὲ τοῖς ἁμαρτάνουσι περὶ μυθολογίαν καθαρμὸς ἀρ-
χαῖος, ὃν Ὅμηρος μὲν οὐκ ᾔσθετο, Στησίχορος δέ.
τῶν γὰρ ὀμμάτων στερηθεὶς διὰ τὴν Ἑλένης κακη-
γορίαν οὐκ ἠγνόησεν ὥσπερ Ὅμηρος, ἀλλ' ἅτε μου-
σικὸς ὢν ἔγνω τὴν αἰτίαν). In other words, Homer
and his muses are amusical, whereas Stesichorus
and the Socratic muses (cf. <u>Phaedrus</u> 259b6-d7)
are truly musical. This adumbrates the private
Socratic victory over the poets in the <u>Symposium</u>,
a victory which depends not only on the truth and
comprehensiveness of the Socratic perspective but
also on the more 'poetic' and more musical Socratic presentation of his perspective. Of course,
the suggestion there, as here in the <u>Phaedrus</u> and
elsewhere, is that the Socratic victory can only
be a private one and never a public victory,
which is inevitably to the so-called but not
truly musical (because not truly philosophical)
poetry of Homer and his tribe.

127Cf. Robert Graves, <u>The Greek myths</u> (Baltimore, 1955), vol. 1, 21.i-m, p. 78. Also cf. <u>Hymn
to Apollo</u> 208.

128κλέος: cf. note 125 above and τοῦ Πυθοκλέους
(<u>Phaedrus</u> 244a1).

116

129Cf. Graves, 21.o, p. 79.

130That Phaedrus is Μυρρινουσίου suggests this, for as Thompson (note ad loc.) rightly suggests, this is a reference to Republic 2.372b5-6, but not (as he wrongly concludes) to the love of festivity, which is alien to the description of the city of sows (ὑῶν πόλιν: 2.372d4) there. Rather the reference is to the city itself, the most compulsory city (ἥ γε ἀναγκαιοτάτη πόλις: 2.369d11), the city which is founded precisely and only to meet needs.

131Cf. Republic 6.509c1-2.

132Cf. Sallis, pp. 133-134.

133Cf. Phaedrus 265c1.

134Cf. Phaedrus 251c8.

135Cf. Cratylus 418c5-d7.

136Cf. Phaedrus 243a2 (καθήρασθαι), 3 (καθαρμός).

137How little Phaedrus will learn from this and the rest of the palinode is indicated in his reply at 268c2-4, especially his use of μαίνεται at c2.

138Cf. Phaedrus 244a5-6: "For if being crazy were simply bad, it would have been spoken beautifully" (εἰ μὲν γὰρ ἦν ἁπλοῦν τὸ μανίαν κακὸν εἶναι, καλῶς ἂν ἐλέγετο).

139Cf. Sallis, pp. 132-133.

140Of course, there is always the possibility that divine craziness generates the biggest goods and the biggest bads, while human craziness generates littler goods and littler bads. Cf. Republic 2.379b1-380c10, esp. 379c2-7.

141The other leg of the διαίρεσις, though, is not forgotten: cf. θείᾳ...δόσει (244a7-8) and ὅταν θείᾳ μοίρᾳ γίγνηται (244c3). Also cf. ἐκ θεοῦ...παρ' ἀνθρώπων (244d4-5), τῷ ὀρθῶς μανέντι (244e4), ἐκ τέχνης (i.e., from art alone, a sober human method: 245a6; cf. 244b3-4, c1-2), and ψυχῆς φύσεως πέρι θείας τε καὶ ἀνθρωπίνης (245c2-3).

142Cf. Timaeus 17a1-3; also Statesman 257a1-b4.

143Cf. Phaedrus 244a7-8, c3, d4-5, 245b1-2, c2-3.

144Cf. 245b3-4; also cf. 244a5, b2, c5, 245a8, b4-5.

145Cf. 244a5-6, b1-2, 7, c1, 2-3, 4, d3-4, 245b1-2; also cf. 245a4.

146Compare 244d2-3 to 245a7.

147Compare 244b3-4 and c1-2 to 245a6-7.

148Cf. 244e4; also cf. 244b4-5. Included here would be self-deception: cf. 245a6-7.

149Cf. 244b7-c4, d1; also cf. 245a4.

150One might also suggest on the basis of this division that Lysias' enscrolled speech is the product of human sobriety, Socrates' Lysian speech of human craziness, and Socrates' Stesichorean speech of divine craziness. Only the category of divine sobriety, if there be any such thing, is missing, although it is possible that the discussion of writing and speaking with which the Phaedrus concludes is meant to be the symmetrically required product of divine sobriety or moderation. On the other hand, as Emily Dickinson suggests ("Much Madness is divinest Sense--/To a discerning Eye--/Much Sense--the starkest Madness--"), divine craziness and divine sobriety may be identical.

151Cf. Cratylus 404d8-406a3: μουσική (=ποίησις here), μαντική, ἰατρική (=λύσις here), τοξική. Cf. Pindar Pythian 5, 11. 60 ff., Hymn to Apollo

130 ff. Also see note 124 above.

152The regular association of Eros (or Cupid) with the bow does not arise until very late in antiquity, although there is the first vague suggestion of it in Euripides, Trojan women, 1. 255 (but there it is in opposition to Apollonian divination).

153Cf. Parmenides Fr. 8, 11. 50-52: "Here I cease my trustable speech and intellectual intuition to you/ about truth; and from here the opinions of mortals/ learn, hearing the deceptive order of my sayings" (ἐν τῶι σοι παύω πιστὸν λόγον ἠδὲ νόημα/ ἀμφὶς ἀληθείης· δόξας δ' ἀπὸ τοῦδε βροτείας/ μάνθανε κόσμον ἐμῶν ἐπέων ἀπατηλὸν ἀκούων). The text is from Parmenides, Parmenides: a text with tr., comm., and critical essays, by Leonardo Tarán (Princeton, 1965); the translation is mine.

154Cratylus 420b7-9: ΣΩ. "Δόξα" δὴ ἤτοι τῇ διώξει ἐπωνόμασται, ἣν ἡ ψυχὴ διώκουσα τὸ εἰδέναι ὅπη ἔχει τὰ πράγματα πορεύεται. ἢ τῇ ἀπὸ τοῦ τόξου βολῇ. ἔοικε δὲ τούτῳ μᾶλλον.

155In other words, it does precisely what Socrates disclaimed: cf. ὤρθωσαν at 244b5 to ἐπανορθοῦσθαι at 229d6.

156This too contains an implicit διαίρεσις: first, there is ψυχή, and then there is ψυχὴ θεία and ψυχὴ ἀνθρωπίνη.

157Cf. ἀποδεικτέον at 245b7, ἀπόδειξις at 245c1, and ἀποδείξεως at 245c4. Also cf. Sallis, pp. 135-136.

158ψυχὴ πᾶσα ἀθάνατος: 245c5. Cf. Vries, note ad loc., on πᾶσα as simultaneously collective (all) and distributive (every).

159Cratylus 399d10-e3, 400a5-b7: /ΣΩ./ οἶμαί τι τοιοῦτον νοεῖν τοὺς τὴν ψυχὴν ὀνομάσαντας, ὡς τοῦτο ἄρα, ὅταν παρῇ τῷ σώματι, αἴτιον ἐστι τοῦ ζῆν αὐτῷ,

119

τὴν τοῦ ἀναπνεῖν δύναμιν παρέχον καὶ ἀναψῦχον, ἅμα
δὲ ἐκλείποντος τοῦ ἀναψύχοντος τὸ σῶμα ἀπόλλυται
τε καὶ τελευτᾷ· ὅθεν δή μοι δοκοῦσιν αὐτὸ "ψυχὴν"
καλέσαι......Τὴν φύσιν παντὸς τοῦ σώματος, ὥστε
καὶ ζῆν καὶ περιιέναι, τί σοι δοκεῖ ἔχειν τε καὶ
ὀχεῖν ἄλλο ἢ ψυχή; ΕΡΜ. Οὐδὲν ἄλλο. ΣΩ. Τί δέ; καὶ
τὴν τῶν ἄλλων ἁπάντων φύσιν οὐ πιστεύεις Ἀναξα-
γόρᾳ νοῦν καὶ ψυχὴν εἶναι τὴν διακοσμοῦσαν καὶ
ἔχουσαν; ΕΡΜ. Ἔγωγε. ΣΩ. Καλῶς ἄρα ἂν τὸ ὄνομα
τοῦτο ἔχοι τῇ δυνάμει ταύτῃ ἡ φύσιν ὀχεῖ καὶ ἔχει
"φυσέχην" ἐπονομάζειν. ἔξεστι δὲ καὶ "ψυχὴν" κομ-
ψευόμενον λέγειν. ΕΡΜ. Πάνυ μὲν οὖν, καὶ δοκεῖ γέ
μοι τοῦτο ἐκείνου τεχνικώτερον εἶναι. ΣΩ. Καὶ γὰρ
ἔστιν· γελοῖον μέντοι φαίνεται ὡς ἀληθῶς ὀνομαζό-
μενον ὡς ἐτέθη. Cf. Sallis, pp. 136-138.

[160]I.e., the self which the self-moving always
is, is movability.

[161]Phaedrus 245c9: πηγή. Cf. Phaedrus 255c1, 2-
7: "then already the fountain of that flow /i.e.,
the flow of beauty/,...which /fountain/ is borne
much toward the lover, on the one hand sank into
him, and on the other hand flows off outside /when/
he is filled; and such as breath or a certain echo
springing from things both smooth and solid is
borne again whence it set out, thus the flow of
beauty /is borne/ again unto the beautiful person
going through the things through which one sees"
(τότ' ἤδη ἡ τοῦ ῥεύματος ἐκείνου πηγή,...πολλὴ
φερομένη πρὸς τὸν ἐραστήν, ἡ μὲν εἰς αὐτὸν ἔδυ, ἡ
δ' ἀπομεστουμένου ἔξω ἀπορρεῖ· καὶ οἷον πνεῦμα ἤ
τις ἠχὼ ἀπὸ λείων τε καὶ στερεῶν ἀλλομένη πάλιν
ὅθεν ὡρμήθη φέρεται, οὕτω τὸ τοῦ κάλλους ῥεῦμα
πάλιν εἰς τὸν καλὸν διὰ τῶν ὀμμάτων ἰόν). In other
words, as a fountain flows back to its source, so
too the ἀρχή of moving moves back upon itself, and
the whole is no less characterized by its eroti-
cally self-reflexive flow than is the soul.

[162]Phaedrus 245d2-3: εἰ γὰρ ἔκ του ἀρχὴ γίγνοιτο, οὐκ ἂν ἐξ ἀρχῆς γίγνοιτο. With Vries (cf.
note ad loc.), but against Burnet (cf. OCT, emended
text and apparatus criticus ad loc.) and Hackforth

(cf. p. 63, n. 1), I accept the manuscript reading
as intelligible. What it suggests is that there is
a source, which is not an ἀρχη, as with a fountain
there is a source which is not the fountain itself,
i.e., there is a source which is beyond an ἀρχη,
as the good is beyond beingness. Cf. Republic 6.
509b6-10: "Then also assert not only having been
recognized to be present to the things which are
recognized by /means of/ the good, but also both
being and beingness in addition to be present to
them by it, since the good is not beingness but
holds itself over beyond beingness by its venera-
bility and power." (Καὶ τοῖς γιγνωσκομένοις τοίνυν
μὴ μόνον τὸ γιγνώσκεσθαι φάναι ὑπὸ τοῦ ἀγαθοῦ παρ-
εῖναι, ἀλλὰ καὶ τὸ εἶναι τε καὶ τὴν οὐσίαν ὑπ'
ἐκείνου αὐτοῖς προσεῖναι, οὐκ οὐσίας ὄντος τοῦ
ἀγαθοῦ, ἀλλ' ἔτι ἐπέκεινα τῆς οὐσίας πρεσβείᾳ καὶ
δυνάμει ὑπερέχοντος.) (For the infinitive φάναι
as the imperative, cf. Adam, note ad Rep. 473a.)

163245d8-e1: πάντα τε οὐρανὸν πᾶσάν τε γένεσιν
συμπεσοῦσαν στῆναι. With Vries (cf. note ad loc.)
and Hackforth (cf. p. 63, n. 2), but against Burnet (cf. OCT, emended text and apparatus criticus
ad loc.), I retain the manuscript reading, which
is intelligible in itself and accords with Timaeus'
usage in the Timaeus, in which ὁ πᾶν and ὁ κόσμος
and ὁ οὐρανός are used interchangeably (cf. Tim.
92c4, 6, 8; 28b2-4 and ff.) and are coupled with
ἡ γένεσις (cf. γένεσιν καὶ τὸ πᾶν at 29d7, and
γενέσεως καὶ κόσμου at 29e4). Also it should be
noted that as above at 245c5, the πάντα and πᾶσαν
are used as simultaneously collective and distributive: cf. Vries, note ad loc.; Hackforth, p. 66,
n. 3; note 158 above.

164This too is consonant with Timaeus' teaching
in the Timaeus. Cf. 30b6-c1: "Therefore indeed in
this way, in accordance with the likely speech, it
is obligatory to speak this cosmos to have become
a living thing having within it, in truth, soul
and intellectual intuition because of the god's
prescience" (οὕτως οὖν δὴ κατὰ λόγον τὸν εἰκότα
δεῖ λέγειν τόνδε τὸν κόσμον ζῷον ἔμψυχον ἔννουν

τε τῇ ἀληθείᾳ διὰ τὴν τοῦ θεοῦ γενέσθαι πρόνοιαν).
Also consider <u>Philebus</u> 30a3-b7.

[165]Again the πᾶν is used as simultaneously collective and distributive.

[166]For a brief discussion of the parallels between this and the treatment of the soul in <u>Laws</u> 10, see Sallis, pp. 139-140, esp. n. 20.

[167]In other words, these two aspects of soul correspond to the discussions of soul found respectively in <u>Republic</u> 4 (nature) and <u>Republic</u> 10 (beingness and speech).

[168]Cf. <u>Timaeus</u> 29b2-3: "Indeed greatest of all is for a beginning to begin in accordance with nature." (μέγιστον δὴ παντὸς ἄρξασθαι κατὰ φύσιν ἀρχήν.)

[169]The elaboration of this problem is central to both the Platonic corpus and the Aristotelian corpus. In a way, this is the central theme of Aristotle's <u>De anima</u>, which begins by treating soul as an οὐσία (Book 1) and ends by treating soul as a nature (Books 2 and 3), which two treatments roughly correspond to the soul as object of study of the dialectician and the soul as object of study of the physicist. Cf. <u>De anima</u> 3.5.430 a10-14; 1.1. et passim.

[170]εἰ δ' ἔστιν τοῦτο οὕτως ἔχον, μὴ ἄλλο τι εἶναι τὸ αὐτὸ ἑαυτὸ κινοῦν ἢ ψυχήν, ἐξ ἀνάγκης ἀγένητόν τε καὶ ἀθάνατον ψυχὴ ἂν εἴη.

[171]For a discussion of the intervening section, see Sallis, pp. 140-144.

[172]<u>Phaedrus</u> 247a8: δαῖτα καὶ...θοίνην. Cf. Kenneth Dorter, "Imagery and philosophy in Plato's <u>Phaedrus</u>," <u>Journal of the history of philosophy</u>, vol. 9, July 1971, p. 280, n. 3: "The <u>Phaedrus</u> abounds in culinary terminology which recurs throughout with the regularity of a leitmotif: 227b6, /̄230d6-8,̄/ 235d1, 236e8, 238a6, b2, 241c8,

243d4, 246e2, 247a8, d2-4, e3, 6, 248b5, 7, c2,
251c8, 255d1, 259c1-4, 260d1, 265e3, 270b6, 276d6."

173Cf. οὐσία ὄντως οὖσα at 247c7, τὸ ὄν at 247
d3, ὅ ἐστιν ὂν ὄντως at 247e2, τἆλλα...τὰ ὄντα ὄντως at 247e2-3.

174Cf. Republic 6.508d4-6: "Thus then also the
one thing of the soul intellectually intuits thus;
whenever it supports itself on this on which truth
and being shine down, it both intellectually intuited and recognized it and it appears to have intellectual intuition" (Οὕτω τοίνυν καὶ τὸ τῆς ψυχῆς ὧδε νόει· ὅταν μὲν οὗ καταλάμπει ἀλήθειά τε
καὶ τὸ ὄν, εἰς τοῦτο ἀπερείσηται, ἐνόησέν τε καὶ
ἔγνω αὐτὸ καὶ νοῦν ἔχειν φαίνεται).

175Phaedrus 247a1-2: μένει γὰρ ῾Εστία ἐν θεῶν
οἴκῳ μόνη.

176Perhaps the closeness of the Phaedrus and
the Cratylus has something to do with Socrates'
assertions in both dialogues that his speech is
the product of inspiration or inspired wisdom: cf.
Cratylus 396d2-e2; also consider 399a1, 409d1-2,
428c6-8. In addition, see Phaedrus 241e1-5, 249
c4-d3, 252e5-253a5, 263d1-3.

177Cratylus 401b1-e1: ΣΩ. "Αλλο τι οὖν ἀφ'
῾Εστίας ἀρχώμεθα κατὰ τὸν νόμον; ΕΡΜ. Δίκαιον
γοῦν. ΣΩ. Τί οὖν ἄν τις φαίη διανοούμενον τὸν ὀνο-
μάσαντα ῾Εστίαν ὀνομάσαι; ΕΡΜ. Οὐ μὰ τὸν Δία οὐδὲ
τοῦτο οἶμαι ῥᾴδιον εἶναι. ΣΩ. Κινδυνεύουσι γοῦν,
ὠγαθὲ ῾Ερμόγενες, οἱ πρῶτοι τὰ ὀνόματα τιθέμενοι
οὐ φαῦλοι εἶναι ἀλλὰ μετεωρολόγοι καὶ ἀδολέσχαι
τινές. ΕΡΜ. Τί δή; ΣΩ. Καταφαίνεταί μοι ἡ θέσις
τῶν ὀνομάτων τοιούτων τινῶν ἀνθρώπων, καὶ ἐάν τις
τὰ ξενικὰ ὀνόματα ἀνασκοπῇ, οὐχ ἧττον ἀνευρίσκε-
ται ὃ ἕκαστον βούλεται. οἷον καὶ ἐν τούτῳ ὃ ἡμεῖς
"οὐσίαν" καλοῦμεν, εἰσὶν οἳ "ἐσσίαν" καλοῦσιν, οἳ
δ' αὖ "ὠσίαν." πρῶτον μὲν οὖν κατὰ τὸ ἕτερον ὄνομα τούτων ἡ τῶν πραγμάτων οὐσία "῾Εστία" καλεῖσθαι ἔχει λόγον, καὶ ὅτι γε αὖ ἡμεῖς τὸ τῆς οὐσίας
μετέχον "ἔστιν" φαμέν, καὶ κατὰ τοῦτο ὀρθῶς ἂν

123

καλοῦτο "'Εστία"· ἐοίκαμεν γὰρ καὶ ἡμεῖς τὸ παλαι-
ὸν "ἐσσίαν" καλεῖν τὴν οὐσίαν. ἔτι δὲ καὶ κατὰ τὰς
θυσίας ἄν τις ἐννοήσας ἡγήσαιτο οὕτω νοεῖν ταῦτα
τοὺς τιθεμένους· τὸ γὰρ πρὸ πάντων θεῶν τῇ 'Εστίᾳ
πρώτη προθύειν εἰκὸς ἐκείνους οἵτινες τὴν πάντων
οὐσίαν "ἐσσίαν" ἐπωνόμασαν. ὅσοι δ' αὖ "ὠσίαν,"
σχεδόν τι αὖ οὗτοι καθ' 'Ηράκλειτον ἄν ἡγοῦντο τὰ
ὄντα ἰέναι τε πάντα καὶ μένειν οὐδέν· τὸ οὖν αἴτιον καὶ τὸ ἀρχηγὸν αὐτῶν εἶναι τὸ ὠθοῦν, ὅθεν δὴ
καλῶς ἔχειν αὐτὸ "ὠσίαν" ὠνομάσθαι. καὶ ταῦτα μὲν
δὴ ταύτῃ ὡς παρὰ μηδὲν εἰδότων εἰρήσθω....

178For the relationship between the soul and
the whole, cf. Phaedrus 270c1-2: "Socrates. Therefore do you believe it to be possible in a way
worthy of speech to intellectually intuit the nature of soul without the nature of the whole?"
(ΣΩ. Ψυχῆς οὖν φύσιν ἀξίως λόγου κατανοῆσαι οἴει
δυνατὸν εἶναι ἄνευ τῆς τοῦ ὅλου φύσεως;)

179Euthyphro 3a7-8: ἀτεχνῶς γάρ μοι δοκεῖ ἀφ'
'Εστίας ἄρχεσθαι κακουργεῖν τὴν πόλιν, ἐπιχειρῶν
ἀδικεῖν σέ. Cf. Burnet, note ad loc.

180Cf. Sallis, pp. 183 ff.

181Cf. Philebus 34c10-35d7.

182Cf. Symposium 199c3-201c9, 201e3-202e2, 203
a9-204b7.

183Cf. Hymn to Aphrodite 22-23, that Hestia was
both first and last of Kronos' children, both oldest and youngest. (See LCL, note ad loc.) In the
Symposium, this range is embodied in the figures
of Phaedrus (cf. 178a9-c3) for whom Eros is the
oldest god and Agathon (cf. 195a8-c7) for whom
Eros is the youngest god. Here again, only in Socrates are the extremes united.

184Cf. Phaedrus 247a6-7: "and the person who is
always both willing and capable follows" (ἔπεται
δὲ ὁ ἀεὶ ἐθέλων τε καὶ δυνάμενος).

185Cf. Republic 4.435e1-441c8, esp. 439e2-440d7.

This represents a revision of the politically appropriate but in other ways inaccurate tripartite account of soul in the Republic by suggesting that it is rather the case (as Glaucon suggests) that spiritedness and desire work together against intellect than (as Socrates suggests) that intellect and spiritedness work together against desire. The revision retains the tripartiteness of soul but it does so by fusing spiritedness and desire (in the sense of the Republic, as the δῆμος of low desires) and interposing a purified erotic part of soul.

186There is an extraordinary density of vision terms at 247c3-252b1: 247c7, d3, 4, 5, 6, e3, 248a4, 6, b4, 6, c3, 6, d2, 249b6, c2, 3, 5, 250a2, 4, 6, b5, 6-7, 8, d3, 4, 6, e3, 3-4, 251a3, 5, 7, b2, c6, e2, 3. This emphasizes the seriousness of blindness as a punishment.

187247c7: οὐσία ὄντως οὖσα.

188Cf. ἀνάμνησις at 249c2, μνήμη at 249c5, and ὑπομνήμασιν at 249c7.

189Cf. Republic 7.514a1 ff. The chained prisoners in the cave are like oysters, the most mindless and most ignorant of living things: cf. Timaeus 92a7-c1; Phaedrus 250c6; Cratylus 400b8-c9.

190Cf. Phaedrus 249c6-d3: "And indeed a man using the suchlike reminders correctly, /a man/ who always is perfected by (is initiated into) the perfect (initiating) perfections (initiations), he alone becomes beingly perfect (initiated); and he, having stood himself outside the human serious things and coming to be near the divine, is set straight in his mind by the many as though he were moving askew, and he has escaped the notice of the many /as/ being inspired." (τοῖς δὲ δὴ τοιούτοις ἀνὴρ ὑπομνήμασιν ὀρθῶς χρώμενος, τελέους ἀεὶ τελετὰς τελούμενος, τέλεος ὄντως μόνος γίγνεται· ἐξιστάμενος δὲ τῶν ἀνθρωπίνων σπουδασμάτων καὶ πρὸς τῷ θείῳ γιγνόμενος, νουθετεῖται μὲν ὑπὸ τῶν πολλῶν ὡς παρακινῶν, ἐνθουσιάζων δὲ λέληθεν τοὺς πολλούς.) Cf. Vries, note ad 249c7-8.

191Phaedrus 249b5-c4: οὐ γὰρ ἥ γε μήποτε ἰδοῦσα τὴν ἀλήθειαν εἰς τόδε ἥξει τὸ σχῆμα. δεῖ γὰρ ἄνθρωπον συνιέναι κατ' εἶδος λεγόμενον, ἐκ πολλῶν ἰὸν αἰσθήσεων εἰς ἕν λογισμῷ συναιρούμενον· τοῦτο δ' ἐστιν ἀνάμνησις ἐκείνων ἅ ποτ' εἶδεν ἡμῶν ἡ ψυχὴ συμπορευθεῖσα θεῷ καὶ ὑπεριδοῦσα ἃ νῦν εἶναί φαμεν, καὶ ἀνακύψασα εἰς τὸ ὂν ὄντως.

192I adapt the distinction between operative and thematic from Eugen Fink, as cited in Richard Zaner, The way of phenomenology (New York, 1970), pp. 115, 160-163.

193The limited scope of the present inquiry makes it impossible to consider exhaustively the remainder of the palinode (250c8-257b6), which as a whole is about the experience of love, but here a few things should be noted at least briefly. First, at 250c8-e1, the hierarchy of the lovable is treated as equivalent to the hierarchy of being, and the criterion for rank in the hierarchy is vivacity (cf. τῆς ἐναργεστάτης at 250d2, ἐναργέστατα at 250d3, ἐναργὲς at 250d5). Second, in the discussion of the corrupt lover (250e1-251a1), homosexuality is explicitly condemned as unnatural, while heterosexuality in the service of procreation is implicitly regarded as natural, for the corrupt lover sows children only because he regards it as a conventional compulsion (250e4-251a1): "but /the corrupt lover/, after he has given himself over to pleasure, takes it in hand to mount /a woman/ and to sow children with respect to the law of a quadruped, and since he has had commerce in addition with insolence he neither has feared nor is ashamed of chasing beside nature pleasure which is beside nature /i.e., both heterosexual acts which are not in the service of procreation and all homosexual acts/" (ἀλλ' ἡδονῇ παραδοὺς τετράποδος νόμον βαίνειν ἐπιχειρεῖ καὶ παιδοσπορεῖν, καὶ ὕβρει προσομιλῶν οὐ δέδοικεν οὐδ' αἰσχύνεται παρὰ φύσιν ἡδονὴν διώκων) (cf. Vries, note ad 251a1, for the double construing of παρὰ φύσιν and for references to related passages in the Laws). Third, the description of the just lover's wing (251a1-c5), its shiver (251a2-7) and

fever 9251a7-b5) and swelling (251b5-7) and boil-
ing (251c1-5), is simultaneously a description of
a phallus in all stages of sexual arousal through
orgasm, i.e., it is a complete somatization of the
psychic, and hence suggests the ease with which a
lover may become corrupted, for in the erotic
things, the step from imaged somatization to behavioral somatization is an easy one to take, i.e.,
the itching (κνῆσις: 251c3) of eros beckons virtually irresistibly to be scratched. And this explains to some extent the enormous power of the
hybristic horse, the virtually irresistible itch
which thymoeidetic epithymia is. As to the rest
of the palinode, cf. Sallis, p. 157: "all that
remains is for Socrates to describe the course
which the development of love follows and then,
finally, to bring the entire speech explicitly to
bear on the question inherited from the speech of
Lysias." Also see Sallis, pp. 157-159.

194Cf. Phaedrus 265c8-d1: "Socrates. The other
things appear to me to have been childish play by
that which is childish play; and of these certain
things which have been uttered from luck /there
are/ two looks which would not be ungratifying if
anyone were capable of grasping their power by
art." (ΣΩ. 'Εμοὶ μὲν φαίνεται τὰ μὲν ἄλλα τῷ ὄντι
παιδιᾷ πεπαῖσθαι· τούτων δέ τινων ἐκ τύχης ῥηθέν-
των δυοῖν εἰδοῖν, εἰ αὐτοῖν τὴν δύναμιν τέχνῃ
λαβεῖν δύναιτό τις, οὐκ ἄχαρι.)

195Phaedrus 265a9-b5: ΣΩ. Μανίας δέ γε εἴδη
δύο, τὴν μὲν ὑπὸ νοσημάτων ἀνθρωπίνων, τὴν δὲ ὑπὸ
θείας ἐξαλλαγῆς τῶν εἰωθότων νομίμων γιγνομένην.
ΦΑΙ. Πάνυ γε. ΣΩ. Τῆς δὲ θείας τεττάρων θεῶν τέτ-
ταρα μέρη διελόμενοι, μαντικὴν μὲν ἐπίπνοιαν
'Απόλλωνος θέντες, Διονύσου δὲ τελεστικήν, Μουσῶν
δ' αὖ ποιητικήν, τετάρτην δὲ 'Αφροδίτης καὶ
"Ερωτος, ἐρωτικὴν μανίαν ἐφήσαμέν τε ἀρίστην
εἶναι.... In the initial classification (244a8-245
c1), only the Muses were mentioned explicitly.

196Republic 10.604a1-607a9.

197The identification is not made until 266c1.

127

198Cf. Timaeus 71d5-72b5: "For the ones composing us, remembering the father's missive, when
he commissioned /them/ to make the mortal class
the best possible unto their power, thus indeed
they correcting even the mean thing of us, so that
in some way it should in addition touch the truth,
set up_in this the divinative. And a sufficient
sign /of/ how the god_has given divination to human thoughtlessness /is this/; for no one in his
mind touches upon inspired and true divination, but
/only/ either having been shackled /in/ the power
of his prudence either in accordance with sleep or
because of disease, or having altered because of
some inspiration. But it is for the person in his
senses to conceive the re-remembered things which
have been uttered by divination and inspired nature either adream or awake, and by reckoning to
divide all, as many apparitions as were seen, in
whatever way and to whom they signify when bad or
good is about to be or has already come or is present; and when the crazy person still also remains
in this, it is not his work to judge by himself
the things which appeared and were voiced, but
well and anciently acting and recognizing his own
things and himself are spoken to be fitting to the
moderate person alone. Whence indeed also law has
set up over inspired divinations the class of prophets as judges; which very persons some name diviners, /the namers/ being altogether unrecogni-
zing that these persons are actors-out of assertion through riddles and of appearing, and they
are not in any way diviners, and they would most
justly be named prophets of the things which are
divined." (μεμνημένοι γὰρ τῆς τοῦ πατρὸς ἐπιστολῆς
οἱ συστήσαντες ἡμᾶς, ὅτε τὸ θνητὸν ἐπέστελλεν γένος ὡς ἄριστον εἰς δύναμιν ποιεῖν, οὕτω δὴ κατορ-
θοῦντες καὶ τὸ φαῦλον ἡμῶν, ἵνα ἀληθείας πη προσ-
άπτοιτο, κατέστησαν ἐν τούτῳ τὸ μαντεῖον. ἱκανὸν
δὲ σημεῖον ὡς μαντικὴν ἀφροσύνῃ θεὸς ἀνθρωπίνῃ
δέδωκεν· οὐδεὶς γὰρ ἔννους ἐφάπτεται μαντικῆς ἐν-
θέου καὶ ἀληθοῦς, ἀλλ' ἢ καθ' ὕπνον τὴν τῆς φρονήσεως πεδηθεὶς δύναμιν ἢ διὰ νόσον, ἢ διά τινα ἐν-
θουσιασμὸν παραλλάξας. ἀλλὰ συννοῆσαι μὲν ἔμφρονος
τά τε ῥηθέντα ἀναμνησθέντα ὄναρ ἢ ὕπαρ ὑπὸ τῆς
μαντικῆς τε καὶ ἐνθουσιαστικῆς φύσεως, καὶ ὅσα ἄν

φαντάσματα ὀφθῇ, πάντα λογισμῷ διελέσθαι ὅπῃ τι σημαίνει καὶ ὅτῳ μέλλοντος ἢ παρελθόντος ἢ παρόντος κακοῦ ἢ ἀγαθοῦ· τοῦ δὲ μανέντος ἔτι τε ἐν τούτῳ μένοντος οὐκ ἔργον τὰ φανέντα καὶ φωνηθέντα ὑφ' ἑαυτοῦ κρίνειν, ἀλλ' εὖ καὶ πάλαι λέγεται τὸ πράττειν καὶ γνῶναι τά τε αὑτοῦ καὶ ἑαυτὸν σώφρονι μόνῳ προσήκειν. ὅθεν δὴ καὶ τὸ τῶν προφητῶν γένος ἐπὶ ταῖς ἐνθέοις μαντείαις κριτὰς ἐπικαθιστάναι νόμος· οὓς μάντεις αὐτοὺς ὀνομάζουσίν τινες, τὸ πᾶν ἠγνοηκότες ὅτι τῆς δι' αἰνιγμῶν οὗτοι φήμης καὶ φαντάσεως ὑποκριταί, καὶ οὔτι μάντεις, προφῆται δὲ μαντευομένων δικαιότατα ὀνομάζοιντ' ἄν.)

199Here I can only repeat the following apology: "The very brief discussion of collection and division in the Phaedrus hardly provides a sufficient basis for a thorough consideration, which, instead, must take its bearings primarily from the Sophist and the Statesman." (Sallis, p. 171, n. 37.) He might also have added the Republic.

200This is the briefer of the two because it has already been explicitly discussed: cf. Phaedrus 249b5-c4, and p. 84 above.

201Phaedrus 265d3-7: ΣΩ. Εἰς μίαν τε ἰδέαν συνορῶντα ἄγειν τὰ πολλαχῇ διεσπαρμένα, ἵνα ἕκαστον ὁριζόμενος δῆλον ποιῇ περὶ οὗ ἂν ἀεὶ διδάσκειν ἐθέλῃ. ὥσπερ τὰ νυνδὴ περὶ Ἔρωτος--ὃ ἔστιν ὁρισθέν--εἴτ' εὖ εἴτε κακῶς ἐλέχθη, τὸ γοῦν σαφὲς καὶ τὸ αὐτὸ αὑτῷ ὁμολογούμενον διὰ ταῦτα ἔσχεν εἰπεῖν ὁ λόγος. I have slightly altered Burnet's punctuation.

202Cf. συνορῶντα at 265d3 to σύνοψιν at Republic 7. 537c2. Also consider Republic 7.537c7: "For the synoptic person is dialectical, but the non-synoptic is not." (ὁ μὲν γὰρ συνοπτικὸς διαλεκτικός, ὁ δὲ μὴ οὔ.)

203Cf. Martin Heidegger, Being and time, tr. John Macquarrie and Edward Robinson (New York, 1962), pp. 416 (H365) and 19 (H1). Also see his Discourse on thinking, tr. John M. Anderson and

E. Hans Freund (New York, 1968), pp. 64 ff.

[204]<u>Phaedrus</u> ·265e1–266b1: ΣΩ. Τὸ πάλιν κατ᾽ εἴδη
δύνασθαι διατέμνειν κατ᾽ ἄρθρα ᾗ πέφυκεν, καὶ μὴ
ἐπιχειρεῖν καταγνῦναι μέρος μηδέν, κακοῦ μαγείρου
τρόπῳ χρώμενον· ἀλλ᾽ ὥσπερ ἄρτι τὼ λόγω τὸ μὲν
ἄφρον τῆς διανοίας ἕν τι κοινῇ εἶδος ἐλαβέτην,
ὥσπερ δὲ σώματος ἐξ ἑνὸς διπλᾶ καὶ ὁμώνυμα πέφυκε,
σκαιά, τὰ δὲ δεξιὰ κληθέντα, οὕτω καὶ τὸ τῆς παρα-
νοίας ὡς ἐν ἡμῖν πεφυκὸς εἶδος ἡγησαμένω τὼ λόγω,
ὁ μὲν τὸ ἐπ᾽ ἀριστερὰ τεμνόμενος μέρος, πάλιν τοῦτο τέμνων οὐκ ἐπανῆκεν πρὶν ἐν αὐτοῖς ἐφευρὼν ὀνο-
μαζόμενον σκαιόν τινα ἔρωτα ἐλοιδόρησεν μάλ᾽ ἐν
δίκῃ, ὁ δ᾽ εἰς τὰ ἐν δεξιᾷ τῆς μανίας ἀγαγὼν ἡμᾶς,
ὁμώνυμον μὲν ἐκείνῳ, θεῖον δ᾽ αὖ τινα ἔρωτα ἐφευρὼν καὶ προτεινάμενος ἐπῄνεσεν ὡς μεγίστων αἴτιον
ἡμῖν ἀγαθῶν. I have removed from the text Heindorf's addition of ἕν at 266a2: cf. Burnet, OCT,
apparatus criticus ad loc.

[205]Cf. κατ᾽ εἶδος at 249b7 and Εἰς μίαν...ἰδέαν
at 265d3 to κατ᾽ εἴδη at 265e1, ἕν τι...εἶδος at
265e4, and τὸ...εἶδος at 266a2–3.

[206]Cf. Sallis, p. 170, who adopts this rendering.

[207]Cf. δύνασθαι at e1 to ἐπιχειρεῖν at e2.

[208]τὸ ἄφρον at 265e4, ἡ παρανοία at 266a2, and
ἡ μανία at 266a6. Cf. Sallis, p. 170, n. 36.

[209]Cf. William Blake, <u>Songs of Experience</u>, "The
Tyger," lines 1–4: "Tyger! Tyger! burning bright/
In the forests of the night,/ What immortal hand
or eye/ Could frame thy fearful symmetry?" (The
complete writings of William Blake with all variant readings, ed. Geoffrey Keynes (New York, 1957),
p. 214.) Although Blake does not explicitly say
so, the tiger is taken as symmetrical because it
is seen from the front.

[210]Cf. <u>Symposium</u> 191a3–5: "and he /i.e., Apol-
lo/ left behind a few /wrinkles/, the ones around
the belly itself and the navel, to be a memorial

130

of the ancient affection." (ὀλίγας δὲ κατέλιπε,
τὰς περὶ αὐτὴν τὴν γαστέρα καὶ τὸν ὀμφαλόν, μνη-
μεῖον εἶναι τοῦ παλαιοῦ πάθους.) In addition,
consider the suggestion at <u>Philebus</u> 35b1-d7 that
desire is memory.

211Cf. <u>Symposium</u> 191b5 ff. Also consider Iago's
loathsomely rich remark: "your Daughter and the
Moore, are making the Beast with two backs."
(William Shakespeare, <u>Othello</u>, a new variorum
edition, ed. Horace Howard Furness (New York,
1963), I.1.128-129.) In connection with Aristophanes' speech, one could raise the question whether Apollo was a good butcher or a bad butcher.

212<u>Symposium</u> 191a5-b1: ἐπειδὴ οὖν ἡ φύσις δίχα
ἐτμήθη, ποθοῦν ἕκαστον τὸ ἥμισυ τὸ αὐτοῦ συνῄει,
καὶ περιβάλλοντες τὰς χεῖρας καὶ συμπλεκόμενοι
ἀλλήλοις, ἐπιθυμοῦντες συμφῦναι, ἀπέθνησκον ὑπὸ
λιμοῦ καὶ τῆς ἄλλης ἀργίας διὰ τὸ μηδὲν ἐθέλειν
χωρὶς ἀλλήλων ποιεῖν.

213Therefore, as Aristophanes presents Eros
(cf. <u>Symposium</u> 189d1-3), far from being a "healer
of these things which, when they have been healed,
would be the greatest happiness for the human race"
(ἰατρὸς τούτων ὧν ἰαθέντων μεγίστη εὐδαιμονία ἂν
τῷ ἀνθρωπείῳ γένει εἴη), it is that which infects
the human race with an ineradicable disease and is
thereby productive of the greatest unhappiness.
The darkness of Aristophanean comedy is exceeded
only by the darkness of the Platonic comedy which
presents so darkly comic a figure.

214Cf. <u>Philebus</u> 57a9 ff., where λόγος is perso-
nified as διαίρεσις.

215<u>Statesman</u> 269b5-c1: ΞΕ. Ταῦτα τοίνυν ἔστι
μὲν σύμπαντα ἐκ ταὐτοῦ πάθους, καὶ πρὸς τούτοις
ἕτερα μυρία καὶ τούτων ἔτι θαυμαστότερα, διὰ δὲ
χρόνου πλῆθος τὰ μὲν αὐτῶν ἀπέσβηκε, τὰ δὲ διεσπαρμένα εἴρηται χωρὶς ἕκαστα ἀπ' ἀλλήλων. ὁ δ'
ἐστὶν πᾶσι τούτοις αἴτιον τὸ πάθος οὐδεὶς εἴρηκεν.
νῦν δὲ δὴ λεκτέον.

216Cf. Seth Benardete, "Eidos and diaeresis in
Plato's Statesman," Philologus, vol. 107, 1963,
p. 203: "The myth gives the conditions under
which the diaeresis would be true." He also refers to the "myth as the perfection of the diaeresis" (p. 204).

217Phaedo 60b1-c7: ὁ δὲ Σωκράτης ἀνακαθιζόμενος
εἰς τὴν κλίνην συνέκαμψέ τε τὸ σκέλος καὶ ἐξέτριψε
τῇ χειρί, καὶ τρίβων ἅμα, Ὡς ἄτοπον, ἔφη, ὦ
ἄνδρες, ἔοικε τι εἶναι τοῦτο ὃ καλοῦσιν οἱ ἄνθρωποι ἡδύ· ὡς θαυμασίως πέφυκε πρὸς τὸ δοκοῦν ἐναν-
τίον εἶναι, τὸ λυπηρόν, τὸ ἅμα μὲν αὐτὼ μὴ 'θέλειν
παραγίγνεσθαι τῷ ἀνθρώπῳ, ἐὰν δέ τις διώκῃ τὸ
ἕτερον καὶ λαμβάνῃ, σχεδόν τι ἀναγκάζεσθαι ἀεὶ
λαμβάνειν καὶ τὸ ἕτερον, ὥσπερ ἐκ μιᾶς κορυφῆς
ἡμμένω δύ' ὄντε. καί μοι δοκεῖ, ἔφη, εἰ ἐνενόησεν
αὐτὰ Αἴσωπος, μῦθον ἂν συνθεῖναι ὡς ὁ θεὸς βουλό-
μενος αὐτὰ διαλλάξαι πολεμοῦντα, ἐπειδὴ οὐκ ἐδύ-
νατο, συνῆψεν εἰς ταὐτὸν αὐτοῖς τὰς κορυφάς, καὶ
διὰ ταῦτα ᾧ ἂν τὸ ἕτερον παραγένηται ἐπακολουθεῖ
ὕστερον καὶ τὸ ἕτερον.

218Cebes seems to understand that Socrates'
usage of myth as genetic account makes Aesop's
tales no longer myths but rather λόγοι, and hence
he refers to them in his interruption as Aesop's
speeches (τοὺς τοῦ Αἰσώπου λόγους, 60d1), even
though when Socrates next refers to them, he refers to them as myths (μύθους...τοὺς Αἰσώπου, 61
b6) in the context of their general accessibility,
as though to emphasize that these things which
are generally regarded as myths differ from Socrates' own myths.

219Cf. Philebus 16b5-17a5 and ff.

220In this sense, one could say that the result
of the synoptic συναγωγή is the good.

221In this sense, one could say that the constant shifting of the sophist from γένος to γένος,
which makes it impossible to capture him, is
grounded in his artful ability to render himself

immune to any considerations rooted in natural
articulations.

222Phaedrus 266b3-c1: Τούτων δὴ ἔγωγε αὐτός τε
ἐραστής, ὦ Φαῖδρε, τῶν διαιρέσεων καὶ συναγωγῶν,
ἵνα οἷός τε ὦ λέγειν τε καὶ φρονεῖν· ἐάν τέ τιν'
ἄλλον ἡγήσωμαι δυνατὸν εἰς ἕν καὶ ἐπὶ πολλὰ πεφυ-
κόθ' ὁρᾶν, τοῦτον διώκω "κατόπισθε μετ' ἴχνιον
ὥστε θεοῖο." καὶ μέντοι καὶ τοὺς δυναμένους αὐτὸ
δρᾶν εἰ μὲν ὀρθῶς ἢ μὴ προσαγορεύω, θεὸς οἷδε,
καλῶ δὲ οὖν μέχρι τοῦδε διαλεκτικούς.

223Philebus 15d4-8: ΣΩ. Φαμέν που ταὐτὸν ἕν
καὶ πολλὰ ὑπὸ λόγων γιγνόμενα περιτρέχειν πάντη
καθ' ἕκαστον τῶν λεγομένων ἀεί, καὶ πάλαι καὶ νῦν.
καὶ τοῦτο οὔτε μὴ παύσηται ποτε οὔτε ἤρξατο νῦν,
ἀλλ' ἔστι τὸ τοιοῦτον, ὡς ἐμοὶ φαίνεται τῶν λόγων
αὐτῶν ἀθάνατόν τι καὶ ἀγήρων πάθος ἐν ἡμῖν. This
would suggest that what immortality we have is the
immortality of this πάθος in us which manifests
itself in speeches, i.e., the immortality of an
affection of Λόγος. And such a possibility must be
kept in the back of one's mind when reading the
demonstrations of the immortality of human soul in
the Phaedo.

224Philebus 14d8-e4: τις ἑκάστου τὰ μέλη τε καὶ
ἅμα μέρη διελὼν τῷ λόγῳ, πάντα ταῦτα τὸ ἕν ἐκεῖνο
εἷναι διομολογησάμενος, ἐλέγχῃ καταγελῶν ὅτι
τέρατα διηνάγκασται φάναι, τό τε ἕν ὡς πολλά ἐστι
καὶ ἄπειρα, καὶ τὰ πολλὰ ὡς ἕν μόνον.

225One would ultimately have to consider whether any of the other references to gods in the
Platonic corpus are also to be taken not as simple
adoptions of Hellenic theological figures but rather as idealized human types or idealized individual humans. Cf. John Milton, "Lycidas," in which
the poet invokes (line 15) what appear to be the
traditional muses, although soon thereafter he
says (lines 19-20), "So may som gentle Muse/ With
lucky words favour my destin'd Urn," he indicates
that by a muse he means the poet himself. (John
Milton, Milton's Lycidas; the tradition and the
poem, ed. C.A. Patrides (New York, 1961), p. 2.)

133

In addition, even when a contrast is drawn between ἄνθρωποι and θεοί, one would have to consider whether the ultimate distinction is between
merely human (ἄνθρωποι) and truly human (θεοί):
cf. Timaeus 68d4-7: "the god is sufficiently both
knowing and capable to mix together the many into
one and again to dissolve from one into many, and
no one of humans either is now or ever will be at
any time hereafter sufficient for either of these
things." (θεὸς μὲν τὰ πολλὰ εἰς ἓν συγκεραννύναι
καὶ πάλιν ἐξ ἑνὸς εἰς πολλὰ διαλύειν ἱκανῶς ἐπιστάμενος ἅμα καὶ δυνατός, ἀνθρώπων δὲ οὐδεὶς οὐδέ-
τερα τούτων ἱκανὸς οὔτε ἔστι νῦν οὔτε εἰς αὖθίς
ποτε ἔσται.) Also cf. Timaeus 53d6-7: "and in
addition a god and whoever of men be friendly to
that /god/ has envisioned the ruling-beginnings
which are above these." (τὰς δ' ἔτι τούτων ἀρχὰς
ἄνωθεν θεὸς οἶδεν καὶ ἀνδρῶν ὅς ἂν ἐκείνῳ φίλος
ᾖ.)

226Cf. Charmides 174d3-7, 167a1 ff., 169e2-7 et
passim.

227Cf. Phaedrus 270e2-5: "/Socrates./ but it is
clear how, if anyone gives speeches to anyone by
art, he will show precisely the beingness of the
nature of this in regard to which he will bear
forth the speeches; and this will be somehow soul.
(ἀλλὰ δῆλον ὡς, ἄν τῳ τις τέχνῃ λόγους διδῷ, τὴν
οὐσίαν δείξει ἀκριβῶς τῆς φύσεως τούτου πρὸς ὃ
τοὺς λόγους προσοίσει· ἔσται δέ που ψυχὴ τοῦτο.)

228Cf. "the art of the beingly rhetorical and
persuasive person" (τὴν τοῦ τῷ ὄντι ῥητορικοῦ τε
καὶ πιθανοῦ τέχνην, 269c9-d1), "a perfect compe-
titor" (ἀγωνιστὴν τέλεον, 269d2; cf. ἀτελῆς, 269
d6), "the most perfect of all in regard to rhetoric" (πάντων τελεώτατος εἰς τὴν ῥητορικὴν, 269
e1-2), "work-perfecting" (τελεσιουργὸν, 270a2),
"and whoever else seriously gives the rhetorical
art" (καὶ ὅς ἂν ἄλλος σπουδῇ τέχνην ῥητορικὴν
διδῷ, 271a4-5), "perfectly" (τελέως, 272a7).

229If there is, then, such a most perfect art,
its method must be informed by and lead toward

the most perfect, and the most perfect is the
good; cf. <u>Philebus</u> 20c8-d11, 60b7-c5.

230Cf. "he will make /others/ see soul" (ποιήσει ψυχὴν ἰδεῖν, 271a6).

231Cf. πιθανοῦ at 269c9; πειθώ at 270b8, 271a2;
πείθεται...ἀπειθεῖ at 271b4-5; εὐπειθεῖς at 271d6;
δυσπειθεῖς at 271d7; πείθεται at 271e3; πειθώ at
272a3; πειθόμενος at 272b2.

232Cf. διδάσκουσιν at 269c8, διδάσκων at 271b3,
ψυχαγωγία at 271c10, διδάσκων at 272b1.

233Cf. γράφουσιν at 269c8, γράφει at 271a5,
γραφήσεται at 271b8, οἱ νῦν γράφοντες at 271c1,
γράφωσι and γράφειν at 271c4, γράφειν at 271c7,
γράφων at 272b1, ὁ συγγραφεύς at 272b2-3.

234Cf. <u>Phaedrus</u> 274b6-7: "<u>Socrates</u>. And the
thing about appropriateness and inappropriateness
of writing, /namely/ in what way it coming to be
would be beautiful and in what way inappropriate,
is left." (ΣΩ. Τὸ δ' εὐπρεπείας δὴ γραφῆς πέρι καὶ
ἀπρεπείας, πῇ γιγνόμενον καλῶς ἂν ἔχοι καὶ ὅπῃ
ἀπρεπῶς, λοιπόν.)

235Cf. τῆς τέχνης at 269c7, τέχνην at 269d1,
τέχνη at 269d6, τῶν τεχνῶν at 269e4, τέχνης at
270b1, τέχνη at 270b6, τεχνικοὶ at 270d2, τέχνῃ at
270e1, τέχνην at 271a5, τέχνη at 271b8, τέχνας at
271c2, τέχνῃ at 271c4, τεχνικῶς at 271c7, τέχνῃ at
272b1, τέχνης at 272b4, τέχνῃ at 272e2, τεχνικοὶ
at 273a3, τεχνικὸν at 273b3, τέχνῃ at 273c5, τεχ-
νην at 273c7, τέχνης at 273d7, τεχνικὸς at 273e3,
τέχνης τε καὶ ἀτεχνίας at 274b3.

236Cf. φύσει at 269d4, εὐφυὴς at 270a3, τὰς
φύσεις at 273e1.

237Cf. φύσεως πέρι at 270a1, φύσιν...ὧν δὴ πέρι
at 270a5-6, φύσιν at 270b4 and c1, φύσεως at 270c2,
περὶ φύσεως at 270c9, περὶ ὁτουοῦν φύσεως at 270d1,
σκοπεῖν τὴν δύναμιν αὐτοῦ, τίνα πρὸς τι πέφυκεν...

ἔχον (to consider its power, what it has by nature) at 270d3-4, πέφυκεν at 270d7, τῆς φύσεως at 270e3-4, φύσιν at 271a7, αὕτη ἡ φύσις περὶ ἧς at 272a1, φύσει at 272d6.

[238]Cf. τὴν ουσίαν δείξει...τῆς φύσεως at 270 e3-4, and φύσιν...δεικνύναι at 271a7-8.

[239]Phaedrus 273d5-6, 8-e4: πανταχοῦ ὁ τὴν ἀλή-θειαν εἰδὼς κάλλιστα ἐπίσταται εὑρίσκειν /τὰς ὁμοιότητας/. ὥστ'...ἐὰν μὴ τις τῶν τε ἀκουσομένων τὰς φύσεις διαριθμήσηται, καὶ κατ' εἴδη τε διαι-ρεῖσθαι τὰ ὄντα καὶ μιᾷ ἰδέᾳ δυνατὸς ᾖ καθ' ἓν ἕκαστον περιλαμβάνειν, οὔ ποτ' ἔσται τεχνικὸς λό-γων πέρι καθ' ὅσον δυνατὸν ἀνθρώπῳ.

[240]Cf. Phaedrus 273d4: ὁμοιότητα τοῦ ἀληθοῦς.

[241]Phaedrus 271a4-b5: ΣΩ. Δῆλον ἄρα ὅτι...ὃς ἄν ...σπουδῇ τέχνην ῥητορικὴν διδῷ, πρῶτον πάσῃ ἀκρι-βείᾳ γράφει τε καὶ ποιήσει ψυχὴν ἰδεῖν, πότερον ἓν καὶ ὅμοιον πέφυκεν ἢ κατὰ σώματος μορφὴν πολυειδές· τοῦτο γάρ φαμεν φύσιν εἶναι δεικνύναι. ΦΑΙ. Παντά-πασι μὲν οὖν. ΣΩ. Δεύτερον δέ γε, ὅτῳ τί ποιεῖν ἢ παθεῖν ὑπὸ τοῦ πέφυκεν. ΦΑΙ. Τί μήν; ΣΩ. Τρίτον δὲ δὴ διαταξάμενος τὰ λόγων τε καὶ ψυχῆς γένη καὶ τὰ τούτων παθήματα δίεισι πάσας αἰτίας, προσαρμόττων ἕκαστον ἑκάστῳ καὶ διδάσκων οἷα οὖσα ὑφ' οἵων λό-γων δι' ἣν αἰτίαν ἐξ ἀνάγκης ἡ μὲν πείθεται, ἡ δὲ ἀπειθεῖ. Cf. 271c10 ff.

[242]Phaedrus 271c10. Cf. Republic 7.518b6 ff.

[243]Cf. Phaedrus 261a8: ψυχαγωγία τις διὰ λόγων.

[244]Cf. 261a8-9: "not only in courts of justice and as many other convocations as are public, but also in private /places/" (οὐ μόνον ἐν δικαστηρί-οις καὶ ὅσοι ἄλλοι δημόσιοι σύλλογοι, ἀλλὰ καὶ ἐν ἰδίοις.

[245]Phaedrus 261a8, 271c10.

[246]Republic 7.518b6 ff.

247Phaedrus 272b5-6: καίτοι οὐ σμικρόν γε φαίνεται ἔργον.

248Phaedrus 274a1-2: δεσπόταις ἀγαθοῖς τε καὶ
ἐξ ἀγαθῶν (cf. 273e7). This is the same phrase
which Socrates uses to describe the souls of gods
in his mythic palinode (246a8). Also cf. 274b9.

249See above pp. 89, 91 ff. Also consider Philebus 18b6-7.

250'Ακοήν, 274c1. The word ἀκοή is the closest
Platonic equivalent to our 'tale,' but whether a
given tale in the Platonic corpus is a λόγος or a
μῦθος depends on how else the tale is characterized. However, I believe that one could formulate
the general rule of thumb that when an ἀκοή is not
otherwise characterized as a μῦθος--and it is not
here--it is to be regarded as a λόγος.

251Philebus 18c7-d2: καθορῶν δὲ ὡς οὐδεὶς ἡμῶν
οὐδ' ἂν ἓν αὐτὸ καθ' αὑτὸ ἄνευ πάντων αὐτῶν μάθοι,
τοῦτον τὸν δεσμὸν αὖ λογισάμενος ὡς ὄντα ἕνα καὶ
πάντα ταῦτα ἕν πως ποιοῦντα μίαν ἐπ' αὐτοῖς ὡς
οὖσαν γραμματικὴν τέχνην ἐπεφθέγξατο προσειπών.

252Phaedrus 274e9: βλάβης τε καὶ ὠφελίας. Cf.
above pp. 33 ff.

253Cf. Epistles 7.341e1-342a1, and above pp. 33
ff.

254Cf. εὐηθείας at Phaedrus 275b8, c7.

255Phaedrus 275b8: δρυὸς καὶ πέτρας.

256Apol. Socr. 34d4-5: οὐδ'...ἀπὸ δρυὸς οὐδ'
ἀπὸ πέτρης.

257Cf. Republic 8.544d7-8.

258Cf. Protagoras 329a3-4: "as books, they
themselves have nothing to answer or to ask" (ὥσπερ βιβλία οὐδὲν ἔχουσιν οὔτε ἀποκρίνασθαι οὔτε
αὐτοὶ ἐρέσθαι).

137

[259]Phaedrus 275e3: οὐκ ἐπίσταται λέγειν οἷς
δεῖ γε καὶ μή.

[260]Phaedrus 276a5-6: ΣΩ. Ὃς μετ' ἐπιστήμης
γράφεται ἐν τῇ τοῦ μανθάνοντος ψυχῇ. Cf. Vries,
note ad loc.

[261]Cf. Protagoras 347e1-348a6: "And thus also
the suchlike beings-together, if they get hold of
men of the very sort which the many of us assert
ourselves to be, in no way are in need of another
sort of sound or even of poets, whom it is not
even possible to ask about the things which they
speak, and the many leading them /i.e., the poets/
in, in their speeches, the ones assert the poet to
intellectually intuit these things, and the ones
/assert the poet to intellectual intuit/ other
things, they conversing about a business which
they are incapable of refuting; but they /i.e.,
our sort/ bid goodbye to the suchlike beings-
together, and they themselves are together with
themselves through themselves, taking and giving
in their own speeches a test of each other. It
seems to me to be useful for both me and you rather to imitate the suchlike persons, /we/ putting aside the poets themselves to make the speeches through ourselves to each other, taking a
test of the truth and ourselves" (οὕτω δὲ καὶ αἱ
τοιαίδε συνουσίαι, ἐὰν μὲν λάβωνται ἀνδρῶν οἷοί-
περ ἡμῶν οἱ πολλοί φασιν εἶναι, οὐδὲν δέονται
ἀλλοτρίας φωνῆς οὐδὲ ποιητῶν, οὓς οὔτε ἀνερέσθαι
οἷον τ' ἐστὶν περὶ ὧν λέγουσιν, ἐπαγόμενοί τε
αὐτοὺς οἱ πολλοὶ ἐν τοῖς λόγοις οἱ μὲν ταῦτά
φασιν τὸν ποιητὴν νοεῖν, οἱ δ' ἕτερα, περὶ πράγματος διαλεγόμενοι ὃ ἀδυνατοῦσι ἐξελέγξαι· ἀλλὰ
τὰς μὲν τοιαύτας συνουσίας ἐῶσιν χαίρειν, αὐτοὶ
δ' ἑαυτοῖς σύνεισιν δι' ἑαυτῶν, ἐν τοῖς ἑαυτῶν
λόγοις πεῖραν ἀλλήλων λαμβάνοντες καὶ διδόντες.
τοὺς τοιούτους μοι δοκεῖ χρῆναι μᾶλλον μιμεῖσθαι
ἐμέ τε καὶ σέ, καταθεμένους τοὺς ποιητὰς αὐτοὺς
δι' ἡμῶν αὐτῶν πρὸς ἀλλήλους τοὺς λόγους ποιεῖσ-
θαι, τῆς ἀληθείας καὶ ἡμῶν αὐτῶν πεῖραν λαμβά-
νοντας).

[262]In a way, this final ὦ φίλε vocative cul-

minates the movement of the dialogue, which can
be schematized around Socrates' three such voca-
tives: ᾮ φίλε Φαῖδρε (227a1, 230c5, 238c5; cf.
276e4), ὦ φίλε Ἔρως (257a3), ᾮ φίλε Πάν (279b8).
The dialogue deals with the soul's movement from
aisthetic radiance by means of divine erotic craziness to a vision of the all, speech about the
all, and speech about the speech about the all
(cf. Cratylus 408c5-d4).

263Cratylus 408d2-3: ἔστιν ἤτοι λόγος ἢ λόγου
ἀδελφός.

264Cf. in the Cratylus, διφυῆ at 408b8, and δι-
φυῆς at 408d1 and context.

265Cf. Diogenes Laertius III.38; Robin, "Notice,"
pp. vi-vii.

266Of course, this classification is not--and
indeed no classification can be--composed of mutu-
ally exclusive categories but of distinct yet
occasionally overlapping categories. For example,
a given διαίρεσις clearly requires a pre-estab-
lished συναγωγή which one can then divide, and a
given συναγωγή requires a pre-delineated manifold
which is then brought together. However, as with
all categories, their interpenetration does not
invalidate them as categories, any more than the
difficulty, say, of determining whether a given
person is sane or crazy invalidates the categories
of sanity and craziness, or of determining whether
a given person is healthy or sick invalidates the
categories of health and sickness.

267In addition--see p. 30, n. 10--an account
may also be designated either as a διήγησις in the
narrow sense or a μίμησις.

THE REPUBLIC TETRALOGY[1]

The dramatic sequence of dialogues initiated by the Republic contains the longest myths in the Platonic corpus. Not only is the bulk of the Timaeus, for whatever varying reasons, universally and correctly acknowledged to be a myth,[2] but the suggestions are very strong, as we will see, that the bulk of the Republic is also to be regarded as a myth.

But first, we must establish to our own satisfaction at least the dramatic connection between the Republic and what Cornford calls "the Timaeus trilogy,"[3] and we must do so precisely because so influential a commentator as Cornford himself denies such a connection.[4] On the other hand, Henri Martin presupposes the connection: "In Plato's dialogue titled Πολιτεία, i.e., Republic, or rather State, Socrates finding himself in Athens with Critias, Timaeus, Hermocrates, and a fourth person, who is not named, had related to them a philosophical conversation which had taken place the day before in the Piraeus between Glaucon, Polemarchus, Thrasymachus, Adeimantus, Cephalus, and Socrates himself."[5]

Let me now, in agreement with Martin,[6] but against Cornford,[7] indicate the evidence which I believe compels one to treat the Republic and the Timaeus as connected both dramatically and hence substantively. First, there is the massive fact that the speeches of the day before[8] which Socrates summarizes--and he emphasizes that it is a summary[9]-- are the same as or at the very least equivalent to the discussion in Books 2-5 of the Republic.[10]

In addition, as its form indicates, the Republic is a dialogue narrated by Socrates to an indeterminate audience, an audience which Socrates goes out of his way in the Timaeus to make numerically determinate (17a1-2): "One, two, three; and indeed where, o friend Timaeus, is our fourth?" And the words 'meal-guest' (ὁ δαιτυμῶν) and 'hearth-feast-host' (ὁ ἑστιάτωρ), which occur in Socrates' first speech, occur in the Platonic corpus only there and in the Republic (respectively at 1.345c5 and 4.421b3). And finally, there is the description of Timaeus himself:

> For also this Timaeus, being of the most-goodly-lawed city of Locris in Italy, and being last to none of those there by property (=beingness) or by class, has taken in hand the greatest ruling-offices and honors of those in the city, and in turn, in accordance with my opinion, has come upon the height of all philosophy.[11]

In short, Timaeus is a philosopher-ruler, i.e., he is "among the men who are both philosophers and politically skilled,"[12] and as such he is the embodiment of the third wave[13] with which Socrates completes the founding of the best city in the Republic, namely the coincidence of political power and philosophy, but which he omits from his summary in the Timaeus here. And since not only is Timaeus described as a philosopher-ruler, but also "since he is the person of the /group/ who is most skilled in astronomy and who has especially made it his work to have envisioned about the nature of the all,"[14] he seems the perfect person to provide the necessary cosmological foundation for the best city, a cosmological foundation which is as utopian in its way as the best city. And the utopian character of the whole enterprise is emphasized by Plato's selection of a utopian, i.e., a 'non-historically-existent,' spokesman.[15]

But the Republic and the Timaeus have more substantive themes in common. In particular, they

142

both, the one in the service of political stability (the best city) and the one in the service of cosmic stability (the best cosmos), employ τέχνη as the model and they both systematically suppress the one force that is most destructive of stability, namely ἔρως. In other words, both the best city and the best cosmos which is its ground depend upon an elevation of τέχνη and a denigration of ἔρως,[16] or an elevation of mathematized body and a denigration of the lived human body. In the Republic, this is present throughout, for example, in Book 1 in Cephalus' freedom from τὰ ἀφροδίσια (1.329a1 ff.) and the pervasiveness of examples from the arts (1.332c5 ff.); in Book 2 in the basis of the founding of the city in speech in needs from which procreation is conspicuously absent (2.369c9-e1), and in the founded city as a city of artisans (2.369e2 ff.); in Book 3 in the genic falsehood (3.414b8 ff.) which substitutes autochthony for sexual generation and in which knowledge of soul is reduced to assaying of metals; in Book 4 in the assertion of the superiority of spiritedness to desire (4.440b3-4 and context) and in the positing of the principle 'one person, one work' (4.423d2 ff.); in Book 5 in the elimination of privacy from the way of life of the guardians, a way of life which is characterized by communism and equality of the sexes;[17] in Book 7 in the presentation of the philosopher's leaving the cave as an external compulsion[18] rather than as an internal and natural desire or ἔρως for the truth; in Book 8 in the nuptial number (8.546a1 ff.) which simultaneously represents the complete mathematization of ἔρως and the impossibility of the complete mathematization of ἔρως; in Book 9 in the presentation of the tyrant as the complete erotic πανοῦργος (cf. 9.571c7-8 and context) and ἔρως as the complete tyrant (cf. 9.573b6-7, d4); and in Book 10 in the description of the εἴδη as made. The Timaeus reproduces these motifs on the cosmic level, for example, in its virtual elimination of the so-called sacred;[19] in its assertion that the κόσμος (οὐρανός or τὸ πᾶν) is made (cf. 28c3 et passim);[20] in its assertion of the superiority of spiritedness to desire (70a2-c1); in its explanation that the human body was made only to keep the head from rolling around on the ground (44d3-45a3); in its assertion that the genitals were created as almost an afterthought (91a1-d6); in its presentation of the receptacle (cf. 49a6, 51a5) as a χώρα (52a8, b4, d3; cf. Rep. 3.414e3), which is the mother (cf. Tim. 50d3, 51a4-5) of the cosmos in a way analogous to the way in which the earth as the land in the genic falsehood is the mother (cf. Rep. 3.414e2, 3) of the city.[21] In short, then, the parallel between the city and the human (cf. Rep. 2.368c7-4. end) is matched by the parallel between the cosmos and the ζῷον; and just as the founding of the city arises out of the needs of the body (Rep. 2.369c9 ff.), i.e., out of a city-human body parallel, only to culminate in a psychology, i.e., in a city-human soul parallel, so too Timaeus' account moves from a somatology (31 b4-34a7) to a psychology (34a8 ff.).

So, one must conclude, it seems, that since the substantive links between the Republic and the Timaeus so strongly support the dramatic link between them, the two dialogues--or rather the total sequence of dialogues which they establish--must be read together. Therefore, let us now turn to this sequence insofar as it bears on the problem of myth in Plato, and let us begin briefly with the Timaeus.

Timaeus' account of the genesis of the all[22] is as a whole a likely myth,[23] but what this means needs to be sufficiently explained. The tendency among commentators is to explain it to mean that physics is likely because it is a myth or a myth because it is likely, or else it is simply assumed to be a thinly disguised scientific treatise.[24] As to the latter, since it ignores the dialogue form and the dramatic context, and since Timaeus-- even though he speaks uninterrupted from 27d7 to the end of the dialogue--repeatedly alludes to his interlocutors and their common task,[25] even if its scientific analysis of the scientific content of the dialogue is sound, it still does not clarify

he dramatic status of that content, and insofar
s dramatic status is an essential component of
ubstantive status, it does not clarify its sub-
tantive role in the Platonic corpus, although it
-along with dramatic considerations--is a prere-
uisite for understanding that role. As to the
ormer, on the other hand, it implicitly accuses
lato--or, to be more precise, Timaeus--of a most
nilluminating redundancy. What, then, is meant
y the designation 'likely myth'? Clearly its
ikeliness does not derive from its being a myth.
e have already seen that in the seventh epistle
lato calls his myth "a certain true speech." In
he second place, throughout the <u>Timaeus</u> itself,
here are repeated references to a likely λόγος,[26]
nd it is not by chance that all but one of these
ccurs in that part of Timaeus' account (53b7-58
2) which is obviously a classificatory descrip-
ion of bodies, while in the next section (58a2
f.), which is about the genesis of compound bo-
ies, i.e., about the change and motion from which
lemental bodily compounds arise, Timaeus refers
o the standard of "likely myths":

> And in addition it is in no way intricate to
> reckon through the other suchlike things, cha-
> sing after the look of likely myths; with re-
> spect to which /look/ whenever for the sake
> of resting up anyone having put down the spee-
> ches about the things which always are, behold-
> ing the likely /myths/ about genesis, possesses
> an unregrettable pleasure, he would make in his
> lifetime a measured and prudent childlike-play-
> ing. Indeed in this way we having hurled forth
> also the things now will go through with respect
> to the thing after this the successive likeli-
> hoods about them in this way.[27]

o, either a μῦθος or a λόγος may be likely, and
ikeliness is not an automatic characteristic of
yths, but rather is one of the characteristics
along with ὀρθός, ἀληθής, ἄτοπος, τέλειος[28]) of
όγος. Therefore, since a μῦθος is not analyti-
ally 'likely,' i.e., since εἰκός is not a super-
luous adjectival addition, what is meant by

145

'likely myth'? I would suggest the following. A
μῦθος, as we have seen, is an account of a genesis, and Timaeus' account of the cosmos is emphatically that, and as such it illustrates the
definition on a grand scale.[29] Therefore, insofar
as Timaeus' account is genetic, it is a myth. But
why is it likely? It is likely, I believe, because
it presents the cosmos as made, and insofar as it
does so, its likeliness is falseness, i.e., it is
"a tool of understanding" or a "blueprint."[30] In
other words, Timaeus' account is as much a construct as is the cosmos of which his account is,
and insofar as it is a construct, a πλασθείς,[31]
it is only likely, but not insofar as it is a
myth.

And the difference between μῦθος and λόγος is further made clear by the ways in which accounts in
general and the accounts of Socrates, Timaeus, and
Critias in particular are designated.

In Timaeus' account (27b7 to the end of the dialogue), there are usages of Λόγος in the sense of
any verbal utterance,[32] of λόγος in the sense of
classificatory description or delimiting or dividing or reckoning,[33] and of μῦθος in the sense of
a synagogic genetic account.[34] And this is a cate-
gorization of which the interlocutors seem well
aware. For Critias' story is referred to exclusively as a λόγος,[35] and in the <u>Critias</u> itself the word
μῦθος occurs nowhere.[36] In addition, in the introductory section of the <u>Timaeus</u> (to 27b6), we find
the same variety of usages: Λόγος,[37] λόγος,[38] ἀκοή
as equivalent to λόγος,[39] and μῦθος.[40] One occurrence of μῦθος needs to be singled out here, namely
the description of the <u>Republic</u> as a μῦθος, because
it completes a suggested classification of the
whole tetralogy:

<u>Republic</u>:	μῦθος τῆς πόλεως[41]
<u>Timaeus</u>:	μῦθος τοῦ κόσμου
<u>Critias</u>:	λόγος τῆς πόλεως
<u>Hermocrates</u>:	λόγος τοῦ κόσμου

I have filled in the missing fourth and designated

146

it in accordance with what seems to be required
to complete the pattern:[42] (1) a genetic account
of the best city; (2) a genetic account of the
best cosmos; (3) a descriptive account of the best
city; (4) a descriptive account of the best cosmos.
And in order to descriptively bring the best city
to life (cf. Tim. 19b3 ff.), so to speak, Socrates
asks that it be set in motion or sent to war (cf.
Tim. 19b8, c4-5). Presumably, then, Hermocrates'
task would have been to set the cosmos in motion
or send the cosmos to war. In the case of the cosmos, this would mean a Heracleiteanism, in which
the following assertions would be the basis for
the account:

> War is the father of all things, and king of
> all things.[43]
> It is useful to have envisioned war being the
> with /everything/, and strife being the right
> way /of everything/, and all things coming to
> be in accordance with strife and use.[44]
> Somewhere Herakleitus speaks that all things
> advance and nothing remains, and likening
> forth the beings to the flow of a river, he
> speaks how one would not step into the same
> river twice.[45]

To show an embodiment of such a view in action, as
it were, seems impossible. So, perhaps Socrates
was wrong in asking for the city to be transformed
from peace or rest (ἡσυχία: cf. Tim. 19b7) to war
or motion. For not only is ἡσυχία equivalent to
εἰρήνη and opposed to πόλεμος (cf. Rep. 9.575b2-3)
which is equivalent to κίνησις (cf. Laws 7.790d6-
7), but it is also opposed to seriousness (σπουδή:
cf. Xenophon, Hellenica 6.2.28). Perhaps, then,
Socrates should have asked for the playful Timaean
cosmos to be transformed into the serious cosmos,
but that is forbidden, as we have seen, by the
prescriptions of the seventh epistle. The dilemma
which is adumbrated here may suggest why the Critias is incomplete and the Hermocrates is missing.
For beings at war behave unaccountably (ἀλόγως),
as Tolstoy so clearly saw:

> The actors of 1812 have long since left the
> stage, their personal interests have vanished
> leaving no trace, and nothing remains of that
> time but its historic results.
> The cause of the destruction of the French
> army in 1812 is clear to us now. No one will
> deny /what/ that cause was.... But no one at
> that time foresaw (what now seems so evident)
> that this was the only way an army of eight
> hundred thousand men--the best in the world
> and led by the best general--could be de-
> stroyed in conflict with a raw army of half
> its numerical strength, and led by inexperi-
> enced commanders as the Russian army was.
> Not only did no one see this, but on the
> Russian side every effort was made to hinder
> the only thing that could save Russia, while
> on the French side, despite Napoleon's expe-
> rience and so-called military genius, every
> effort was directed...to doing the very thing
> that was bound to lead to destruction.
> /It/ was not the result of any plan, for no
> one believed it to be possible; it resulted
> from a most complex interplay of intrigues,
> aims, and wishes among those who took part in
> the war and had no perception whatever of the
> inevitable, or of the one way of saving Russia.
> Everything came about fortuitously.[46]

War and chance, then, go hand in hand, and it
would seem as though no true likeness of chance
is possible. Only a universal motion picture came-
ra could reproduce such motion, and hence Seth
Benardete is correct when he says that Socrates'
"desire to see a living animal move does not differ from the desire to see a picture of an animal
move,"[47] although he seems not wholly correct in
emphasizing that "the clearest example of two-
dimensional kinematics is geometrical construction,"[48] rather than motion pictures, the possibility of which is implicit in the projected
images on the wall in the image of the cave. And
the making of a motion picture is, in a very literal sense, a λόγος, a διαίρεσις, a breaking down

of a one into a many, although not simply, since a
three-dimensional moving one is broken down into a
motionless two-dimensional many which is then projected to produce a two-dimensional apparently
moving one:

> Therefore the nature of the living thing chanced
> to be perpetual, and indeed it was not possible
> altogether perfectly to fasten this to the gene-
> rated thing; and he was of a mind to make a cer-
> tain movable likeness of the perpetual, and
> simultaneously with thoroughly ordering heaven,
> of the perpetual which remains in one he makes
> a perpetual likeness hurtling in accordance with
> number, this /perpetual likeness/ which indeed
> we have named 'time'......and the was and the
> will be are time's looks which have come to be,
> bearing which indeed upon the perpetual being-
> ness we do not correctly escape our own notice.
> ......but these have come to be /as/ looks imita-
> ting the perpetual and circling in accordance
> with number.[49]

Hence the Republic and the Timaeus are the film
script for a motion picture (a movable likeness)
that it is impossible ever to film, i.e., the sub-
stitution of artificial wholeness for true wholeness renders precision of speech impossible.
Therefore, it is no accident that the Critias
breaks off at precisely that moment when direct
speech is about to be articulated and that the
Hermocrates cannot even begin.

Let us now turn to the Republic which, it is suggested, is as a whole a myth.[50] And certainly the
entire account at least from Book 2 through Book
10 is a genetic account of political life from
its origin in human needs through the best city
to the de-generation of the best city. But also,
insofar as the city is a big individual human
(cf. Rep. 2.368c7-369b4), it is a genetic account
of the individual human lifetime. So, the Republic as a whole can be taken as a myth both of the
city and of the individual. And not only is the

whole _Republic_ a myth, but some of its parts are myths of whose parts in turn some are also myths. For example:

    (1) Glaucon's account of Gyges' ancestor is a myth.[51]
    (2) The account of the education of the guardians is a myth.[52]
    (3) The guardians' education consists of myths.[53]
    (4) The genic falsehood is a myth.[54]
    (5) The genesis of soul types is a myth.[55]
    (6) Er's account is a myth.[56]

The _Republic_, then, is composed of myths within myths within myths,[57] and it culminates in the γένεσις of all γενέσεις, the good, "the beginning of the all" or "the beginning which is the all."[58]

Glaucon is concerned with origins, and insofar as the _Republic_ treats justice to a large extent through its genesis, Glaucon is responsible. And this is evident in the myth with which he illustrates his objections to Socrates' procedure in the first book, a myth which he takes from Herodotus (I.8-13) and alters to suit his purposes. In Herodotus, the hero is Gyges himself, but in Glaucon's version, the hero is one of Gyges' ancestors, and this change is consistent with Glaucon's tendency to go back to the origins, to see things genetically. And according to Glaucon's hypothetical account,[59] no one is voluntarily just, but only by convention, i.e., justice is that which is agreed upon by those who are not capable of avoiding suffering injustice and electing to do injustice after they have entered into a compact with each other (_Rep._ 2.358e5-359a5). That is, justice is the established advantage of the weak, even though everyone, if he could, would elect to do injustice with impunity (_Rep._ 2.359a5-b4). And the Gyges' ancestor story shows that justice has its genesis in the fear of being visible at, i.e., punishable for, doing injustice by showing that anyone who is given invisibility, i.e., impunity, will do injustice.[60] And it shows that the desire for injustice is all-pervasive. For Gyges' ancestor acquires the ring of invisibility by stealing it from a corpse before he knows its special power, i.e., he is a simple thief, a tomb robber.[61] So, although prior to the earthquake fear as a rule kept him from doing injustice, as soon as the opportunity arose to do injustice unseen,[62] he seized it without hesitation. The ring, then, simply gives him the power to do all the time what he did only occasionally before and what and more he would have done all the time if he had had the power to do so.[63] This account has its analogue in the myth of Er when the first lot falls to the man of habitual virtue from an ordered regime, and he chooses the greatest tyranny (cf. Rep. 10.619b6-d1). And in the myth it is strongly suggested that what Glaucon had presented as merely hypothetical is in fact the case and not at all hypothetical, except that there the assertion that no one is voluntarily just is refined into the assertion that no one is voluntarily just except the philosopher.[64]

Next, the education of the guardians is a myth because it shows the genesis of habitual virtue through an education based on a θεολογία from which a θεογονία is generated. In other words, the education of the guardians is doubly genetic: it shows the genesis of habitual virtue and it shows the genesis of the proper theogony which as a genetic or genealogic account is itself also to be regarded as consisting of myths.

In addition, the founding falsehood of the best city (2.414b8-415d8) is a myth, a genetic account, which is both γενναῖον and a ψεῦδος. Clearly its being a μῦθος does not make it, as we have seen, a ψεῦδος. Therefore, its mythical character must have something to do with its being γενναῖον. In what sense? The adjective γενναῖος has an enormous range of meaning. In the Republic alone, it is used to describe the type of naivete which Thrasymachus regards justice to be (1.348c12), the perfect simple just man whom Glaucon constructs (2.

361b7), Homer and Hesiod (2.363a8), loaves of
barley and wheat (2.372b4), bred dogs (2.375e1-2),
the good judge (3.409c2), comportment in the face
of adversity (4.440d1), the power of the contra-
dicting art (5.454a1), bred birds (5.459a3), the
big and vigorous but inept shipowner (6.488c4),
the philosophic nature in its imminent corruption
(6.494c6), tyranny (8.544c6), and democracy (8.
558c2). What unifies this range which γενναῖος has
is its fundamental meaning, "reflective of its genesis or birth" (cf. LSJ), and in that sense every
μῦθος is γενναῖος, a designation which implies nothing either way about its truth or falsity. And
the γενναῖον ψεῦδος is both true and false.[65]

Finally, let us turn to the great soul myths which
conclude the Republic, Book 9.588b1-592b6 and Book
10.614a5-621d3, the former of which is meant to be
the mythical prologue to the latter. As Nettleship
has observed:

> The first half of Book X is disconnected from
> the rest of the Republic, and the transition to
> the subject of art and poetry...is sudden and
> unnatural......It does not bear in any way on
> the last section of Book X, in which the immor-
> tality of the soul is treated, and which would
> naturally follow at the end of Book IX, form-
> ing a fitting conclusion to the whole work.[66]

Although Nettleship is correct in emphasizing the
direct connection between the end of Book 9 and
the second half of Book 10, and in emphasizing
the abruptness of the reintroduction of the subject of poetry, he is incorrect in saying that
the discussion of poetry does not bear on the
last section of Book 10. To show that it does, a
brief review of the overall context appears necessary. The initial discussion of poetry was carried
on in a politico-educational context, in the context of the founding of the city, which leads
through false myths (of which the foundation is
the genic falsehood) for the purpose of inculca-
ting habitual virtue[67] and through a partitive
political psychology in the service of habitual

virtue (cf. Rep. 4.430c2-3) to a discussion of
the institutions of the best city which culminates in philosophy. The introduction of philosophy then impels a refining of what had previously
been discussed, beginning at the image of the
cave with a new discussion of education, of philosophic education, going through a recompletion
of the founding of the city (7.540d1-541b5), a
new psychology in terms of a manifold of soul
types and their genesis, a new discussion of poetry (this time from the perspective of the ancient quarrel between philosophy and poetry[68]),
a non-partitive psychology, and culminating in a
true myth, a transpolitical philosophic myth.

Let us now look at the final myths themselves, beginning with Socrates' account of the genesis of
soul types, without which account one cannot begin
to penetrate the obscurities of the myth of Er.
Socrates fashions an image of the soul of a human
in this way:[69]

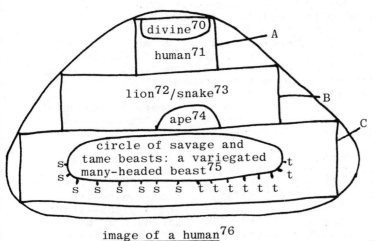

image of a human[76]

Socrates enumerates the following natural[77] types
of soul on the basis of this schema:

153

(1) <u>A dominant</u>:
    (a) A_h or A_d dominating B and C: produced by τὰ καλά (cf. 589c8-d2)
    (b) A dominating C and making B and C friends or allies of each other: the just soul (cf. 589a6-b7)
    (c) A lulls and gentles B and C_s, thus freeing C_t for habituation to virtue: the unjust soul punished (cf. 591b1-8)
(2) <u>B and C dominant</u>:
    (a) B and C feast and become strong, while A starves and is weak: the unjust soul (cf. 588e3-589a5)
        (i) A follows B and C anywhere
        (ii) A does not habituate B and C
        (iii) A fails to reconcile B and C,
    which battle and bite and eat each other
    (b) B_1 and B_s strengthened by stubbornness and irascibility ally with C: the uncontrolled soul I (cf. 590a5-b2)
    (c) B_1 and B_s weakened or made cowardly by luxury and softness ally with C: the uncontrolled soul II (cf. 590a5-8, b3-5)
(3) <u>C dominant</u>:
    (a) C_s dominating C_t, B, and A: love of gold, produced by τὰ αἰσχρά (cf. 589d2-590a4)
    (b) C dominating B from flattery and unfreedom: B_1 metamorphoses into B_a (cf. 590 b6-c1)
    (c) C dominating A weakened by mechanical and manual art so as to learn only what flatters it (cf. 590c2-7)

Several things should be noted about this psychology. First, it is not literally true--any more than that Socrates is literally an openable statue (cf. <u>Symp.</u> 216d2-217a2) or that souls literally have metal in them (cf. <u>Rep.</u> 3.414b8-415d8) or that humans are literally chained in a cave (cf. <u>Rep.</u> 7. beg.)--that the human is fashioned by putting three parts together and then placing the image of a human around them. Second, it is an attempt to give in imagistic shorthand, as it were, a matrix for understanding types of human behavior (e.g., just acts or unjust acts or stubbornness or softness or greed and so on). So, if someone asserts that a human has the look (ἰδέα) of a snake, he does not mean that the human is literally a snake, but that he acts like a snake. Similarly, if someone asserts that the soul of a human leaves a human body and enters the body of a beast, that is not to be taken at face value as a belief in transmigration of souls, but rather as a way of describing an alteration in his patterns of behavior. As Alfarabi so judiciously remarks:

> For there is no difference between seeing a man who possesses the most perfect bestiality and performs the most perfect activities thereof, and assuming that he is dead and transformed into that beast and its shape. Thus there is no difference between a man who acts like a fish, and a fish with a shape like that of a man: his only virtue is his human shape and the fact that he acts like a perfect fish, nor is there any difference between this and his shape's being like a fish, and yet calculating his actions well like a man. For in all this he does not possess humanity except insofar as the calculation, by which he performs the activity of that beast well, is the calculation of a man. He /i.e., Plato/ explained that the more perfectly one performs the activity of the beast, the further he is from being human; had the activities of that beast proceeded from some animate body having the shape of that beast along with man's calculation about these activities, such activities would be nothing but the most perfect activity that can proceed from that beast —the more perfectly and effectively the animate body performs the activities of that beast, the further it is from being human. [78]

It is in this sense that Thrasymachus, for example, acts "as a beast" [79] or that "a misologist...and unmusical person...acts in regard to everything by violence and savageness as a beast." [80] And it is in accordance with this that the myth of the transformation of a person into a tyrant is the para-

155

digm both for the regime/soul transformations down from the best city[81] and for all the other transformations in the Republic[82] and elsewhere in Plato:[83]

> "Therefore what is the beginning of the change from an outstanding leader to a tyrant? Or is it clear that it is whenever the outstanding leader begins to do the same thing as the thing in the myth which is spoken in respect to the temple of Wolfian Zeus in Arcadia?"
>
> "What?" he /i.e., Adeimantus/ asserted.
>
> "How then /for/ the person who has tasted the human innard, the one which has been cut up among other /innards/ of other sacred victims, indeed there is a compulsion for this person to become a wolf......Then indeed is there a compulsion after this for the suchlike person and has he been destined either to perish at the hands of his personal enemies or to be a tyrant and to become from a human a wolf?"
>
> "There is much compulsion," he asserted.....
>
> "And let us again bespeak that armed camp which the tyrant is, /an armed camp/ which is beautiful and big and variegated and never the same, whence it will be nurtured."......
>
> "By Zeus, then, already then," he said, "such a populace will recognize the sort of nurtured-creature which it generating has welcomed and caused to increase...."[84]

And the wolf which is the tyrant is one of the savage heads of the many-headed beastlike part (cf. Rep. 9.571c5) of the human soul. Therefore, whenever in a Platonic dialogue there is an ostensible transformation from a human into a beast or from a beast into a human or even from a beast into a beast, this must not be taken literally, but rather it must be taken as an imagistic way of delineating an internal transformation within a human from one type of behavior to another.[85]

And the same rule must apply to every account of transmigration of souls, such as the account which is found within the myth of Er. The myth has the following outline:

> (1) 614a5-616b1: introduction
>> (a) 614a5-b1: the theme adumbrated
>> (b) 614b2-8: whose it is and the circumstances
>> (c) 614b8-615a4: Er's account of the souls
>> (d) 615a4-c4: Socrates' interruption and summary
>> (e) 615c5-616b1: Er's account of Ardiaios the great (dialogue)
> (2) 616b1-617d1: Er's account: cosmography
>> (a) 616b1-c4: pillar of light
>> (b) 616c4-617b4: spindle of compulsion and the whorls
>> (c) 617b4-7: Sirens
>> (d) 617d1-618b6: Moirai
> (3) 617d1-618b6: Er's account: the lottery of lifetimes
> (4) 618b6-619b1: Socrates' interruption
> (5) 619b2-620d5: Er's account: the electings
> (6) 620d6-621b7: Er's account: the return
>> (a) 620d6-e1: daimons
>> (b) 620e1-4: Klotho
>> (c) 620e4-6: Atropos
>> (d) 620e6-621a1: Compulsion
>> (e) 621a2-b1: plain of forgetfulness and the River Uncaringness
>> (f) 621b1-7: return to earth
> (7) 621b8-d3: conclusion: Socrates directly discoursing to Glaucon

At first (614a5-b1) Socrates adumbrates the theme of the myth in an apparently straightforward manner, but it is not as straightforward as it seems. He says that his account will detail the "prizes and wages and gifts" (614a1) of justice for a person when he has come to his end as opposed to the previous account of the wages[86] of a person when he is living. And the stress is on rewards for justice. But the myth as recounted belies this, for the emphasis is on punishments for injustice and there is comparatively little about rewards for justice.[87] And Socrates gives this account be-

cause it is owed by the speech,[88] i.e., it is a
paying back in speech to speech what is owed by
speech to speech, i.e., it is an act of justice
in the Cephalean sense and it brings to bear the
entire conventional apparatus[89] of the underworld
and the afterlife. But the model for the philosophic understanding of that conventional apparatus
is not pious acceptance, which would be the salutary model for the many, but rather it is the
onomatology which Socrates practices in the <u>Cra-
tylus</u> with regard to the conventional apparatus
of names and naming. In addition, it is important
that the repayment of debt is internal to speech,
i.e., it is self-repayment, because by analogy
the election of lifetimes and the so-called transmigration of souls will also need to be understood
internally as an imagistic way of describing internal transformations of a human in this lifetime.[90] And although the distinction which Socrates makes between the living and the ended
appears to be--and is imagistically treated as--a
distinction between the living and the dead, his
use for what is usually regarded as the person
who is dead of the participle τελευτήσαντα,[91] the
person who has come to his end, instead of the
participle ἀποθανόντα or τεθνηκότα, the person who
has died, suggests another distinction, the distinction between the person in his potentiality
and the person in his actuality or ἐντελέχεια,
i.e., the person in the state of having reached
that for which he would by nature strive, of having reached, in other words, his τέλος, even if
that τέλος and the desire which would initiate his
movement toward it are belied by his habitual actions. And as though to emphasize the connection
between τελευτήσαντα and τέλος, Socrates uses the
adverb τελέως in the very next phrase.

Socrates then describes whose account it is, and
as in the case of the palinode in the <u>Phaedrus</u>,
the description is composed of names on which
there are puns:

> "But yet," I said, "I will not say to you
> the account of Alkinoos then, but that of a man

with defensive strength, Er the /son/ of Armenios, a Pamphylian with respect to his race."92

The account of Alkinoos which Socrates' myth is
not is Odysseus' narrative of his experiences after leaving Troy in Books 9-12 of the Odyssey
(cf. Adam, note ad loc.). However, such a denial
clearly invites comparison, especially since the
soul of Odysseus himself appears in the myth (620
c3-d2) as the person who has received the last
lot, since we meet the Sirens in a purified form
(617b4-7), and since the soul of Aias is the twen-
tieth soul in both the Odyssey93 and Er's tale.94
And if one considered the structure of Odysseus'
narrative and Er's account, I believe that one
would see that Er's account is an inverted Odysse-
an narrative, as the following table of correspondences may show:

Odyssey	Republic
(1) Kalypso (promise of immortality and arrival at Phaiakia), 12. 447-453 (and 7.240-297)	Introduction, 614a5-616b1
(2) Helios' cattle, 12.260-446	Pillar of light, 616 b1-c4
(3) Skylla and Charybdis, 12.201-259	Spindle of compulsion and the whorls, 616 c4-617b4
(4) Sirens, 12.144-200	Sirens, 617b4-7
(5) Circe II, 12.1-143	Moirai, 617b7-d1
(6) Underworld II (men and demigods), 11.385-640	Lottery of lifetimes, 617d1-618b6
(7) Alkinoos' and Arete's interruption, 11.333-384	Socrates' interruption, 618b6-619b1
(8) Underworld I (Teiresias and women), 11. 1-332	Electings, 619b2-620 d5
(9) Circe I (enchanted beasts), 10.133-574	Daimons, 620d6-e1
(10) Laistrygones (cannibalism), 10.80-132	Klotho, 620e1-4

(11) Aiolian island (bag of winds), 10.1-79	Atropos, 620e4-6
(12) Cyclopes (lawless savagery), 9.105-566	Compulsion, 620e6-621a1
(13) Lotos eaters (drugged forgetfulness and uncaringness), 9.67-104	Plain of forgetfulness and the River Uncaringness, 621a2-b1
(14) Sack of the Kikonian city, 9.39-66	Return to earth, 621 b1-7
(15) Prologue (departure from Troy), 9.1-38	Conclusion, 621b8-d3

The more obvious connections at (1), (2), (3), (4), (7), (12), and (13) make one suspect that the less obvious connections are as parallel as the obvious ones, but to fully explore these correspondences would require a work unto itself, so I simply offer this as a suggestion and a program for future study.

And there is the paronomasia 'Αλκίνου...ἀλκίμου, strong intellect...strong, so that one could render Socrates' introduction thus: "I will not say to you the account of a strong intellect but that of a man who is /nonetheless/ strong." And this strong man is a man at the time of life when he has to make the choice of the lifetime which he will lead, i.e., he is a man in the spring of his lifetime, ἦρ being a contraction of ἔαρ (spring: cf. LSJ). And he is of the Pamphylian race, i.e., he is of every tribe, which means that he is not a Greek, and even though Greek examples predominate, the myth is directed not at Greeks as Greeks but rather at humans as humans.[95]

Now, let us turn to Er's account itself, and since we cannot treat it all exhaustively, let us focus upon certain key passages.

When the souls come to the daimonic place,[96] the judges place signs upon them:

> And /he asserted/ judges to be seated between these /chasms/ whom, since they thoroughly

> judged, /he asserted/ to bid the just persons
> to proceed /in their way/ to the right and up-
> wards through the heaven, having fastened ᵗ
> around /them/ signs in front, /signs/ of the
> things which have been judged, and the unjust
> persons /to proceed in their way/ to the left
> and downwards, these too having signs in back,
> /signs/ of all the things which they acted.⁹⁷

So, the signs for the just indicate only their
justice but not their actions, while the signs for
the unjust indicate only their actions but not
their injustice. Is the reason for this that a
just person may act unjustly without impairing his
justice, while an unjust person never acts except
unjustly? Or is it that justice need not manifest
itself in actions, while injustice necessarily
eventuates in actions, all of which are unjust? Or
is it that the primary behavioral manifestation of
justice is in refraining from certain actions
(i.e., justice is behaviorally negative but psychically positive), while the primary behavioral
manifestation of injustice is in performing certain actions (i.e., injustice is behaviorally
positive, but psychically negative), a distinction which might explain the relative attractiveness of injustice, the advantages of which one
wears, as it were, on one's sleeve,⁹⁸ and unat-
tractiveness of justice, the advantages of which
are hidden, as it were, in one's heart?⁹⁹

Then, in Socrates' interruption and summary (615
a4-c4), several things should be emphasized.
First, as throughout the myth, his presentation
is skewed toward injustice and the wages of injus-
tice.¹⁰⁰ Second, wages or salaries, μισθοί, is a
neutral term and may designate rewards or punishments, i.e., it designates the appropriate remu-
neration for the act. Third, Socrates implies
that private injustice is more reprehensible than
public injustice, because killing someone by
one's own hand is in the class of acts which receive greater wages for injustice (615c2-4),
while indirectly causing many to be killed politically (615b2-5) is implicitly in the class of

acts which receive lesser wages for injustice.
Finally, in the whole Socratic parenthesis here,
there is no reference to the gods as inflicting
the punishments or dispensing the rewards, i.e.,
the philosophical version of the account would
require stripping away the conventional theological causal explanation.

Er's account of Ardiaios the great[101] (615c5-616
b1) is a dialogue between two anonymous souls at
which Er is present, and the character of the inquiry delineated is perplexing with respect to
person 1, the inquiring soul. There are several
possible explanations for his inquiry. Perhaps
person 1 knows only that Ardiaios was a ruler, but
does not know anything about his character. But if
this were so, it would be difficult to explain his
curiosity about Ardiaios, for surely there would
have been others whom he would know better and
about whom he would be curious. And this especially seems unlikely both since Er clearly knows of
Ardiaios, even a thousand years after Ardiaios
lived, and since the two anonymous souls, who are
just returning from having completed their thousand year sojourn, would have been contemporaries
of Ardiaios (cf. 615c7-8). Perhaps, then, person 1
knows that Ardiaios was a patricide and fratricide
and unholy tyrant, but does not regard these necessarily as bads[102] or is not sure whether they
are bads, perhaps because he regards political
crimes as somehow excusable, which would explain
person 2's emphasis on the political character
(cf. 615d6-7) of these incurable or virtually incurable souls. Or perhaps--and this is not incon-
sistent with the preceding alternative--person 1
knows Ardiaios' character as vicious, but is un-
sure whether indeed vice is punished. In any case,
presumably person 1's sojourn was in heaven, so
that he would not have encountered Ardiaios. However, person 2's sojourn was under the earth (cf.
615d5) where he did encounter Ardiaios.

Er's cosmography (616b1-617d8) is perhaps the most
difficult passage in the entire myth, but this
much is clear, that although it purports to be a

description of ἐκεῖ, it is in fact a description
of ἐνθάδε:

> And /̄he asserted/̄ the nature of the whorl to be
> suchlike; with respect to its shaped-surface, _
> /̄its nature/̄ is of the very sort as the /̄nature/̄
> of the /̄whorl/̄ here....[103]

So, the description of the things there is an indirect description of the things here.[104] But
which things here? A partial answer may be con-
tained in the hymning of the Moirai:

> And /̄he asserted/̄ three others being seated
> around through an equal /̄distance/̄, each in a
> throne, daughters of Compulsion, Fates, being
> clad in white, having wreaths over their _
> heads, Lachesis and Klotho and Atropos, /̄--he
> asserted them/̄ to hymn in regard to the Si-
> rens' harmony, Lachesis /̄hymning/̄ the things
> which have come to be, and Klotho the things
> which are, and Atropos the things which are
> about to be.[105]

This echoes Socrates' introduction to his discussion of narrating:

> Then do not however many of all things as are
> spoken by mythologizers or poets chance to be
> a narrating either of things which have come
> to be or of things which are or of things
> which are about to be?[106]

This suggests perhaps that in one sense at least
the Moirai are the deities who preside over narrating. And if so, the Ἀνάγκη who is the mother
of the Moirai could be understood as the logographic compulsion to which Socrates refers in the
Phaedrus (264b7) and hence what is presented as a
cosmography would be in fact a logography.[107] And
hence a properly constructed writing would be
like a series of concentric whorls, presenting
different colors at different levels to different
persons and moving at different speeds at diffe-

rent levels to different persons, i.e., a properly
constructed writing would be written so that one
person might hear the one sound or tone of one
Siren and another that of another, and so that
another perhaps might even hear the harmony which
all the Sirens produce together. And that harmony
is the unity behind the variegated structure of
the writing, and that unity is especially adumbrated here by the pillar of light, whose function as
co-bond here is analogous to the function as co-
bond of being seen and seeing or of being and
knowing of the sun and the good in the analogy between them. And if the Timaeus establishes that
the cosmos is a ζῷον and the Phaedrus that a writing is a ζῷον, then the Republic suggests that a
writing is a cosmos.[108]

Then, in the lottery of lifetimes (617d1 ff.), we
turn--or rather return--to the problem of soul
types. And that Lachesis, the fate of the past,
presides over the lottery, which includes all
lifetimes, i.e., the lifetimes of all beasts and
all humans (cf. 618a3-4), implies that all lifetimes that are have already been and that no new
lifetimes will arise. In other words, it seems as
though the zoic γένη are fixed in number--however
large the number may be--for all time.

In addition, there is here a significant shift in
emphasis from the bulk of the Republic.[109] For
throughout the Republic, it had been assumed that
there were a small finite number of human natures
which fitted some humans for one thing and others
for other things, and that these natures were
predetermined for each person. And in terms of
responsibility for one's lifetime, this would
have meant--although this was not stated explicit-
ly--that no one is responsible for himself, that
if one were not perfectly just, one could not be
blamed, because one simply had a nature of which
perfect justice was not a part.[110] But here (617
e1-5) it is asserted that each person, each soul,
elects both its daimon and its lifetime (with
whatever degree of virtue that lifetime contains);
hence, each person is the cause of, bears the re-

164

ponsibility for, his own nature. In other words, whereas the bulk of the <u>Republic</u> depends on the assumption that we simply are what we are, the myth of Er asserts that we are what we choose to be.[111] But this shift produces a perplexity. For if we are to choose <u>freely</u>, our souls must be without a τάξις (618b2-4), i.e., they must be empty, and yet if we are to <u>choose</u> freely, our souls must contain all possibilities at least as possibilities (618b4-6), i.e., they must be full. And this problem is the problem of learning, so it is not surprising that when Socrates interrupts the narrative at precisely this point (618b6), he takes up the question of learning:

> Indeed there, as is likely, o friend Glaucon, is all the risk for a human, and because of these things one must take care especially, so that each of us having been uncaring for other learnings will be both a seeker and a learner of this learning, if somewhere he is such as to learn and to find out who will make him, thoroughly recognizing both the useful and the vicious lifetime, capable and knowledgeable of electing always everywhere the better _/lifetime/_, from the possible _/lifetimes/_.[112]

So, the learning is the learning and seeking of the learning and finding out[113] who will make one an infallible elector of the better possible lifetimes by enabling one to recognize the criteria for distinguishing useful lifetimes from vicious lifetimes. In other words, the learning is a learning of a learning about a teacher, i.e., the learning is a learning of who is the best teacher of decency. And presumably Plato himself has engaged in such a learning and has determined that the best such teacher is Socrates. Therefore, his dialogues revivify Socrates, so that others may learn through writings about Socrates what Plato himself learned through direct being together with Socrates. And the Socratic assertion that to acquire such a learning is to equip oneself to elect a good lifetime forms the prologue to Er's

account of the electings, an account which to a
great extent shows what can happen when one lacks
this learning.

Er begins his account of the electings with the
prophet's speech which outlines the terms of the
electings. According to the prophet (619b2-6),
the electing of one's nature takes the form of
choosing a lot which does nothing more than establish the numerical order in which lifetimes are
chosen. And apparently one's numerical position,
whether one is first or n^{th}, is in no way decisive, because somehow there are enough lifetimes,
so that in principle at least everyone could
choose a good lifetime. In other words, no one
would be prevented by numerical order from choosing a good lifetime.

The description of the person who received the
first lot, who is numerically first to elect, is
of great importance:

> he asserted the person who had obtained the
> first lot straightway having gone up to elect
> the biggest tyranny....and /he asserted/ him
> to be of the persons having come from heaven,
> having spent his lifetime in his earlier life-
> time in an ordered regime, having partaken of
> virtue by habit without philosophy.[114]

So, the first lot and electing fell to someone who
before had only habitual virtue, demotic virtue,
and who resided in an ordered regime, and this
person chooses the worst tyranny, and his choosing
this in haste is no excuse (619b8-c6). Clearly,
then, there can be no adequate solution to the
problem of virtue on the political plane, the
plane of habituation to virtue, and just as clearly, insofar as the person of habitual virtue alone
represents virtually everyone but the philosopher,
the lesson of Glaucon's account of Gyges' progenitor's ring, that all humans by nature desire to do
injustice with impunity, prevails, and that means
that in actual political life, in political life
in deed, there will be no cessation of bads. So,

the myth asserts that the city in speech is only in speech, and it brings to the surface the anti-utopianism which has been the constant subsurface aspect of the surface utopianism of the bulk of the Republic. In other words--and all the discussions in the Republic would have to be read with an eye to this--the Republic is at one and the same time a great utopian book and a great anti-utopian book.

And why does the first lot make the choice that he does? He makes it because as a reward for his virtue he went to heaven. This seems paradoxical, so Er interrupts his narrative to discuss (619d1-7) the two paths, the heavenly path and the subearthly path. And he asserts that the path of heaven is too easy, that those who travel to heaven are not exercised in toils, and hence the majority of them made senseless and gluttonous choices in haste. The subearthly path, on the other hand, is filled with toils, and hence the majority of those who travel that path made better and less hasty choices. So, the first soul chooses as he does because without true virtue he was corrupted by the easy life in heaven, and he did not have philosophy as an antidote to heaven. And the very radical and paradoxical teaching of the Republic, then, is that without philosophy, there is no true virtue, or--to put it inversely--knowledge is virtue. "Because of which indeed also /he asserted/ there to come to be a change of bads and goods for the many of the souls and because of the luck of the lot."[115] In other words, the bad souls from the subearthly path as a rule choose good life-times, while the good souls from heaven as a rule choose bad lifetimes, and the reason for this is the path from which they came and the lot which they happened to choose. This latter requirement is odd, because the lottery was presented initially as little more than a convenience, yet here it is suggested that it does play a role, an assertion which clearly calls for interpretation. And Socrates interrupts to answer that call in direct discourse:

167

since if someone always, when he should come to
his lifetime here, should philosophize healthily
and /if/ the lot of his electing should not fall
among the ones at the end, on the basis of the
things which are messaged from there he runs the
risk not only of being happy here, but also of
proceeding not the subterranean and rough journey from here to there and here again but the
smooth and heavenly /journey/.[116]

So, Socrates repeats the second factor in the
electing but only with respect to the philosophers. As Socrates interprets this, then, a certain exhaustion of lifetimes occurs which is not
decisive for non-philosophers (whose choices are
grossly irrational in any case), but which is decisive for philosophers. What is the meaning of
this qualification? At the least, since in the
choices enumerated here, there is available at the
very end the lifetime of the just man as defined
earlier in the Republic (cf. 620c6-7), we can in-
fer that the life of such a just man is not what
the philosopher would choose. The philosopher
whose lot is at the end, then, would wish to
choose a lifetime which is not available at the
end. But which one? If we stick strictly to the
myth as presented, it would have to be one of the
possibilities which have been selected before
Odysseus' turn comes:[117]

(1) swan (κύκνος), chosen by a musical man
(Orpheus) who hates women (620a3-6)
(2) nightingale (ἀηδών), chosen by a musical
man (Thamyros), who lost his voice and memory because he rivalled the Muses (620a6-7; cf. Iliad
2.594-600)
(3) lion, chosen by a disgruntled warrior
(Aias) (620b1-3)
(4) eagle, chosen by a king turned misan-
thrope (Agamemnon) (620b3-5)
(5) athlete, chosen by an athlete (Atalanta)
from love of honors (620b5-7)
(6) artisan woman, chosen by a boxer and
builder (Epeios) (620b7-c2)
(7) ape, chosen by a laughmaker (Thersites)

168

(620c2-3).

Since the philosopher in the Platonic corpus is
Socrates, let us re-ask our question thus: which
lifetime would Socrates choose? Let us first eli-
minate which he would not choose. He would not
choose any of the lifetimes in which θυμός is a
dominant factor, and those would be the lifetimes
characterized by or elected out of anger and
hatred and indignation and love of honors, namely
he would not choose lifetimes (1) (hatred), (2)
love of honors), (3) (anger: the lion is the thymoeidetic beast; cf. Rep. 9.588b1-592b6, esp. 588
d3, e6, 589b4, 590a9-b1, b9), (4) (hatred), (5)
(love of honors), (7) (indignation: the ape is an
auxiliary thymoeidetic beast; cf. Rep. 9.590b9,
Iliad 2.212 ff.). Therefore, it seems as though
the lifetime which Socrates would choose if he
could would be (6), a choice which is certainly
appropriate--from the points of view of both the
lifetime elected and the elector--to the Socrates
of the Republic at least, because it is the lifetime of an artisan elected by an artisan,[118] because the electing of a woman's lifetime assumes
the equality of the sexes (i.e., man-artisan becomes woman-artisan), because the elector is the
progeny of comprehensiveness of vision,[119] and because this is the only case in which the electing
soul elects a nature.[120]

Finally, after the preceding denigration of the
heavenly way, Socrates restores the desirability
of the way, but within very severe limits, the limits of healthy philosophizing. In other words,
the heavenly path should be restricted to healthy
philosophers alone, which means that only healthy
philosophy is true justice.

When Er's account resumes, he indirectly reempha-
sizes what Socrates has said: "For /he asserted
them/ to elect the many things in accordance with
the habituation of their earlier lifetime."[121]
Their vision,[122] then, is dimmed by habituation
of which only the philosopher is free. And the
operation of vision dimmed by habituation can be

169

seen throughout the electings. For example, for
Orpheus (620a3-6)·, his misogyny eventuates in his
unwillingness to be a human again and his musical
skill eventuates in his election of a musical
beast, the swan (cf. Phaedo 84e3-85b7). And in
Orpheus' case, the phrase ψυχὴν...τὴν ποτε 'Ορφέως
γενομένην, "the soul which once came to be Orpheus'," is striking for several reasons. First, it
apparently mirrors the continuity of the cycle,
i.e., the soul was once Orpheus' soul but before
that it was the soul of another and another. But
it can also mean 'the soul when it came to be
Orpheus',' i.e., when Orpheus made it his own, as
it were, a sense which does not require transmigration. It could also mean that it is not now Orpheus' soul, although its present possessor is un-
identified,[123] and this would suggest how strong
is the persistence of habituation, i.e., it is
virtually ineradicable. And the foolishness of the
choice is suggested by the subsequent assertion
that a swan and musical animals generally elect
the lifetime of humans, which means that Orpheus'
desire not to be human again will in all likelihood be thwarted.

And for Aias (620b1-3), his misanthropy eventuates
in his avoidance of being human, while his habituation as a warrior eventuates in his electing the
lifetime of a lion, i.e., the lifetime of θυμός
incarnate. And in the case of Atalanta, an athlete
elects to be an athlete; and in the case of Epeios
--as we have seen--an artisan elects to be an artisan. Finally, Thersites' becoming an ape culminates the pattern of habituation-compelled meta-
morphoses, in that his passage into an ape is the
only metamorphosis which is not called an electing: "and /he asserted himself/ to see far among
the last the /soul/ of laughter-making Thersites
sinking into an ape."[124] And the emphasis that
the choices are determined by habit and not made
freely surfaces in the addendum (620d2-5), where
it is asserted that the unjust changed into wild
beasts and the just into tame beasts. Therefore,
the so-called freedom is merely an illusion.

The last to elect is Odysseus, and he having
toiled and having freed himself from love of
honor makes a considered choice of a lifetime
which had been neglected by the others, i.e., of
a lifetime which οὖτις (no one) wants.[125] And the
toils which enable him to make such a choice must
be toils which he has experienced on the subearthly path,[126] rather than any experiences which he
underwent while he was alive.[127] And this would
mean that the Odysseus who elects is an unjust
man[128] who has been converted to justice.

The account, then, opened with a discussion of an
incurably unjust man (Ardiaios) and it ends with
a curably--indeed cured--unjust man. But the cure
eventuates in abstention from politics, which
means that there can be no solution to the problem
of human virtue and happiness on the political
plane.

NOTES

[1]By the _Republic_ tetralogy I mean the dramatic
sequence of dialogues which consists of the _Repub-
lic_, the _Timaeus_, the incomplete _Critias_, and the
projected _Hermocrates_. I include the last of
these, because the internal references to it are
sufficient to make it a necessary consideration at
least as an abandoned projection, and such a consideration may lead to some understanding of the
reasons for its abandonment. I examine the dramatic connection between these dialogues, about
which there has been some controversy, in the
body of the text.

[2]Cf., e.g., R.G. Bury, "Introduction to the
Timaeus," in the LCL, p. 3: "the literary genius
displayed in the style and diction of its central
Myth has compelled...admiration." Frutiger, pp.
209-211, treats the _Timaeus_ as one of what he
calls Plato's "mythes parascientifiques." J.A.
Stewart, _The myths of Plato_ (Carbondale, Ill.,
1960), p. 273, remarks that "the whole Discourse
delivered by Timaeus is a Myth." Léon Robin, _Pla-
ton_ (Paris, 1968), p. 143, refers to "le mythe
cosmologique du _Timée_." Also consider Pierre-
Maxime Schuhl, _La fabulation platonicienne_ (Paris,
1968), p. 108: "La biologie de Platon s'insère
dans sa cosmologie qui, tout entière, présente un
aspect mythique." Paul Friedlaender, _Plato; an in-
troduction_, tr. Hans Meyerhoff (New York, 1958),
p. 248: "the _Timaeus_ was to have the form...of a
myth." Plato, _Plato's cosmology: the Timaeus of
Plato_, tr. with comm. by F.M. Cornford (Indianapolis, n.d.), p. 37: "the _Timaeus_ is a 'myth' or
'story' (μῦθος)." One could multiply such citations.

[3]Cornford, _Cosmology_, p. 5.

[4]Cornford, _Cosmology_, pp. 4-5. Cornford goes so
far as to say (p. 5): "The design of the present

172

trilogy is thus completely independent of the Republic.

[5]Henri Martin, Études sur le Timée de Platon
(Paris, 1841), tome 1, p. 1: "Dans le dialogue de
Platon intitulé Πολιτεία, c'est-à-dire la Répub-
lique, ou plutôt l'Etat, Socrate se trouvant à
Athènes avec Critias, Timée, Hermocrate et un
quatrième personnage, qui n'est pas nommé, leur
avait raconté une conversation philosophique qui
avait eu lieu la veille au Pirée entre Glaucon,
Polémarque, Thrasymaque, Adimante, Céphale et
Socrate lui-même...." Also consider A.E. Taylor,
A commentary on Plato's Timaeus (Oxford, 1928), p.
27, who discusses "the connexion between the Timaeus and the Republic." And cf. Plato, ΠΛΑΤΩΝΟΣ
ΤΙΜΑΙΟΣ: the Timaeus of Plato, ed. with intro. and
notes by R.D. Archer-Hind (London, 1888), initial
note: "Sokrates meets by appointment three of the
friends to whom he has on the previous day narrated the conversation recorded in the Republic.
After the absence of the fourth member of the par-
ty has been explained, he proceeds to summarize
the social and political theories propounded in
that dialogue. It will be observed that the unusually long introductory passage...has its appli-
cation not to the Timaeus only, but to the whole
trilogy, Republic, Timaeus, Critias. The recapitulation of the Republic indicates the precise
position of that work in the series...... The
supposed date of the present discussion is two
days after the meeting in the house of Kephalos
...... On the following day Sokrates reports to
the four friends what passed at the house of Kephalos; and on the next the present dialogue
takes place." And cf. Stewart, p. 252: "The assumed chronological order of the pieces is Republic, Timaeus, Critias...... But, of course,
the logical order is Timaeus, Republic, Critias."

[6]Also consider the notes of Bury (LCL) ad 17c
ff.

[7]Even Cornford begrudgingly cites the Republic
in his note ad 18c (p. 10, n. 1), and he asserts

(p. 3, italics mine): "Socrates, we are told, had been describing the institutions of a city on the lines of the Republic." But it is striking in Cornford that he very uncharacteristically derives substantive disconnection from dramatic disconnection rather than simply relying on his apparently preternatural ability to see into Plato's motives: "we may regard his doctrine simply as Plato's own" (p. 3), "Plato's design" (p. 4, cf. p. 5), "No doubt Plato was thinking of" (p. 4), and so on. Cornford (pp. 4-5) also adduces the festival to which reference is made in the Timaeus (21a2-3, 26e3) as evidence against the connection between the Republic and the Timaeus. For, as is universally and correctly agreed, the Republic takes place on the day of the festival of the Thracian goddess Bendis (cf. Rep. 1.327a1-5). But what festival would have taken place two days later (see note 5 above)? It is clear that it would have to be a festival in honor of "the goddess who is both a lover of war and a lover of wisdom" (φιλοπόλεμός τε καὶ φιλόσοφος ἡ θεὸς οὖσα, Timaeus 24c7-d1), namely Athena, who is in a way the goddess who implicitly presides over the central books of the Republic which indeed deal with both war and wisdom. It has been widely assumed that the festival must be the Lesser Panathenaea: cf. Martin, p. 1; Archer-Hind, p. 66, note ad ἐν τῇ πανηγύρει; and Cornford, Cosmology, loc. cit. But whereas Martin and Archer-Hind see this as no obstacle to a closeness of dramatic date between the dialogues, Cornford points out--and he cites (p. 4, n. 1) Proclus in support--that the Lesser Panathenaea was at least two months after the Bendidea (cf. Taylor, note ad 17a1), and he concludes from this that the Timaeus cannot be the dramatic sequel to the Republic. Even though Cornford seems right about the relative dates of the Bendidea and the Lesser Panathenaea, it still does not follow that the Timaeus could not have taken place two days after the Republic. For Cornford is incorrect when he says (p. 5, n. 1) that the word πανήγυρις (literally, 'a gathering of all,' from πᾶς + ἄγυρις: cf. LSJ; Timaeus 21a2) "implies an important festival," because it is used in a much lesser

sense by Socrates at <u>Rep.</u> 4.421b2, 10.604e4, 614
e3. Therefore, it seems best to agree with Taylor
(note ad 17a1): "It has been suggested that Plato
has made an oversight, but this is not likely. A
modern writer would hardly be capable of making
Epiphany and Good Friday, or Trinity Sunday and
Michaelmas, fall in the same week. It is more natural to suppose that the reference...is not to
the lesser Panathenaea but to some other festival
connected with Athena." And we need to go no further than this, I believe, in identifying the festival, which, it is plausible to assume, is as
non-historically existent as the dialogue's major
interlocutor (see note 15 below).

[8]At the beginning of the <u>Timaeus</u>, the extraordinary density of occurrences of χθές (yester-
day), which seem to echo cavernously the χθές
which is the second word of the <u>Republic</u>, suggests
a connection between the two dialogues. Cf. <u>Tim.</u>
17a2, b2, c1, 19a7, 20b1, c6, 25e2, 26a4, 7, b4,
c8, e7. The only other Platonic dialogue which has
an initial χθές equal in prominence to that of the
<u>Republic</u> is the <u>Sophist</u> 216a1, from which the re-
ference back is clearly to the <u>Theaetetus</u> and to
which there is no subsequent χθές referring back
as there is in the <u>Timaeus</u> to the <u>Republic</u>. Finally, there is a χθές at the very beginning of
the <u>Euthydemus</u> (271a1), but there the prominent
word is the interrogative Τίς which Crito uses out
of his curiosity to discover the identity of Socrates' conversational interlocutor of the previous
day.

[9]Cf. τὸ κεφάλαιον at 17c2 and ἐν κεφαλαίοις at
19a8.

[10]The reference back to the <u>Republic</u> is conti-
nued in the <u>Critias</u> as well: cf. <u>Critias</u> 110c3-d4,
esp. χθές at <u>d3</u>.

[11]<u>Timaeus</u> 20a1-5: Τίμαιός τε γὰρ ὅδε, εὐνομωτά-
της ὢν πόλεως τῆς ἐν Ἰταλίᾳ Λοκρίδος, οὐσίᾳ καὶ
γένει οὐδενὸς ὕστερος ὢν τῶν ἐκεῖ, τὰς μεγίστας

μὲν ἀρχάς τε καὶ τιμὰς τῶν ἐν τῇ πόλει μετακεχείρισται, φιλοσοφίας δ' αὖ κατ' ἐμὴν δόξαν ἐπ' ἄκρον ἁπάσης ἐλήλυθεν.

[12]Timaeus 19e5-6: ἅμα φιλοσόφων ἀνδρῶν ᾗ καὶ πολιτικῶν. Cf. Republic 5.473c11-e2, 474b3-c3.

[13]Cf. Republic 5.472a1-7, 473c6-8.

[14]Timaeus 27a3-5: ἅτε ὄντα ἀστρονομικώτατον ἡμῶν καὶ περὶ φύσεως τοῦ παντὸς εἰδέναι μάλιστα ἔργον πεποιημένον.

[15]Cf. Cornford, Cosmology, pp. 2-3: "There is no evidence for the historic existence of Timaeus of Locri...... The very fact that a man of such distinction has left not the faintest trace in political or philosophic history is against his claim to be a real person. The probability is that Plato invented him...." Cf. Martin, p. 50. The utopianism of the best city, the best cosmos, and of Timaeus himself is further matched by the utopianism of Atlantis: cf. Frutiger, pp. 244 ff. In addition, one could add that the two major non-historically existent speakers in the Platonic dialogues, Diotima and Timaeus, both have names containing the stem τιμ-.

[16]Cf. Leo Strauss, The city and man (Chicago, 1964), pp. 110-113, 116-118, 128, 133, 138; Allan Bloom, "Interpretive Essay," in Plato, The Republic of Plato, tr. with notes and an interpretive essay by Allan Bloom (New York, 1968), p. 378 et passim.

[17]The case for the equality of the sexes is made on the basis of an undeniable psychic equality and a suppression of any somatic difference: cf. 454c1-5, where the somatic difference between the sexes is reduced to the difference between the hairy and the bald (but also cf. 455e1 ff.). And in the discussion of procreation, the guardians are bred as beasts are bred and there is no mention of the period of pregnancy. It is as though

176

the political implementation of the psychic equality of the sexes requires an extremely sophisti-
cated eugenic technology, in which the foetus is
removed from the womb after conception only to be
returned for nursing--and even that in a very
limited way (cf. 460c8-d7)--when it reaches full
term. What is clearly required, then, is a suppression of erotic compulsions by geometric compulsions (cf. 458d5), a redefinition of the sacred
as the politically beneficial or useful (cf. 458
e4). Cf. Bloom, p. 468 ff., n. 5.

18Cf. ἀναγκάζοιτο at 515c6, ἀναγκάζοι at 515e1,
ἕλκοι at 515e6, μὴ ἀνείη πρὶν ἐξελκύσειεν at 515
e7-8, ἑλκόμενον at 516a1.

19Consider Timaeus' perfunctory and compulsory
invocation at 27c4-d1; also cf. 40d6-41a3 (italics
mine): "And about the other daimons /i.e., other
than the planets and stars/ to speak and to recognize their genesis is bigger than in accordance
with us, and one must be persuaded by the persons
who have spoken before, since they are, as they
asserted, progenies of gods, and since somehow
they distinctly have envisioned their own progeni-
tors at any rate; therefore it is impossible to
distrust the children of gods, although they speak
without likely and compulsory showings-forth, but
we following the law must trust them as we would
persons declaring themselves to announce household
things. Therefore in this way let the genesis of
these gods hold and be spoken for us in accordance
with them. Ocean and Tethys, the children of Earth
and Heaven, were generated, and of these Phorkys
and Kronos and Rhea and as many as are with these
/were generated/, and from Kronos and Rhea /were
generated/ Zeus and Hera and all whom we know to
be spoken as their siblings, and still other progenies of these" (Περὶ δὲ τῶν ἄλλων δαιμόνων εἰπεῖν καὶ γνῶναι τὴν γένεσιν μεῖζον ἢ καθ' ἡμᾶς,
πειστέον δὲ τοῖς εἰρηκόσιν ἔμπροσθεν, ἐκγόνοις μὲν
θεῶν οὖσιν, ὡς ἔφασαν, σαφῶς δέ που τούς γε αὐτῶν
προγόνους εἰδόσιν· ἀδύνατον οὖν θεῶν παισὶν ἀπισ-
τεῖν, καίπερ ἄνευ τε εἰκότων καὶ ἀναγκαίων ἀπο-
δείξεων λέγουσιν, ἀλλ' ὡς οἰκεῖα φασκόντων ἀπαγ-

γέλλειν ἐπομένους τῷ νόμῳ πιστευτέον. οὕτως οὖν
κατ' ἐκείνους ἡμῖν ἡ γένεσις περὶ τούτων τῶν θεῶν
ἐχέτω καὶ λεγέσθω. Γῆς τε καὶ Οὐρανοῦ παῖδες Ὠκε-
ανός τε καὶ Τηθὺς ἐγενέσθην, τούτων δὲ Φόρκυς Κρόνος τε καὶ Ῥέα καὶ ὅσοι μετὰ τούτων, ἐκ δὲ Κρόνου
καὶ Ῥέας Ζεὺς Ἥρα τε καὶ πάντες ὅσους ἴσμεν
ἀδελφοὺς λεγομένους αὐτῶν, ἔτι τε τούτων ἄλλους
ἐκγόνους). That this is the only place in Timaeus'
narration where the traditional Greek pantheon is
even alluded to makes the 'godlessness' of the
dialogue stand out all the more. In other words,
the perspective of Timaeus--and presumably his interlocutors as well--is one of complete religious
enlightenment.

[20]The possibility that the all is ἀγενές (27c5)
is mentioned only to be immediately forgotten. And
the cosmos is presented as the work of a δημιουργός
(cf. 28a6 et passim) of whose beautiful cosmos
(cf. 29a2) the kallipolis of the Republic (7.527c2)
is an analogue, and of whom each citizen of the
best city is an analogue (cf. Rep. 3.395c1).

[21]In a sense, Timaeus' entire account is a
lengthy cosmic elaboration of the founding lie of
Socrates' best city.

[22]29c4-5: πέρι...τῆς τοῦ παντὸς γενέσεως. He
says here that it is also about the gods (πέρι
θεῶν, 29c4), but as becomes clear later, by the
gods he means first and foremost the planets and
stars and not the traditional Greek pantheon: see
note 19 above.

[23]Cf. τὸν εἰκότα μῦθον at 29d2. Also cf. τῶν
εἰκότων μύθων at 59c6, and τὸν εἰκότα μῦθον at
68d2.

[24]Cornford's position (Cosmology, pp. 30-31)
is that it is likely because it is poetic and it
is a myth because there is no certainty in physics
and because it is a myth or story: "The cosmology
of the Timaeus is poetry" (p. 30); "The Timaeus
is a poem" (p. 31); "There are two senses in which
the Timaeus is a 'myth' or 'story' (μῦθος). One...

178

no account of the material world can ever amount
to an exact and self-consistent statement of un-
changeable truth. In the second place, the cosmology is cast in the form of a cosmogony, a 'story'
of events spread out in time" (p. 31). Cf. Frutiger, pp. 173-175, 210-211. Also consider Taylor,
general note ad 27d5-29d3, pp. 59-61. And cf.
Friedlaender, p. 248: "The cosmos that /Plato's/
scientific method tried to penetrate was, at the
same time, the object of his aesthetic admiration
and of his religious awe," "We cannot speak with
exactness about the world of change," "About
changing nature we can, at the utmost, give 'plausible accounts'." Also cf. G. Vlastos, Plato's
universe (Seattle, 1975), p. 49: "The creation
story of the Timaeus, despite its allegorical
tincture, attests Plato's assimilation of the results obtained by this science /i.e., empirically
oriented science, esp. astronomy/ in which theory
and practice were now successfully interacting."
It is striking that on the whole in these commentaries one could form the impression that the major interlocutor of the Timaeus is Plato himself
and not Timaeus of Locris.

[25]He speaks frequently in the first person plural and refers back on occasion to the speech as a
whole, e.g., 40d7, 48e1, 69a6-b2, 90e1-3, and so
on.

[26]Cf. κατὰ λόγον τὸν εἰκότα at 30b7, κατὰ τὸν
...εἰκότα λόγον at 53d5-6, κατὰ τὸν εἰκότα λόγον
at 55d5, τὸν εἰκότα λόγον at 56a1, κατὰ τὸν...λό-
γον...εἰκότα at 56b4, εἰκότι λόγῳ at 57d6.

[27]59c5-d3: τἄλλα δὲ τῶν τοιούτων οὐδὲν ποικίλον
ἔτι διαλογίσασθαι τὴν τῶν εἰκότων μύθων μεταδιώ-
κοντα ἰδέαν· ἣν ὅταν τις ἀναπαύσεως ἕνεκα τοὺς
περὶ τῶν ὄντων ἀεὶ καταθέμενος λόγους, τοὺς γενέσεως πέρι διαθεώμενος εἰκότας ἀμεταμέλητον ἡδονὴν
κτᾶται, μέτριον ἂν ἐν τῷ βίῳ παιδιὰν καὶ φρόνιμον
ποιοῖτο. ταύτῃ δὴ καὶ τὰ νῦν ἐφέντες τὸ μετὰ τοῦτο
τῶν αὐτῶν πέρι τὰ ἑξῆς εἰκότα δίιμεν τῇδε.

[28]Cf. Respectively 56b4, 26e4-5, 20d7, 92c4. It

179

should be noted here that in the Timaeus no λόγος
is described as καλός.

29The word γένεσις occurs in the Timaeus at
27a6, d6, 28b6, 29c3, 5, d7, e4, 34c4, 37e3, 38a2,
6, c4, 39e3, 40e4, 41e3, 42c1, 3, 48a1, b4, 6,
49c7, e7, 52b1, 53e3, 54b7-8, d3, 58a2, c3, 59c8,
61c7, d4, 62a2, 73b3, 75b8, 76e4, 77c3, 90a8,
90d2, 91a1, d5.

30Cf. Seth Benardete, "On Plato's Timaeus and
and Timaeus' science fiction," Interpretation; a
journal of political philosophy, vol. 2, no. 1,
Summer 1971, pp. 22, 32, 40.

31Cf. Timaeus 26e4-5, which contains a double
opposition, of πλασθέντα to ἀληθινὸν and of μῦθον
to λόγον. But this does not mean that one could
not have an ἀληθινὸς μῦθος or a πλασθεὶς λόγος.
For we have already examined the ἀληθινὸς μῦθος in
the seventh epistle, and one may fashion a λόγος
(cf. πλάττοντι λόγους at Apol. Socr. 17c5).

32Cf. 27b8, 29b8, c6, 46d4, 47c5, 6, 49a4, 51c5,
53c1, 62a6, 69a7, 70a4-5 (twice), b3, 71a3, 5, d4,
75e3, 87b1, 91b1, 92c4.

33Cf. 28a1, 29a6, b4, 30b7, 32b5, 37e6-38a1,
48d2, 49a3, b5, 51b6, c7, e3, 52c6, d3, 53d5-6,
54b1, 55d5, 7, 56a1, b4, 57d6, 59c7-8, 67d2, 68b7,
70d5, 74e4, 76e4-5, 77b4, 80d1, 83c4, 87c4, 88e4,
89e3, 90e5, 8, 91b6. One could add here the
phrase ἀνὰ λόγον at 29c2, 53e4, 56c7, 69b5, 82b3-4.

34Cf. 29d2, 59c6, 68d2.

35Cf. 19c3, 20b3, d1, 7, 21a7, c5, d3, 6-7,
26a5, d7, e5 (explicitly in opposition to μῦθος,
e4).

36It is puzzling, therefore, that there is such
widespread agreement among commentators (cf. Frutiger's list, pp. 129-130; Cornford's allusion to it
as "romance" and "legend," Cosmology, pp. 4 and 18;
Taylor, note ad Tim. 25a1; Archer-Hind, p. 78;

Stewart's list, pp. 100-101; Friedlaender, pp.
200-203; Martin's description of it as "fable," I.
p. 258; and Couturat, De platonicis mythis (Paris,
1896), pp. 28 ff.) that the account of Atlantis is
a μῦθος when it is emphatically treated as a λόγος.
In other words, the account of the war between
Athens and Atlantis is not a genetic account of
either Athens or Atlantis but a descriptive account of the best city (ancient Athens) in motion
(cf. Tim. 19b8), i.e., engaged in the greatest of
its great and wondrous deeds (cf. Tim. 20e4-6). In
the Critias, the word μυθολογία occurs once, but
only in a general remark, and does not refer specifically to the account of Atlantis: "For mythology and the re-seeking of the ancient things come
upon cities simultaneously with leisure, when they
/i.e., mythology and re-seeking/ see the compulsory things for a lifetime already having been
prepared for them /i.e., for the cities/, but not
before." (110a3-6: μυθολογία γὰρ ἀναζήτησίς τε τῶν
παλαιῶν μετὰ σχολῆς ἅμ' ἐπὶ τὰς πόλεις ἔρχεσθον,
ὅταν ἴδητόν τισιν ἤδη τοῦ βίου τἀναγκαῖα κατεσκευ-
ασμένα, πρὶν δὲ οὔ.) And if μυθολογία and ἀναζήτησις τῶν παλαιῶν are identical, then when the natural compulsions have been met, i.e., when the so-
called useful arts have come to be, searching out
the originary things arises, i.e., philosophy
arises.

37Cf. 17c1-2 (of the Republic), 19c7 (of interpreting), 19e1 (opp. ἔργον), 7 (opp. ἔργον), 20c1,
21e6 (of the way the Hellenes talk), 26e7 (of the
Republic), 27a8. In addition, the generic use of
λόγος at 22a5 is then specified as μῦθος by the
equation between γενεαλογεῖν and μυθολογεῖν (b1-2),
between a particular kind of genetic account and
genetic accounts as a whole (cf. 23b3-5).

38Cf. 27b1, 6, and note 35 above.

39Cf. 20d1, 21a6, 22b8 (of originary accounts),
23a2 (of accounts of great deeds), 25e1.

40Cf. 22c7 (of genetic accounts), 23b5 (of ge-
nealogies which are childlike), 26e4 (opp. λόγος),

26c8 (of the account of the genesis of the best city and its citizens in the Republic).

[41]Cf. Couturat, p. 48.

[42]In this connection, I would add that Seth Benardete, "Plato's Timaeus," p. 51, is on the right track when he says: "Timaeus' speech is an attempt to give the cosmological equivalent to the Phaedrus myth." But he seems to mean by the Phaedrus myth Socrates' palinode, and hence goes off the track. The correct parallel, I believe, is between Socrates' Lysian speech (a myth) with its combination of calculation and compulsion and Timaeus' speech with its combination of intellect and compulsion, and between Socrates' mythic palinode (the motion of the soul) and the missing Hermocrates (the cosmos in motion).

[43]Herakleitos, DK[5] 53B: Πόλεμος πάντων μὲν πατήρ ἐστι, πάντων δὲ βασιλεύς....

[44]Herakleitos, DK[5] 80B: εἰδέναι δὲ χρὴ τὸν πόλεμον ἐόντα ξυνόν, καὶ δίκην ἔριν, καὶ γινόμενα πάντα κατ' ἔριν καὶ χρεών.

[45]Cratylus 402a8-10: λέγει που 'Ηράκλειτος ὅτι πάντα χωρεῖ καὶ οὐδὲν μένει, καὶ ποταμοῦ ῥοῇ ἀπεικάζων τὰ ὄντα λέγει ὡς δὶς ἐς τὸν αὐτὸν ποταμὸν οὐκ ἂν ἐμβαίης. (I have deleted the quotation marks from Burnet's text as unnecessary.)

[46]Leo Tolstoy, War and peace, tr. Louise and Aylmer Maude (New York, Norton Critical Ed., 1966), Book 10, ch. 1, pp. 761, 761-762, 763.

[47]Benardete, "On Plato's Timaeus," p. 26. Cf. Republic 10.596d8-e4 to Timaeus 19b4-c1. Also cf. Rep. 10.598b8-c4.

[48]Benardete, "On Plato's Timaeus," p. 26.

[49]Timaeus 37d3-7, e3-5, 38a7-8: ἡ μὲν οὖν τοῦ ζῴου φύσις ἐτύγχανεν οὖσα αἰώνιος, καὶ τοῦτο μὲν δὴ τῷ γεννητῷ παντελῶς προσάπτειν οὐκ ἦν δυνατόν·

εἰκὼ δ' ἐπενόει κινητόν τινα αἰῶνος ποιῆσαι, καὶ διακοσμῶν ἅμα οὐρανὸν ποιεῖ μένοντος αἰῶνος ἐν ἑνὶ κατ' ἀριθμὸν ἰοῦσαν αἰώνιον εἰκόνα, τοῦταν ὃν δὴ χρόνον ὠνομάκαμεν..... καὶ τό τ' ἦν τό τ' ἔσται χρόνου γεγονότα εἴδη, ἃ δὴ φέροντες λανθάνομεν ἐπὶ τὴν ἀίδιον οὐσίαν οὐκ ὀρθῶς...... ἀλλὰ χρόνου ταῦτα αἰῶνα μιμουμένου καὶ κατ' ἀριθμὸν κυκλουμένου γέγονεν εἴδη.

[50]Socrates says (2.376d9-10): "Come therefore, let us, as persons mythologizing in a myth and having leisure, educate the men in speech." ("Ἴθι οὖν, ὥσπερ ἐν μύθῳ μυθολογοῦντές τε καὶ σχολὴν ἄγοντες λόγῳ παιδεύωμεν τοὺς ἄνδρας.) The mythologizing is the giving an account of the guardians' education. And the myth in which that mythologizing occurs is clearly meant to be the Republic as a whole. Also consider Socrates' reference to "the regime which we mythologize in speech" (ἡ πολιτεία ἣν μυθολογοῦμεν λόγῳ, 6.501e4). As a whole, then, the Republic corresponds to Phaedrus' remark (Phaedrus 276e1-3): "You bespeak, o Socrates, an altogether beautiful...childlike-playing... in speeches, /namely/ mythologizing about both justice and the other things of which you speak" (Παγκάλην λέγεις...παιδιάν, ὦ Σώκρατες,...ἐν λόγοις..., δικαιοσύνης τε καὶ ἄλλων ὧν λέγεις πέρι μυθολογοῦντα).

[51]Cf. μυθολογοῦσιν at Rep. 2.359d6.

[52]Cf. Rep. 2.376d9-10, and note 50 above.

[53]Cf. μῦθον at 2.377c1; μῦθοι at 2.378e5; μύθων at 3.386b8-9; μύθοις at 2.377a6, c4, 7; μύθους at 2.377a4, b6, d5, 379a4, 381e3, 3.391e12; μυθολογοῦντα at 2.380c2; μυθολογεῖν at 2.379a2, 3.392b6; μεμυθολογημένα at 2.378e3; μυθολογητέον at 2.378 c4; μυθοποιοῦς at 2.377b11; μυθολογίας at 3.394 b9-c1; μυθολογίαις at 2.382d1; μυθολόγῳ at 3.398 b1; and μυθολόγων at 3.392d2. And the myths of the best city will be based on, will perfect, a θεολογία (cf. 2.379a5-6), a λόγος or classificatory description of the gods (which is formulated in outline at least into two laws, Rep. 2.379a5-383c7,

and then elaborated in Book 3). In other words, the best city will educate not through a groundless θεογονία, but rather through a θεογονία grounded in a θεολογία. And although the myths of the best city may still be falsehoods, they are falsehoods grounded in truth, and they are useful or beneficial falsehoods (cf. χρήσιμον at 2.382c6-7, d3; ὠφελίᾳ at 3.389b8). Therefore, one can falsify in such a way as to adumbrate the truth which is being falsified. Cf. Rep. 2.382b9-c1: "since the /falsehood/ in speeches at any rate is a certain imitation of the affection in the soul and /it is/ a look-alike which has come to be later, it is not an altogether unmixed falsehood /i.e., it is a falsehood mixed with the truth/" (ἐπεὶ τό γε ἐν τοῖς λόγοις μίμημά τι τοῦ ἐν τῇ ψυχῇ ἐστιν παθήματος καὶ ὕστερον γεγονὸς εἴδωλον, οὐ πάνυ ἄκρατον ψεῦδος).

[54]Cf. μύθου at 3.415a2, μυθολογοῦντες at 3.415 a3, and μῦθον at 3.415c7.

[55]Cf. μυθολογοῦνται at 9.588c2.

[56]Cf. μῦθος at 10.621b8.

[57]Cf. Eva Brann, "The music of the Republic," ΑΓΩΝ, vol. 1, no. 1, April 1967, pp. 1-2, esp. the diagrammatic representation of the structure of the Republic (p. 2) as a series of concentric circles, except that the circles which she labels "Logos" and "Ergon" should be labelled as deepening layers of "Myth."

[58]Republic 6.511b7: τὴν τοῦ παντὸς ἀρχήν. The genitive here can be taken as either a genitive of contents/material or an objective genitive or both simultaneously: cf. Smyth, Greek grammar (Cambridge, Mass., 1973), sections 1323, 1328, 1331-1334.

[59]That this is purely hypothetical is indicated by Glaucon's assertion that the position which he takes does not represent his own opinion: cf. Rep. 2.358b7-d6, esp. c6, ἔμοιγε...οὔ τι δοκεῖ οὕτως.

In a sense, then, one could also say that insofar as the rest of the Republic is a response to Glaucon's interruption here, it too is purely hypothetical.

60The sophist's version of invisibility is his chameleon-like shifting from city to city: cf. Tim. 19e2-8.

61Clearly if Gyges' ancestor, and not Leontios (cf. Rep. 4.439e6-440a3), had come upon the corpses outside the wall of Athens, he would have stripped them of all their valuables instead of debating within himself whether to look or not.

62And the opportunity is provided by a natural event. I.e., through an upheaval, nature cooperates in giving him the means to act invisibly in accordance with his previously invisible nature.

63Clearly his fellow shepherds would have done the same, as their behavior at the conference when Gyges' ancestor vanishes indicates, for no sooner is he "gone" than they begin to converse about him as though he were gone, and we can assume, I believe, that their remarks were not filled with praise but rather were filled in all likelihood with low backbiting.

64And Socrates is the living embodiment of Glaucon's construct, i.e., he is the perfectly just man who has the greatest reputation for injustice: cf. Rep. 2.361b5-d1. It should not be forgotten, however, that the philosopher, at least the philosopher who has learned from Socrates' fate, also must employ a protective ring of invisibility either by sequestering himself in a school or by writing invisibly or by both, as Plato did.

65Cf. Leo Strauss, CM, pp. 102-103; Eva Brann, pp. 10-11.

66Richard Lewis Nettleship, Lectures on the Republic of Plato (New York, 1968), pp. 340-341.

[67]That the education of the guardians was directed to habitual virtue alone is made especially clear at Rep. 7.522a3-b1.

[68]Republic 10.607b5-6: παλαιὰ μέν τις διαφορὰ φιλοσοφίᾳ τε καὶ ποιητικῇ.

[69]I have designated each part by a capital letter so as to simplify the summary which follows. I will also specify the parts within the parts by lower case subscripts as follows: A_d=A-divine, A_h=A-human, B_l=B-lion, B_s=B-snake, B_a=B-ape, C_s=C-savage, C_t=C-tame.

[70]Cf. 589c8-d1, e4, 590c9-d1, 3-4.

[71]Cf. 588d3-4, e6-589a1, a7-b1, c8-d1.

[72]Cf. 588d3, e6, 589b4, 590a9-b1, 9.

[73]Cf. 590b1 and Adam note ad loc.

[74]Cf. 590b9.

[75]Cf. 588c7-10, e5, 589b1-3, c8-d3, e4, 590a6-7, b6-7, c4-5, 591b2, c6.

[76]Cf. 588d10-e2. For the relative sizes of the three parts, see 588d4-5.

[77]Cf. τῆς φύσεως at 589d2.

[78]Alfarabi, Philosophy of Plato and Aristotle, tr. Muhsin Mahdi (Glencoe, Ill., 1962), p. 64. Cf. Aristotle, History of animals 8.1.588a15-b6: "For there are in the most of the other animals too tracks of the manners in respect to the soul, which very things for humans have more apparent differences; for also tameness and savageness, and gentleness and harshness, and courage and cowardice, and fears and boldness, and spirits and roguishnesses and similarities of awareness in respect to thinking are in many of them /i.e., animals/, in accordance with which very things we

bespoke for the parts. For the ones differ /only/
by the more and less in regard to a human, and
the human /differs only by the more and less/ in
regard to many of the animals (for some of the
suchlike things internally underpin the humans
more, and some internally /underpin/ the other
animals more), and the ones differ by analogy;
for as in a human there are art and wisdom and
awareness, thus there is a certain other suchlike
natural power for some of the animals. And about
the things which we bespeak the suchlike is apparent to those who have gazed upon the age of children; for in them /i.e., children/ it is possible
to see tracks and seeds of the aptitudes/attitudes
which will be later, and the soul in accordance
with this time-of-life /i.e., childhood/ differs
in no way from the soul of beasts, so that it is
not unaccountable if some things the same underpin
the other animals, and some things nearly so and
some things analogous. And thus nature crosses
over from the unsouled things to the animals in
accordance with a little, so that their dividing-
line escapes notice by /their/ contiguity and is
the middle of the ones before /them/." ("Ενεστι
γὰρ ἐν τοῖς πλείστοις καὶ τῶν ἄλλων ζῴων ἴχνη τῶν
περὶ τὴν ψυχὴν τρόπων, ἅπερ ἐπὶ τῶν ἀνθρώπων ἔχει
φανερωτέρας τὰς διαφοράς· καὶ γὰρ ἡμερότης καὶ
ἀγριότης, καὶ πραότης καὶ χαλεπότης, καὶ ἀνδρεία
καὶ δειλία, καὶ φόβοι καὶ θάρρη, καὶ θυμοὶ καὶ
πανουργίαι καὶ τῆς περὶ τὴν διάνοιαν συνέσεως ἔν-
εισιν ἐν πολλοῖς αὐτῶν ὁμοιότητες, καθάπερ ἐπὶ
τῶν μερῶν ἐλέγομεν. Τὰ μὲν γὰρ τῷ μᾶλλον καὶ ἧττον
διαφέρει πρὸς τὸν ἄνθρωπον, καὶ ὁ ἄνθρωπος πρὸς
πολλὰ τῶν ζῴων (ἔνια γὰρ τῶν τοιούτων ὑπάρχει μᾶλλον ἐν ἀνθρώποις, ἔνια δ' ἐν τοῖς ἄλλοις ζῴοις
μᾶλλον), τὰ δὲ τῷ ἀνάλογον διαφέρει· ὥσπερ ἐν ἀνθρώπῳ τέχνη καὶ σοφία καὶ σύνεσις, οὕτως ἐνίοις
τῶν ζῴων ἐστί τις τοιαύτη ἑτέρα φυσικὴ δύναμις.
Φανερὸν δὲ περὶ ὧν λέγομεν ἐστὶν τὸ τοιοῦτον ἐπὶ
τὴν τῶν παίδων ἡλικίαν βλέψασιν· ἐν τούτοις γὰρ
τῶν μὲν ὕστερον ἕξεων ἐσομένων ἔστιν ἰδεῖν οἷον
ἴχνη καὶ σπέρματα, διαφέρει δ' οὐθὲν ἡ ψυχὴ τῆς
τῶν θηρίων ψυχῆς κατὰ τὸν χρόνον τοῦτον, ὥστ' οὐδὲν ἄλογον εἰ τὰ μὲν ταῦτα τὰ δὲ παραπλήσια τὰ δ'
ἀνάλογον ὑπάρχει τοῖς ἄλλοις ζῴοις. Οὕτω δ' ἐκ τῶν

ἀψύχων εἰς τὰ ζῷα μεταβαίνει κατὰ μικρὸν ἡ φύσις, ὥστε τῇ συνεχείᾳ λανθάνει τὸ μεθόριον αὐτῶν καὶ τὸ μέσον προτέρων ἐστίν.) I have adopted in most cases, against Bekker (see apparatus criticus ad loc.), the readings of ms. Aᵃ.

[79]Republic 1.336b5: ὥσπερ θηρίον.

[80]Republic 3. 411d7-e1: Μισόλογος...καὶ ἄμουσος ...βίᾳ...καὶ ἀγριότητι ὥσπερ θηρίον πρὸς πάντα διαπράττεται.

[81]This would also suggest that if the transformation of the democrat into the tyrant is a myth, then the entire account of regime/soul transformations may also be a myth.

[82]Such as the transformation of the guardians from dogs into wolves.

[83]Such as the transformation of the philosopher into a dead man in the Phaedo. Cf. Alfarabi, pp. 63-64.

[84]Republic 8.565d4-e1, 566a2-5, 568d4-6, 569a8-b1: Τίς ἀρχὴ οὖν μεταβολῆς ἐκ προστάτου ἐπὶ τύραννον; ἢ δῆλον ὅτι ἐπειδὰν ταὐτὸν ἄρξηται δρᾶν ὁ προστάτης τῷ ἐν τῷ μύθῳ ὃς περὶ τὸ ἐν Ἀρκαδίᾳ τὸ τοῦ Διὸς τοῦ Λυκαίου ἱερὸν λέγεται; Τίς; ἔφη. Ὡς ἄρα ὁ γευσάμενος τοῦ ἀνθρωπίνου σπλάγχνου, ἐν ἄλλοις ἄλλων ἱερείων ἑνὸς ἐγκατατετμημένου, ἀνάγκη δὴ τούτῳ λύκῳ γενέσθαι...... ἆρα τῷ τοιούτῳ ἀνάγκη δὴ τὸ μετὰ τοῦτο καὶ εἵμαρται ἢ ἀπολωλέναι ὑπὸ τῶν ἐχθρῶν ἢ τυραννεῖν καὶ λύκῳ ἐξ ἀνθρώπου γενέσθαι; Πολλὴ ἀνάγκη, ἔφη...... λέγωμεν δὲ πάλιν ἐκεῖνο τὸ τοῦ τυράννου στρατόπεδον, τὸ καλόν τε καὶ πολὺ καὶ ποικίλον καὶ οὐδέποτε ταὐτόν, πόθεν θρέψεται...... Γνώσεταί γε, νὴ Δία, ἦ δ' ὅς, τότ' ἤδη ὁ δῆμος οἷος οἷον θρέμμα γεννῶν ἠσπάζετό τε καὶ ηὖξεν....

[85]To work this out systematically throughout the Platonic corpus--which is beyond the scope of this work--one would have to catalogue all the references to beasts therein in order to compile a

precise set of human equivalences for each such reference.

86It should be noted that in 614a1, wages are central.

87E.g., at 615a4-616b1, the remarks have to do with punishment for injustice, while there is only at 616b1 a perfunctory remark that "doings of good works are in turn antistrophes to these" (καὶ αὖ τὰς εὐεργεσίας ταύταις ἀντιστρόφους). This emphasis on injustice continues through the myth.

88Cf. 614a7-8: τὰ ὑπὸ τοῦ λόγου ὀφειλόμενα.

89There is an analogy here between μῦθος and λόγος, and a difference. In the case of λόγος, which is a descriptive classification of the things which are, one either simply confronts τὰ ὄντα or one confronts speeches (the conventional apparatus) about τὰ ὄντα. But in the case of μῦθος, which is a genetic account, an account of origins (in a double sense, the from which and to which on the basis of which one can see why things which are are what they are), one cannot simply confront the phenomena involved and therefore one must confront speeches about them. And the speeches about them are to a large extent the prevailing codified theology. Therefore, to investigate the origins, one must go through the conventional apparatus. However, this going through the conventional apparatus does not compulsorily entail a belief in that apparatus. And when faced with it in a Platonic dialogue, we must act as Socrates did with respect to the Delphic oracle's pronouncement that no one was wiser than he, namely we must investigate whether it is meant literally or not, and in the case of the myths in Plato this involves an act of mental translation of the conventional apparatus into a non-conventional language.

90Cf. Gorgias 492e8-493a1: "For I would not wonder if Euripides speaks truly in these things, speaking--"And who has envisioned, if living is dying,/ and dying living?" and we beingly are

dead equally" (οὐ γάρ τοι θαυμάζοιμ' ἂν εἰ Εὐριπίδης ἀληθῆ ἐν τοῖσδε λέγει, λέγων--"τίς δ' οἶδεν,
εἰ τὸ ζῆν μέν ἐστι κατθανεῖν,/ τὸ κατθανεῖν δὲ
ζῆν;" καὶ ἡμεῖς τῷ ὄντι ἴσως τέθναμεν).

[91]Cf. 618e3-4: ζῶντί τε καὶ τελευτήσαντι.

[92]Republic 10.614b2-4: 'Αλλ' οὐ μέντοι σοι, ἦν
δ' ἐγώ, 'Αλκίνου γε ἀπόλογον ἐρῶ, ἀλλ' ἀλκίμου μὲν
ἀνδρός, 'Ηρὸς τοῦ 'Αρμενίου, τὸ γένος Παμφύλου.

[93]Except for Teiresias, to whom the prophet of
Lachesis in the myth of Er corresponds, Odysseus
saw the following named souls: (1) Antikleia, his
mother, (2) Tyro, (3) Antiope, (4) Alkmene,
(5) Megara, (6) Epikaste, (7) Chloris, (8) Leda,
(9) Iphimedeia, (10) Phaidra, (11) Prokris,
(12) Ariadne, (13) Maira, (14) Klymene, (15) Eri-
phyle, (16) Agamemnon, (17) Achilleus, (18) Patro-
klus, (19) Antilochus, (20) Aias, (21) Minos,
(22) Orion, (23) Tityos, (24) Tantalos, (25) Si-
syphos, (26) Herakles.

[94]He is explicitly called εἰκοστήν at 620b1.

[95]I am unable to explain the significance of
his being τοῦ 'Αρμενίου, son of Armenios (cf. Adam,
note ad loc.). The difficulty of determining the
meaning of this designation as well as the others
is exacerbated by the fact that each ('Αλκίνοος,
ἀπόλογος, ἄλκιμος, 'Ηρ, 'Αρμένιος, Πάμφυλος) is a
ἅπαξ λεγόμενον in Plato.

[96]614c1: τόπον τινὰ δαιμόνιον.

[97]614c3-d1: δικαστὰς δὲ μεταξὺ τούτων καθῆσθαι,
οὕς, ἐπειδὴ διαδικάσειαν, τοὺς μὲν δικαίους κελεύ-
ειν πορεύεσθαι τὴν εἰς δεξιάν τε καὶ ἄνω διὰ τοῦ
οὐρανοῦ, σημεῖα περιάψαντας τῶν δεδικασμένων ἐν τῷ
πρόσθεν, τοὺς δὲ ἀδίκους τὴν εἰς ἀριστεράν τε καὶ
κάτω, ἔχοντας καὶ τούτους ἐν τῷ ὄπισθεν σημεῖα
πάντων ὧν ἔπραξαν. The use of the word σημεῖα here
suggests, in the light of the traditional σῶμα-σῆμα
word play, that although the myth is ostensibly
about disembodied souls in the afterlife, it is at

190

bottom about embodied souls in this life. Cf.
Cratylus 400b9-c9. Also cf. Gorgias 493a2-3: καὶ
τὸ μὲν σῶμά ἐστιν ἡμῖν σῆμα.

98And hence in front, so that in the judgment,
to redress this the signs are placed in back.

99And hence in back, so that in the judgment,
to redress this the signs are placed in front.

100In the whole fifteen line passage (615a4-c4),
only two lines (b6-c1) deal with wages for justice.

101Cf. Adam, note ad loc.: "'Ἀρδιαῖος is a
purely fictitious personage, no doubt, although
verisimilitude is preserved;" also cf. Bloom, p.
471, n. 15: "Ardiaeus is apparently of Socrates'
invention." And clearly the Pamphylia of which
Ardiaios was tyrant is as fictitious as Ardiaios
himself.

102The theme of the attractiveness of tyranny
pervades the myth.

103616c7-d2: τὴν δὲ τοῦ σφονδύλου φύσιν εἶναι
τοιάνδε· τὸ μὲν σχῆμα οἷάπερ ἡ τοῦ ἐνθάδε....

104Socrates makes the same point in his summary
at the end, 10.621c4-d2: "we will always hold to
the upper road and pursue justice with prudence in
every manner, so that we be friends to ourselves
and the gods, both remaining here and there, and
when we bring in its prizes...both here and in the
thousand year journey" (τῆς ἄνω ὁδοῦ ἀεὶ ἐξόμεθα
καὶ δικαιοσύνην μετὰ φρονήσεως παντὶ τρόπῳ ἐπιτη-
δεύσομεν, ἵνα καὶ ἡμῖν αὐτοῖς φίλοι ὦμεν καὶ τοῖς
θεοῖς, αὐτοῦ τε μένοντες ἐνθάδε, καὶ ἐπειδὰν τὰ
ἆθλα αὐτῆς κομιζώμεθα...καὶ ἐνθάδε καὶ ἐν τῇ χιλι-
έτει πορείᾳ).

105617b7-c5: ἄλλας δὲ καθημένας πέριξ δι' ἴσου
τρεῖς, ἐν θρόνῳ ἑκάστην, θυγατέρας τῆς 'Ανάγκης,
Μοίρας, λευχειμονούσας, στέμματα ἐπὶ τῶν κεφαλῶν
ἐχούσας, Λάχεσίν τε καὶ Κλωθὼ καὶ "Ατροπον, ὑμνεῖν
πρὸς τὴν τῶν Σειρήνων ἁρμονίαν, Λάχεσιν μὲν τὰ

γεγονότα, Κλωθῶ δὲ τὰ ὄντα, Ἄτροπον δὲ τὰ μέλ-
λοντα.

106Republic 3.392d2-3: ἆρ' οὐ πάντα ὅσα ὑπὸ
μυθολόγων ἢ ποιητῶν λέγεται διήγησις οὖσα τυγχάνει
ἢ γεγονότων ἢ ὄντων ἢ μελλόντων;

107This may partially account for the fact that
"this conception of close-fitting concentric whorls
...appears to be unique in ancient astronomy."
(Adam, note ad 616D,E.)

108I would not assert that this is the only
thing that Er's cosmography suggests, although I
would assert that it is not meant to be taken as a
'scientific' cosmography.

109The myth is filled with such shifts.

110One could even say that the entire program
of eugenics of the best city was designed to in-
sure that such natures would be bred out of the
citizenry.

111In a way, the emphasis on punishment in the
myth also reflects this shift.

112618b6-c6: ἔνθα δή, ὡς ἔοικεν, ὦ φίλε Γλαύκων, ὁ
πᾶς κίνδυνος ἀνθρώπῳ, καὶ διὰ ταῦτα μάλιστα ἐπιμε-
λητέον ὅπως ἕκαστος ἡμῶν τῶν ἄλλων μαθημάτων ἀμε-
λήσας τούτου τοῦ μαθήματος καὶ ζητητὴς καὶ μαθητὴς
ἔσται, ἐάν ποθεν οἷός τ' ᾖ μαθεῖν καὶ ἐξευρεῖν τίς
αὐτὸν ποιήσει δυνατὸν καὶ ἐπιστήμονα, βίον καὶ
χρηστὸν καὶ πονηρὸν διαγιγνώσκοντα, τὸν βελτίω ἐκ
τῶν δυνατῶν ἀεὶ πανταχοῦ αἱρεῖσθαι.

113The two yoke pairs, καὶ ζητητὴς καὶ μαθητὴς
and μαθεῖν καὶ ἐξευρεῖν, indicate that one must
not only be guided to this by another but one must
also and to an equal degree exert one's own efforts.

114619b7-8, c6-d1: τὸν πρῶτον λαχόντα ἔφη εὐθὺς
ἐπιόντα τὴν μεγίστην τυραννίδα ἑλέσθαι....εἶναι δὲ
αὐτὸν τῶν ἐκ τοῦ οὐρανοῦ ἡκόντων, ἐν τεταγμένῃ

:ολιτείᾳ ἐν τῷ προτέρῳ βίῳ βεβιωκότα, ἔθει ἄνευ
ιλοσοφίας ἀρετῆς μετειληφότα.

115619d5-7: διὸ δὴ καὶ μεταβολὴν τῶν κακῶν καὶ
ῶν ἀγαθῶν ταῖς πολλαῖς τῶν ψυχῶν γίγνεσθαι καὶ
ιὰ τὴν τοῦ κλήρου τύχην.

116619d7-e5: ἐπεὶ εἴ τις ἀεί, ὁπότε εἰς τὸν ἐν-
▪άδε βίον ἀφικνοῖτο, ὑγιῶς φιλοσοφοῖ καὶ ὁ κλῆρος
▪ὑτῷ τῆς αἱρέσεως μὴ ἐν τελευταίοις πίπτοι, κιν-
▪υνεύει ἐκ τῶν ἐκεῖθεν ἀπαγγελλομένων οὐ μόνον ἐν-
▪άδε εὐδαιμονεῖν ἄν, ἀλλὰ καὶ τὴν ἐνθένδε ἐκεῖσε
▪αὶ δεῦρο πάλιν πορείαν οὐκ ἂν χθονίαν καὶ τραχεῖ-
▪ν πορεύεσθαι, ἀλλὰ λείαν τε καὶ οὐρανίαν.

117I exclude tyranny here because it is presen-
.ed as the electing of a person without philosophy.
 also leave out the human lifetimes of unspeci-
ʾied character chosen by musical animals, because
.hey are unspecified and because Socrates is nei-
:her musical nor a beast, and I retain only those
vhich are specified.

118Epeios was the builder of the Trojan horse:
)dyssey 8.493.

119Epeios is the son of Panopeus, υἱὸς Πανοπῆος
ʾIliad 23.665): cf. Rep. 10.620c1, τοῦ Πανοπέως.

120Cf. Republic 10.620c2: φύσιν.

121Republic 10.620a2-3: κατὰ συνήθειαν γὰρ τοῦ
ϊροτέρου βίου τὰ πολλὰ αἱρεῖσθαι.

122In the account of the soul's electings, the
emphasis is on vision: cf. τὴν θέαν at 619e6;
.δεῖν at 619e6, 620a3, 6, 7, c1, 2; ἰδοῦσαν at
₃20d1; κατιδοῦσαν at 620b6.

123In this case the situation would be this:
(soul of Orpheus)———▶(soul of x)——▶(soul of swan).
But this is merely a suggestive undertone.

124Republic 10.620c2-3: πόρρω δ' ἐν ὑστάτοις

193

ἰδεῖν τὴν τοῦ γελωτοποιοῦ Θερσίτου πίθηκον ἐνδυο-μένην. This also stresses the diminishing degree of freedom of choice as one nears the end.

[125]Cf. <u>Odyssey</u> 9.366-367: "'No one' is my name; and my mother and father and all my other comrades call me 'No one.'" (Οὖτίς ἐμοί γ' ὄνομα· Οὖτιν δέ με κικλήσκουσι/ μήτηρ ἠδὲ πατὴρ ἠδ' ἄλλοι πάντες ἑταῖροι.)

[126]Cf. τῶν...πόνων at 620c5 to πόνων at 619d3 and πεπονηκότας at 619d4.

[127]If the reference were to be made strongly to the experiences of the <u>Odyssey</u>, the word would not have been οἱ πόνοι but rather τὰ πάθη, as in the case of Agamemnon (620b5).

[128]Cf. Graves, vol. 2, 161.o. ff., pp. 299-300.

A NON-MYTH AND MYTHS

Since the scope of the present work makes an exhaustive analysis of all Platonic myths unfeasible, I will at least briefly sketch the remaining ones.

But before doing so, it is necessary to examine a non-myth which is almost always referred to as a myth,[1] namely the λόγος at the end of the Gorgias (522e1-527e7). This virtually universal tendency to call it a myth persists despite Socrates' explicit and emphatic statement that it is not a μῦθος but a λόγος (Gorgias 523a1-2; cited p. 13 above), a statement which Socrates reiterates at the end of the first section of his account (italics mine):

> These things, o Callicles, are things which I
> having heard trust to be true; and on the basis
> of these speeches I reckon something suchlike
> to come along.[2]

Why does Socrates make these remarks? This question must be faced, because Socrates casually calls those accounts myths to which the Gorgias account is most frequently compared, the accounts at the end of the Republic and toward the end of the Phaedo, and his designation of them as such is just as casually accepted by his interlocutors. But the Gorgias is different. How does it differ? In terms of externals alone, it differs in that while the final underworld myths of the Republic and the Phaedo contain cosmographies, the final underworld λόγος of the Gorgias does not. But the difference goes beyond externals, in that while the final myths of the Republic (as we have seen) and of the Phaedo (as we will see) are genetic accounts, the final λόγος of the Gorgias is a descriptive account. And it is a descriptive account despite its use of personages and trappings which our prejudices would lead us to label as mythical. But if it is a descriptive account, what does it describe? It describes--and this is not surprising in the Platonic dialogue which deals most exclusively with forensic rhetoric[3]--the defects of forensic rhetoric and its practitioners. In particular, the figures of Minos, Rhadamanthus, and Aiakos are representative of Gorgias, Polus, and Callicles. For Gorgias and Polus are described as teacher and pupil in a way analogous to the way in which Minos and Rhadamanthus are described as teacher and pupil in the Minos.[4] And Callicles is strongly identified with Alcibiades,[5] whose ancestry could be traced back to Aiakos (cf. Alc. I 121a1-2, b1-4). And Socrates enjoins upon them that they become dead to the allure of the body, which is the clothing of the soul,[6] so as to substitute for their own cosmetic rhetoric a true rhetoric spoken from soul to soul. And although Socrates' kolastic reprimand is through images, it is remarkably direct,[7] and it is not a myth.

However, there is a myth in the Gorgias, the myth of the soul as a sieve and wine jar:

> Socrates. But indeed also, as at any rate you speak, a lifetime is a formidable thing. For I would not wonder if Euripides speaks truly in these things, speaking--"and who has envisioned if living is dying,/ and dying living?" and we beingly are dead equally; for already I at least also heard a certain one of the wise /speaking/ how we now are dead and the body is our tomb/sign, and /how/ this /part/ of the soul, in which desires are, chances to be such as to be repeatedly persuaded and to teeter upwards and downwards, and /how/ then some elegant mythologizing man, perhaps some Sicilian or Italian, bringing this along by the name, named /it/, because of its being both persuadable and persuasive,

'wine jar,' and /he named/ the mindless 'uninitiates,' and this /part/ of the soul of the
mindless, /the part/ in which desires are, the
uncontrollable and not watertight /part/ of it,
he having likened it forth because of its un-
fillableness, /spoke/ how it would be a perforated wine jar. Indeed this shows the contrary
to you, o Callicles, how of those in /the do-
main/ of Hades--bespeaking indeed the unseeable
--these uninitiates would be most wretched and
would bear water into the perforated wine jar
by another, a suchlike perforated sieve. And
then, as the person speaking to me asserted,
/the mythologizer/ speaks the sieve to be the
soul; and to a sieve he likened forth the soul
of the mindless as perforated, since it is not
capable of being watertight because of untrust-
ingness and forgetfulness. These things likelily
are in some way under /the category of/ eccen-
tric things, yet it should clarify what I wish
to show to you, if somehow I am able, /so as/
to persuade /you/ to change, to elect instead
of the lifetime which is unfillable and uncontrollable the lifetime which is orderly and
sufficient by means of the things which are
always present to it and competent. But do I
persuade you in any way to change over to the
orderly /as/ being happier than the uncontrollable, or will you rather not change in any
way, if I mythologize many other suchlike
things?
     Callicles. You have spoken this /latter/
more truly, o Socrates /i.e., I will not
change/.[8]

So, Socrates presents three accounts, the account
of a poet (492e7-493a1), of a wise man (493a1-5),
and of a mythologizer (493a5-b3, b7-c3) as related
by the wise man. Socrates, also a mythologizer
(493d3), interrupts the third account (493b3-7)
and appends his own conclusion (493c3-d3). The
accounts of the poet and the wise man describe
our condition, while the mythologizer provides an
account of the origin of our condition in a bipar-
tite account of soul. The soul, then, is a sieve,

fundamentally a perforated sieve. What does a
sieve do? It discriminates, refines,separates.
And clearly different souls have different capa-
cities for discrimination. We all begin, as children, with a perforated sieve, but the mindless
remain in this condition and hence are at the mer-
cy of their desires, i.e., they are unsatisfied
and unfilled. Presumably as a soul becomes mind-
ful, it blocks the perforations, its capacity for
fine discriminations increases, and it can be satisfied and filled. But for persons in whom this
does not happen, the result is uncontrollable desire which is the auditor of rhetoric, and as
such may be either led astray (by sham rhetoric)
or led aright (by true rhetoric). And the uncontrollable desire for power is, in terms of the
image, no different in kind from the uncontrollable desire for punishment, a theme which resur-
faces in the final λόγος. And Socrates tries here,
as in the final λόγος, to admonish Callicles and
those like him, but Callicles is unfillable, as
the sequel in which Socrates elaborates the myth
a bit indicates by reemphasizing Socrates' goal of
persuading:

> /Socrates./ Do I speaking these things per-
> suade you in any way to concede the orderly
> lifetime to be better than the uncontrollable
> /lifetime/, or do I not persuade?
>   Callicles. You do not persuade, o Socrates.[9]

So, Socrates fails in his use of the correct rhetoric, which as mythology is the gymnastic of the
soul:

> Socrates. Indeed bear with me, let me speak
> to you another image from the same gymnasium as
> the /image/ now.[10]

Clearly, then, the final λόγος, which calls for
soul stripping by speaker and auditor, must be
supplemented by the gymnastic art of mythmaking.

In the Protagoras, we have a clear case of a μῦθος
(320c8-324d1) and a λόγος (324d1-328d4) side by

side, i.e., a descriptive account of virtue and its teachability in cities follows an account of the genesis[11] of virtue.[12] By the time that Protagoras concludes, "I have spoken to you, o Socrates, the suchlike myth and speech, how virtue is teachable,"[13] we can see that his usage of the terms μῦθος and λόγος is consistent with the general Socratic-Platonic usage of the terms.[14]

In the Phaedo, there are two myths, the myth of the genesis of the concomitance of the pleasant and the painful (Phaedo 60b1-c7), which we have already discussed (see above pp. 89-90 and n. 218, p. 132), and the myth of the beautiful earth (Phaedo 110a8-111e5), which we must now consider. And first one must see precisely what in Socrates' final account (107c1-114c6) is myth and what is not. Indeed Socrates is very careful in drawing the dividing lines, beginning with the remark prefatory to the account:

> Socrates asserted, "Well, o Simmias, you bespeak well not only these things but also then our first hypotheses, and if they are trustable to you, nevertheless they must be considered more distinctly; and if you divide them sufficiently, as I believe, you will follow the speech, in accordance with as much as it is possible especially for a human to follow; and if this very thing becomes distinct, you will seek in no way beyond it." "You speak truly," /Simmias/ asserted.[15]

So, Socrates will begin his further consideration with a λόγος,[16] a διαίρεσις,[17] a classificatory description of souls and of the forms of the true earth's places. Having concluded this initial λόγος (at 110a7), Socrates remarks and Simmias replies:

> "And those things in turn would appear still much more to differ from the things among us; for if indeed it is beautiful to speak a myth also, it is worth hearing, o Simmias, of what sorts the things on the earth under the heaven

> chance to be." "But, o Socrates," Simmias as-
> serted, "we would hear this myth then plea-
> santly."[18]

The myth, then, consists only of the account of
the things on the earth, not of the things under
the earth. And since it is a myth, it is synagogic
or synoptic, i.e., it presents "the earth itself
/as seen/ if someone should behold it from above,"[19]
and it is genetic, causal.[20] And when Socrates has
concluded the myth proper, which began and was go-
verned throughout by λέγεται (110b5), he signals
his return to a λόγος by shifting at 111e5 from
indirect discourse to direct discourse. And although the λόγος which follows (111e5-114c6) pro-
mises itself as a causal account,[21] the promise is
not fulfilled and no cause is ever given for the
continual oscillation. Instead, the account--as
we expect for a λόγος--is a classificatory description of the subterranean streams (Ocean,
Acheron, Pyriphlegethon, and Cocytus) and of human
types (persons with neutral lives, incurable criminals, curable criminals, persons with holy lives,
and philosophers).

Finally, although we do not propose to examine the
Phaedo account in detail, this much should be remarked, that there is a descent from the heavenly
account in the first λόγος through the account of
the earth's surface in the μῦθος to the subterranean account in the second λόγος, a descent into
body as such,[22] however beautified, and therefore
it stands as an encomium to body which should
serve as a warning to those readers of the Phaedo
who would take at face value the apparent denigration of the body which the Phaedo perhaps more
than any other Platonic dialogue ostensibly presents.

In the Theaetetus, the Protagorean conventionalist epistemological position is presented in a
way which is analogous to the presentation of the
Protagorean conventionalist political position in
the Protagoras, namely a Protagorean μῦθος (Theaetetus 155e3-164e4) followed by a Protagorean

λόγος (Theaetetus 164e4-168c2).[23] The μῦθος of
which Protagoras is the father (cf. 164e2-3) describes the genesis of the Protagorean account of
the sensing which is knowledge out of the Herakleitean ἀρχή (cf. 156a3, 152e2-4, 160d5-e2) that
"the all was moving and nothing other besides
this,"[24] i.e., it is about the generation of sensing out of motion (cf. 156a3-c3). In addition,
the Theaetetus is concerned with the generation of
accounts (λόγοι),[25] i.e., it is as concerned with
accounts as with the phenomena of which the accounts are, and hence it ends with a λόγος which
is a classificatory διαίρεσις of Λόγος (206c7-210
b3). Three types of Λόγος are divided off as different from one another. The first (206d1-e3) is
that Λόγος means any verbal utterance: this is
what we have throughout called Λόγος in the broad
or generic signigication. The second (206e4-208
b12), which is the technical[26] division of something itself into its parts, and the third (208
b12-210a9), which is the division by its diffe-
rentness[27] of something from other things--these
two together constitute what throughout we have
called λόγος in its narrow signification as a
διαίρεσις. The possibility of a λόγος as a genetic
account is not even considered. But this is intelligible in the light of the consistent usage
throughout the Platonic corpus by both Socrates
and others of the term μῦθος to designate a genetic account. Perhaps, then, if Theaetetus (at 201
c9-d1) had defined knowledge as ἡ μετὰ λόγου τε
καὶ μύθου ἀληθὴς δόξα (true opinion with a speech
and a myth), he would have been closer to the mark.

This concludes our survey of myth as such in the
Platonic corpus,[28] but there is one type of account which is left to consider, because it is
at least etymologically connected with myth, namely the paramyth, to which we will turn in the next
chapter.

NOTES

[1]Cf. Søren Kierkegaard, The concept of irony, tr. Lee M. Capel (New York, 1965), p. 130, note: "there are in Plato three νεκυιαν /sic/, i.e., myths about the underworld: in the Phaedo, Gorgias, and Republic." It was reading this note which initially propelled me on the journey toward Platonic myth. Also cf. E.R. Dodds, note ad Gorgias 523a2-3: "the Gorgias myth is called a λόγος because it expresses in imaginative terms a 'truth of religion'": it is remarkable that Dodds' prejudgment is so deeply imbedded that he unthinkingly explains away its explicit designation as a λόγος on the basis of that prejudgment. Also cf. Friedlaender, pp. 181, 184-185, 186; Frutiger, pp. 29-30; Stewart, pp. 100-101; Robin, Platon, pp. 126, 142, 148; Voegelin, pp. 39 ff.

[2]Gorgias 524a8-b2 (italics mine): Ταῦτ' ἔστιν, ὦ Καλλίκλεις, ἃ ἐγὼ ἀκηκοὼς πιστεύω ἀληθῆ εἶναι· καὶ ἐκ τούτων τῶν λόγων τοιόνδε τι λογίζομαι συμβαίνειν.

[3]In the early stages of the dialogue, Gorgias is gradually led by Socrates to reduce his definition of rhetoric to forensic rhetoric: compare 452 e1-4, where Gorgias describes rhetoric as "persuading...by speeches judges in a court of justice and councillors in a council and assemblymen in an assembly and in every other convocation which becomes a political convocation" (Τὸ πείθειν...τοῖς λόγοις καὶ ἐν δικαστηρίῳ δικαστὰς καὶ ἐν βουλευτηρίῳ βουλευτὰς καὶ ἐν ἐκκλησίᾳ ἐκκλησιαστὰς καὶ ἐν ἄλλῳ συλλόγῳ παντί, ὅστις ἂν πολιτικὸς σύλλογος γίγνηται), to 454b5-6, where he describes it as "persuasion...in courts of justice and in the other mobs" (τῆς πειθοῦς...τῆς ἐν τοῖς δικαστηρίοις καὶ ἐν τοῖς ἄλλοις ὄχλοις).

[4]Cf. Minos 318c4-321d10, esp. 320b8-c3: "And Rhadamanthus was a good man; for he was educated

by Minos. Yet he was educated not in the whole
basilic art, but in an underling to the basilic
/art/, as much as to oversee in the courts of justice; whence also he was spoken to be a good
judge." ('Ραδάμανθυς δὲ ἀγαθὸς μὲν ἦν ἀνήρ· ἐπεπαίδευτο γὰρ ὑπὸ τοῦ Μίνω. ἐπεπαίδευτο μέντοι οὐχ
ὅλην τὴν βασιλικὴν τέχνην, ἀλλ' ὑπηρεσίαν τῇ βασι-
λικῇ, ὅσον ἐπιστατεῖν ἐν τοῖς δικαστηρίοις· ὅθεν
καὶ δικαστὴς ἀγαθὸς ἐλέχθη εἶναι.)

[5]Cf. Gorgias 519a7-b2: "And perhaps they will
take hold of you, if you do not take good hold of
yourself /i.e., if you are not careful/, and of my
comrade Alcibiades, when they destroy even their
originary things in addition to the things which
they have acquired, not of /you both/ being causes
of the bads but perhaps co-causes." (σοῦ δὲ ἴσως
ἐπιλήψονται, ἐὰν μὴ εὐλαβῇ, καὶ τοῦ ἐμοῦ ἑταίρου
'Αλκιβιάδου, ὅταν καὶ τὰ ἀρχαῖα προσαπολλύωσι πρὸς
οἷς ἐκτήσαντο, οὐκ αἰτίων ὄντων τῶν κακῶν ἀλλ'
ἴσως συναιτίων.)

[6]Cf. Cratylus 403b5-6: ἡ ψυχὴ γυμνὴ τοῦ σώματος.

[7]Since Socrates speaking to Gorgias, Polus, and
Callicles here is analogous to Zeus speaking to
Minos, Rhadamanthus, and Aiakos, there is a suggestion that in the greater triad--and the Gorgias
is pervaded by triads--of Zeus, Poseidon, and Pluto, Socrates corresponds to Zeus. It is also possible to construe--and this is highly speculative
--Poseidon as Alcibiades (cf. Alcibiades' oath to
Poseidon at Symp. 214d6) and Pluto as Homer (compare the description of Pluto as "a perfect sophist" at Crat. 403e4 and its context to Rep. 10.
596d1, where the pan-mimic is called "an altogether wondrous sophist" and its context, which
focusses especially on Homer, e.g., at 595b10,
597e6, 598d7-8, 599b9-c1 ff., 600b6-c1, c2 ff.,
e4, 605c10-11, 606e1-607a3, d1). Also cf. Iliad
15.184-199. One might add that Diotima too is
referred to as a perfect sophist (cf. Symp. 208c1).
And since her name means 'honored by Zeus,' then
insofar as Socrates is identified with Zeus, and
insofar as Diotima is a poeticized philosopher (a

203

Homerized philosopher), Socrates (Zeus) may be
regarded as honoring Homer.

[8]Gorgias 492e7-493d4: ΣΩ. Ἀλλὰ μὲν δὴ καὶ ὡς
γε σὺ λέγεις δεινὸς ὁ βίος. οὐ γάρ τοι θαυμάζοιμ'
ἂν εἰ Εὐριπίδης ἀληθῆ ἐν τοῖσδε λέγει, λέγων--
"τίς δ' οἶδεν, εἰ τὸ ζῆν μέν ἐστι κατθανεῖν,/ τὸ
κατθανεῖν δὲ ζῆν;" καὶ ἡμεῖς τῷ ὄντι ἴσως τέθναμεν·
ἤδη γάρ του ἔγωγε καὶ ἤκουσα τῶν σοφῶν ὡς νῦν
ἡμεῖς τέθναμεν καὶ τὸ μὲν σῶμά ἐστιν ἡμῖν σῆμα,
τῆς δὲ ψυχῆς τοῦτο ἐν ᾧ ἐπιθυμίαι εἰσὶ τυγχάνει ὂν
οἷον ἀναπείθεσθαι καὶ μεταπίπτειν ἄνω κάτω, καὶ
τοῦτο ἄρα τις μυθολογῶν κομψὸς ἀνήρ, ἴσως Σικελός
τις ἢ Ἰταλικός, παράγων τῷ ὀνόματι διὰ τὸ πιθανόν
τε καὶ πειστικὸν ὠνόμασε πίθον, τοὺς δὲ ἀνοήτους
ἀμυήτους, τῶν δ' ἀνοήτων τοῦτο τῆς ψυχῆς οὗ αἱ
ἐπιθυμίαι εἰσί, τὸ ἀκόλαστον αὐτοῦ καὶ οὐ στεγανόν,
ὡς τετρημένος εἴη πίθος, διὰ τὴν ἀπληστίαν ἀπεικά-
σας. τοὐναντίον δὴ οὗτος σοι, ὦ Καλλίκλεις, ἐνδείκ-
νυται ὡς τῶν ἐν Ἅιδου--τὸ ἀιδὲς δὴ λέγων--οὗτοι
ἀθλιώτατοι ἂν εἶεν, οἱ ἀμύητοι, καὶ φοροῖεν εἰς
τὸν τετρημένον πίθον ὕδωρ ἑτέρῳ τοιούτῳ τετρημένῳ
κοσκίνῳ. τὸ δὲ κόσκινον ἄρα λέγει, ὡς ἔφη ὁ πρὸς
ἐμὲ λέγων, τὴν ψυχὴν εἶναι· τὴν δὲ ψυχὴν κοσκίνῳ
ἀπῄκασεν τὴν τῶν ἀνοήτων ὡς τετρημένην, ἅτε οὐ
δυναμένην στέγειν δι' ἀπιστίαν τε καὶ λήθην. ταῦτ'
ἐπιεικῶς μέν ἐστιν ὑπό τι ἄτοπα, δηλοῖ μὴν ὃ ἐγὼ
βούλομαί σοι ἐνδειξάμενος, ἐάν πως οἷός τε ὦ, πεῖ-
σαι μεταθέσθαι, ἀντὶ τοῦ ἀπλήστως καὶ ἀκολάστως
ἔχοντος βίου τὸν κοσμίως καὶ τοῖς ἀεὶ παροῦσιν
ἱκανῶς καὶ ἐξαρκούντως ἔχοντα βίον ἑλέσθαι. ἀλλὰ
πότερον πείθω τί σε καὶ μετατίθεσθαι εὐδαιμονεσ-
τέρους εἶναι τοὺς κοσμίους τῶν ἀκολάστων, ἢ οὐδ'
ἂν ἄλλα πολλὰ τοιαῦτα μυθολογῶ, οὐδέν τι μᾶλλον
μεταθήσῃ; ΚΑΛ. Τοῦτ' ἀληθέστερον εἴρηκας, ὦ Σώκρατες.

[9]494a3-6: ⌊ΣΩ.⌋ πείθω τί σε ταῦτα λέγων συγχω-
ρῆσαι τὸν κόσμιον βίον τοῦ ἀκολάστου ἀμείνω εἶναι,
ἢ οὐ πείθω; ΚΑΛ. Οὐ πείθεις, ὦ Σώκρατες.

[10]493d5-6: ΣΩ. Φέρε δή, ἄλλην σοι εἰκόνα λέγω
ἐκ τοῦ αὐτοῦ γυμνασίου τῇ νῦν.

[11]Cf. αἰτία at Prot. 323a4.

[12]For a discussion of the Protagorean account, see my "The Platonic Godfather: a note on the Protagoras myth," Journal of value inquiry, vol. XV, 1981.

[13]Protagoras 328c3-4: Τοιοῦτόν σοι...ὦ Σώκρατες, ἐγὼ καὶ μῦθον καὶ λόγον εἴρηκα, ὡς διδακτὸν ἀρετή.... Cf. Protagoras' opening remark in this section, 320c2-4: "'But, o Socrates,' he asserted, 'I will not begrudge /you this/; but am I, as an older person to younger persons, to show off to you either speaking a myth or having narrated by a speech?'" ('Αλλ', ὦ Σώκρατες, ἔφη, οὐ φθονήσω· ἀλλὰ πότερον ὑμῖν, ὡς πρεσβύτερος νεωτέροις, μῦθον λέγων ἐπιδείξω ἢ λόγῳ διεξελθών;)

[14]It is perhaps to emphasize this consistency that there is in this segment of the dialogue an extraordinary density of the vocative ὦ Σώκρατες in Protagoras' account: cf. 320c2, 322d6, 323a4, 324c8, 325c4, 326e3.

[15]Phaedo 107b4-10: Οὐ μόνον γ', ἔφη, ὦ Σιμμία, ὁ Σωκράτης, ἀλλὰ ταῦτά τε εὖ λέγεις καὶ τάς γε ὑποθέσεις τὰς πρώτας, καὶ εἰ πισταὶ ὑμῖν εἰσιν, ὅμως ἐπισκεπτέαι σαφέστερον· καὶ ἐὰν αὐτὰς ἱκανῶς διέλητε, ὡς ἐγῷμαι, ἀκολουθήσετε τῷ λόγῳ, καθ' ὅσον δυνατὸν μάλιστ' ἀνθρώπῳ ἐπακολουθῆσαι· κἂν τοῦτο αὐτὸ σαφὲς γένηται, οὐδὲν ζητήσετε περαιτέρω. 'Αληθῆ, ἔφη, λέγεις.

[16]Cf. τῷ λόγῳ at 107b7.

[17]Cf. διέλητε at 107b7.

[18]Phaedo 110a8-b4: ἐκεῖνα δὲ αὖ τῶν παρ' ἡμῖν πολὺ ἂν ἔτι πλέον φανείη διαφέρειν· εἰ γὰρ δὴ καὶ μῦθον λέγειν καλόν, ἄξιον ἀκοῦσαι, ὦ Σιμμία, οἷα τυγχάνει τὰ ἐπὶ τῆς γῆς ὑπὸ τῷ οὐρανῷ ὄντα. 'Αλλὰ μήν, ἔφη ὁ Σιμμίας, ὦ Σώκρατες, ἡμεῖς γε τούτου τοῦ μύθου ἡδέως ἂν ἀκούσαιμεν.

[19]110b6: ἡ γῆ αὐτή...εἴ τις ἄνωθεν θεῷτο.

[20]Cf. αἴτιον at 110e2.

[21]Cf. αἰτία at 112b1.

[22]As Seth Benardete has correctly remarked, in lectures which he gave at the Graduate Faculty of the New School in the Spring of 1971 and which I was fortunate enough to attend, the subterranean account uses language and describes functions as though the inside of the earth were the inside of the human body.

[23]See my "The Platonic Godfather," note 17.

[24]Theaetetus 156a5: τὸ πᾶν κίνησις ἦν καὶ ἄλλο παρὰ τοῦτο οὐδέν.

[25]This entails also the problem of the security, as it were, of λόγος and of philosophy, a problem which is forced upon one by the setting of the dialogue. For the brief description of Theaetetus' behavior at the battle of Corinth (Theaet. 142a6-c1) is reminiscent of the lengthy description of Socrates' behavior at the battle of Potidaea (Symp. 219e5-221c1). And since Theaetetus and Socrates are look-alikes (Theaet. 143e7-144a1) and since Theaetetus is at least potentially philosophical in nature (Theaet. 144a1-b7; cf. 155c8-d5), the question arises as to how Socrates could emerge from battle unscathed while a potential alternative Socrates (i.e., Theaetetus) could not. That it is not a question of courage is clear, but of what it is a question is not. I would suggest (cf. Laws 3.690a1-c9, esp. c5-8) that the difference is luck, namely that Socrates was luckier than Theaetetus. And the role of luck or chance points to the precariousness of the perpetuation of philosophy. In this regard, it seems no accident that in the frame dialogue, Theaetetus is presented at the point in his lifetime at which his luck has run out, while in the inner dialogue, Socrates is presented at the point in his lifetime at which his luck has run out (cf. Apol. Socr. 32 d7-8).

[26]Cf. Theaetetus 207c2: τεχνικόν.

27Cf. <u>Theaetetus</u> 209a5: διαφορότητος.

28We have already discussed the <u>Statesman</u> myth
sufficiently for our purposes (see above pp. 88-
89). As for the <u>Laws</u>, since it supports our con-
clusions thus far and since I do not wish to accu-
mulate citations unnecessarily in the body of the
text, I will briefly survey it here. In Book 1,
through a brief reference to the myth of Ganymede
which the Cretans feigned to justify their practice of homosexuality (636b7-e4), we see clearly
that myths can be false in that persons may in-
vent false genetic accounts in order, in this
case, to make behavior respectable, to justify behavior, which otherwise would be neither respectable nor justifiable. Then, in the myth-image of
animals as divine puppets or marionettes (<u>Laws</u>
1.644b6-645c3), of which the strings are pleasure
and pain, opinion of pleasure to come (=hope) and
opinion of pain to come (=fear), and the common
opinion of a city (=reckoning or law), and so on,
--in this image is adumbrated the genesis of virtue (which here clearly means law-abidingness)
and badness out of the interaction of these things
as controlled presumably by the puppeteer-lawgiver
through education. At <u>Laws</u> 3.682a1-683d5 (but esp.
682a1-b1, e4-6, 683c8-d5), the account of the genesis, the founding, of cities is called a myth
(cf. 4.711d6-712a7, 712e9-714b2; 6.751d7-752a4).
Later (4.719a7-720a2), a contrast is drawn between
poets and law-positers, in which reference is made
to the origin of contradictions or equivocations
of poets in their being inspired so as to be out
of their senses; law-positers, on the other hand,
must be absolutely univocal. (One should perhaps
add here that if this mythical account of poetry
were a true account--and it is not--Plato's dialogues would have been produced when he was out of
his senses: cf. 7.811c6-10). At 6.771a5-d1 (esp.
c5-d1), it is asserted that the λόγος (division/
classification/description/cuttings) of the apportionment of the city into twelve would require for
the showing that these are true apportionments a
long myth (πολὺς...μῦθος: c6-7), i.e., a genetic
account. The myth governing marriage (6.773b4-6

207

ff.) declares that the origin of marriage should
be serviceability to the city and not pleasure.
And ancient myths have persuaded the Athenian
Stranger that one could found or generate institutions based on equality of the sexes (7.804d6-
805b4). Then, as in the Republic, the program of
education (Laws 7.809b3-812b1) is called a myth
(812a1-2). Also consider Laws 9.865d3-866a2,
872c7-873b1; 11.926e9-928a2; 12.941b2-c4.

Finally: it was stated at the
outset, that this system would
not be here, and at once, perfected. You cannot but plainly
see that I have kept my word.
But I now leave my cetological
System standing unfinished,
even as the great Cathedral of
Cologne was left, with the
crane still standing upon the
top of the uncompleted tower
.....This whole book is but a
draught--nay, but the draught
of a draught. Oh, Time, Strength,
Cash, and Patience!
    --Herman Melville, <u>Moby Dick</u>
(New York, Norton Crit. Ed.,
1967), ch. 32, pp. 127-128.

PARAMYTHS

In the course of cataloguing all the occurrences
of the word μῦθος and its derivatives in the Platonic corpus, a hitherto unremarked category of
account emerged with sufficient clarity as to de-
serve separate consideration, and that is the consolation or paramyth (ἡ παραμυθία or τὸ παραμύθιον).

And let us begin, as we did with myths, with the
question: what are the characteristics which the
various interlocutors in the Platonic dialogues
attribute to paramyths? They are persuasions[1] of
citizens to tractability,[2] i.e., to lawful behavior.[3] In addition, they are playful[4] teaching de-
vices which are rough but not harsh.[5] They tame

the spirited,[6] make the reticent eager,[7] and are
a form of speechmaking to crowds.[8] But they can
be compulsions from oneself to love and to praise
one's own.[9] And they are trusts ($\pi\acute{\iota}\sigma\tau\epsilon\iota\varsigma$)[10] which
are preparations for initiation,[11] and which
bring ease.[12] And above all, although they are
not incorrect,[13] nevertheless they are lies[14]
which mitigate fears.[15]

What, then, is a paramyth? It is a preparatory,
soothing, trustable lie. And the following accounts in the dialogues are paramyths:

(1) Phaedo 70a6-b4: persistence of soul after
death.[16]
(2) Phaedo 82b10-84b8: separation of soul from
senses.
(3) Republic 5.450d3-451b1: the safe audience.
(4) Republic 5.476e1-480a13: the 'theory of
looks.'
(5) Republic 6.499d10-501a1: the philosopher's
pursuit.
(6) Laws 10.885a6 ff.: warnings against atheism.
(7) Laws 11.922e1-923c4: the city is the true
owner of all possessions.

Since this list contains assertions and accounts
of things which would routinely appear in summa-
ries of Platonic philosophy as among Plato's central teachings, and since these are described as
lies (paramyths), we must seek precisely what the
status of these accounts is. And in this seeking,
two factors must be considered. First, it must be
emphasized that their being lies does not make
them simply or necessarily incorrect, i.e., they
may be lies and still be correct in some sense.
Second, the meaning of $\pi\alpha\rho\acute{\alpha}$ in composition[17] is
'by' (as in 'byproduct,' e.g., $\pi\acute{\alpha}\rho\epsilon\rho\gamma\text{ov}$) or 'beside' (as in 'alongside,' e.g., $\pi\acute{\alpha}\rho\epsilon\iota\mu\iota$) or 'beyond' (as in 'overstep,' e.g., $\pi\alpha\rho\alpha\beta\alpha\acute{\iota}\nu\omega$) or
'aside' (as in 'turn aside,' e.g., $\pi\alpha\rho\alpha\tau\rho\acute{\epsilon}\pi\omega$) or
'over' (as in 'overlook,' e.g., $\pi\alpha\rho\text{o}\rho\acute{\alpha}\omega$). If one
puts all this together, then, one can see, I be-
lieve, that the Platonic usage of paramyth is the
closest to what we ordinarily mean by our usage of

myth as an account which lacks evidence because
it deals with things in regard to which knowledge
is either impossible or virtually impossible to
achieve, things which are somehow outside or beyond rational certitude or one's capacity for rational certitude, and which hence must be adumbrated through an imaginative, largely hypothetical
account. And since the designation of a paramyth
depends upon its addressee, what is a paramyth for
the many (e.g., some of the proemia to the laws in
the <u>Laws</u>) may be a μῦθος or a λόγος for the philosopher, although what is a paramyth for the philosopher would be a paramyth for everyone. For example, the account of the philosopher's pursuit
(<u>Rep.</u> 6.499d10-501a1) is a paramyth for the many
as an antidote to their antipathy toward philosophy and philosophers,[18] an antipathy grounded in
the many's perception that philosophy is destructive of the city, destructive of demotic virtue
(cf. <u>Rep.</u> 6.497d6-498c4), and that antidote consists in showing them how philosophers may become
craftsmen of demotic virtue.[19]

And the paramyth about the safe audience (<u>Rep.</u>
6.450d3-451b1) shows how different persons need
different paramyths. When Glaucon directly con-
soles Socrates, he describes the safe audience by
inversion as discerning and trustable and benevo-
lent,[20] but when Socrates reformulates the consolation so that it really does console him, he describes the safe audience as composed of prudent
friends.[21] So, whereas for Glaucon, they need not
be friends, for Socrates, they need not be benevo-
lent.

In addition, the 'theory of looks' is first presented in the <u>Republic</u> as an antidote for the person of opinion without knowledge to his antipathy
toward philosophers. And it is a drug which must
be administered to him without letting him know
that he is unhealthy:

> "Therefore what if this person, whom we assert
> to opine but not to know, be harsh to us and
> dispute as though we do not speak truly? Will

211

we have something to console and gently persuade him, /we/ hiding /from him/ that he is
not healthy?" "It is indeed obligatory," he
/i.e., Glaucon/ asserted. "Indeed come, consider what we will say to him. Or do you wish us
thus to inquire from him, /we/ speaking how if
he has envisioned something, there is no envy
of him, but we would be pleased to see /him/
having envisioned something. But /we would
say/ speak this to us...."[22]

So, in the sense of paramyth as it is developed
briefly in this passage, a Platonic dialogue is in
one sense a paramyth, namely a gently persuasive
and salutary dialogic lie, which prepares the
transformation from the disease of opinion to the
health of knowledge without revealling that opinion is a disease.

The paramythic proemia of the Laws function analogously except that their preparatory persuasion is
not so gentle and is meant to effect a transformation from one level of opinion to the level of
opinion which the founded colony requires, but
they too are antidotes against atheism, on the one
hand, and against private accumulation, on the
other. Finally, the paramyths of the Phaedo are
antidotes to the fear of death, although the death
whose fear they counter is not the death with
which the philosopher would be concerned. For the
philosopher is concerned not with the death of his
body or soul in any personal sense, but rather
with the death of the Λόγος:

Phaedo. I will say. For I chanced to be sit-
ting beside the couch on a certain low stool on
his right, and he was much loftier than I. Therefore he having stroked my head and having squeezed
the hairs on my neck--for he was accustomed, whenever he should chance to, to play with my hairs--
asserted, "Indeed perhaps tomorrow, o Phaedo, you
may cut off these beautiful locks." "It is likely,
o Socrates," I said. "Not if you are persuaded by
me." "But what?", I said. "Today," he asserted,
"both I /may cut off/ my /hairs/ and you these,

212

> if then our speech comes to its end and we are
> not capable of reviving it. And I then, if I
> should be you and the speech should escape me,
> would swear to do as the Argives /do/, /namely/
> not to let my hair grow earlier than until I
> re-battling will be victorious over Simmias'
> and Cebes' speech."[23]

So, it is the Λόγος which must not come to an end,
and the death to be feared is the death of the Λόγος. And in this sense too, the Platonic dialogues
serve as a paramythic antidote to the fear that
the Λόγος, and philosophy with it, will die. Writing, then, does generate immortality, not primarily one's own immortality, but rather the immortality of Λόγος.

NOTES

[1]Cf. Euthydemus 288b3-c5; Critias 108b8-d8; Laws 10.899d4-6.

[2]Cf. Laws 9.880a6-b1 (=proemia to laws); also cf. Laws 11.922e1-923c4 (esp. 923c2-4), 928a1-2.

[3]Cf. Laws 6.773e5-774a3.

[4]Cf. Sophist 224a1-5, 229e1 ff.; Statesman 267e7-268b7.

[5]Cf. Sophist 224a1-5, 229e1 ff.

[6]Cf. Republic 4.441e4-442a7.

[7]Cf. Laws 2.666a2-3 (=wine) and context.

[8]Cf. Euthydemus 289d8-290a6.

[9]Cf. Protagoras 346b1-5; also cf. 361a3 ff.

[10]Cf. Phaedo 70a6-b4, esp. πίστεως at 70b2.

[11]Cf. Euthydemus 277d1-8.

[12]Cf. Republic 1.329d7-e6 (=wealth); Critias 115a3-b6; Menexenus 247c5-7 (cf. 236e1-237a4); Laws 1.625b1-7, 632d9-633a4, 4.704d3-705a8, 9.853 e10-854b1.

[13]Cf. Epinomis 976a5-b1 and context.

[14]Cf. Laws 10.885a6 ff. (cf. 888c6-7).

[15]Cf. Epistles 7.329d1-e1 (cf. 345e4-5).

[16]Socrates' response to Cebes here (Phaedo 70 b5-7) indicates that a paramyth is not a myth.

[17]See Smyth 1692.4.

18Cf. Republic 6.500d10-e5: "'But if indeed
the many sense that we speak truly about it, will
they indeed be harsh to the philosophers and will
they distrust us when we speak how a city would
not ever otherwise be happy, unless the painters
using the divine paradigm should thoroughly
sketch it?' 'They will not be harsh,' he /i.e.,
Adeimantus/ said, 'if indeed they sense /this/.'"
('Αλλ' ἐὰν δὴ αἴσθωνται οἱ πολλοὶ ὅτι ἀληθῆ περὶ
αὐτοῦ λέγομεν, χαλεπανοῦσι δὴ τοῖς φιλοσόφοις καὶ
ἀπιστήσουσιν ἡμῖν λέγουσιν ὡς οὐκ ἄν ποτε ἄλλως
εὐδαιμονήσειε πόλις, εἰ μὴ αὐτὴν διαγράψειαν οἱ
τῷ θείῳ παραδείγματι χρώμενοι ζωγράφοι; Οὐ χαλεπα-
νοῦσιν, ἦ δ' ὅς, ἐάνπερ αἴσθωνται.)

19Cf. Republic 6.500d4-9: "'Therefore,' I
spoke, 'if some compulsion comes to be for him to
be concerned to put the things which he sees
there into the habits of humans both privately and
publicly, and to fashion not only himself, then do
you believe he will come to be a bad craftsman of
moderation and justice and public virtue all together?' 'Least so,' he /i.e., Adeimantus/ said."
(*Ἂν οὖν τις, εἶπον, αὐτῷ ἀνάγκη γένηται ἃ ἐκεῖ
ὁρᾷ μελετῆσαι εἰς ἀνθρώπων ἤθη καὶ ἰδίᾳ καὶ δημο-
σίᾳ τιθέναι καὶ μὴ μόνον ἑαυτὸν πλάττειν, ἆρα κακὸν δημιουργὸν αὐτὸν οἴει γενήσεσθαι σωφροσύνης τε
καὶ δικαιοσύνης καὶ συμπάσης τῆς δημοτικῆς ἀρετῆς;
"Ηκιστά γε, ἦ δ' ὅς.)

20Cf. 6.450d3-4: οὔτε...ἀγνώμονες οὔτε ἄπιστοι
οὔτε δύσνοι.

21Cf. 6.450d10: φρονίμοις τε καὶ φίλοις.

22Republic 5.476d8-e7: Τί οὖν ἐὰν ἡμῖν χαλεπαί-
νῃ οὗτος, ὅν φαμεν δοξάζειν ἀλλ' οὐ γιγνώσκειν,
καὶ ἀμφισβητῇ ὡς οὐκ ἀληθῆ λέγομεν; ἔξομέν τι
παραμυθεῖσθαι αὐτὸν καὶ πείθειν ἠρέμα, ἐπικρυπτό-
μενοι ὅτι οὐχ ὑγιαίνει; Δεῖ γέ τοι δή, ἔφη. "Ιθι
δή, σκόπει τί ἐροῦμεν πρὸς αὐτόν. ἦ βούλει ὧδε
πυνθανώμεθα παρ' αὐτοῦ, λέγοντες ὡς εἴ τι οἶδεν
οὐδεὶς αὐτῷ φθόνος, ἀλλ' ἄσμενοι ἄν ἴδοιμεν εἰδότα
τι. ἀλλ' ἡμῖν εἰπὲ τόδε....

215

[23]Phaedo 89a9-c4: ΦΑΙΔ. Ἐγὼ ἐρῶ. ἔτυχον γὰρ
ἐν δεξιᾷ αὐτοῦ καθήμενος παρὰ τὴν κλίνην ἐπὶ χα-
μαιζήλου τινός, ὁ δὲ ἐπὶ πολὺ ὑψηλοτέρου ἢ ἐγώ.
καταψήσας οὖν μου τὴν κεφαλὴν καὶ συμπιέσας τὰς
ἐπὶ τῷ αὐχένι τρίχας--εἰώθει γάρ, ὁπότε τύχοι,
παίζειν μου εἰς τὰς τρίχας--Αὔριον δή, ἔφη, ἴσως,
ὦ Φαίδων, τὰς καλὰς ταύτας κόμας ἀποκερῇ. Ἔοικεν,
ἦν δ' ἐγώ, ὦ Σώκρατες. Οὔκ, ἄν γε ἐμοὶ πείθῃ. Ἀλλὰ τί; ἦν δ' ἐγώ. Τήμερον, ἔφη, κἀγὼ τὰς ἐμὰς καὶ
σὺ ταύτας, ἐάνπερ γε ἡμῖν ὁ λόγος τελευτήσῃ καὶ μὴ
δυνώμεθα αὐτὸν ἀναβιώσασθαι. καὶ ἔγωγ' ἄν, εἰ σὺ
εἴην καὶ με διαφεύγοι ὁ λόγος, ἔνορκον ἂν ποιησαί-
μην ὥσπερ Ἀργεῖοι, μὴ πρότερον κομήσειν, πρὶν ἂν
νικήσω ἀναμαχόμενος τὸν Σιμμίου τε καὶ Κέβητος λόγον.

216

CONCLUSION

In the enterprise of understanding Plato's writings in themselves, we can never claim--to use Coleridge's phrase--that we understand Plato's ignorance:

> In the perusal of philosophical works I have been greatly benefited by a resolve, which, in the antithetic form and with the allowed quaintness of an adage or maxim, I have been accustomed to word thus: <u>Until you understand a writer's ignorance, presume yourself ignorant of his understanding</u> ......I have now before me a treatise of a religious fanatic, full of dreams and supernatural experiences. I see clearly the writer's grounds, and their hollowness. I have a complete insight into the causes, which through the medium of his body has acted on his mind; and by application of received and ascertained laws I can satisfactorily explain to my own reason all the strange incidents, which the writer records of himself ......<u>I understand his ignorance</u>.
> On the other hand, I have been re-perusing with the best energies of my mind the <u>Timaeus</u> of Plato. Whatever I comprehend impresses me with a reverential sense of the author's genius; but there is a considerable portion of the work, to which I can attach no consistent meaning. In other treatises of the same philosopher,...I have been delighted with the masterly good sense, with the perspicuity of the language, and the aptness of the inductions. I recollect likewise that numerous passages in this author, which I thoroughly comprehend, were formerly no less unintelligible to me,

than the passages now in question. It would, I
am aware, be quite fashionable to dismiss them
at once as Platonic jargon. But this I cannot
do with satisfaction to my own mind, because I
have sought in vain for causes adequate to the
solution of the assumed inconsistency. I have
no insight into the possibility of a man so emi-
nently wise, using words with such half-meanings
to himself as must perforce pass into no-meaning
to his readers. When in addition to the motives
thus suggested by my own reason, I bring into
distinct remembrance the number and the series
of great men, who after long and zealous study
of these works had joined in honouring the name
of Plato with epithets, that almost transcend
humanity, I feel, that a contemptuous verdict
on my part might argue want of modesty, but would
hardly be received by the judicious, as evidence
of superior penetration. Therefore, utterly baffled in all my attempts to understand the ignorance of Plato, <u>I conclude myself ignorant of
his understanding.</u>[1]

Coleridge was by no means a Platonist, but rather
the example of Plato here is meant to include all
writers who are one's superior in understanding.

How, then, should one study Plato? One must begin
by recognizing the most obvious datum which the
Platonic corpus presents, namely that Plato virtually exclusively wrote dialogues. In addition,
Plato himself is not an interlocutor in any of his
own dialogues.[2] And since Plato is acknowledged to
be a philosopher, and since he is acknowledged to
be such on the basis of the dialogues, we cannot
simply dismiss the dialogic character of the Platonic writings as somehow extraneous to the acknowledged philosophical content which it adumbrates, but we must regard it to be as intrinsically a part of the philosophical import of the
dialogues as any other aspect of them. In other
words, the Platonic dialogues are philosophical
dramas, and they are as truly dramatic as they
are truly philosophical. How, then, does this af-

fect the reading of Plato? In the first place,
Plato does not speak, but his interlocutors
speak. In the second place, insofar as his interlocutors are fully drawn dramatic personages,
what they speak is accompanied by what they do
(which would include also what they neither speak
nor do), and what they speak and do (together
with what they neither speak nor do) is a reflec-
tion of what they are. And this totality of their
intra-dialogic being, speaking, and doing for
themselves is the totality of their speaking for
us. Now, it is to the totality of the dialogue's
speaking for us that our speaking to the dialogue,
on the basis of which our speaking about (commentary upon) the dialogue is formulated, must be
addressed. So, what Plato means by the totality of
the dialogue's speaking for us must be discerned
not only through that speaking for us, but in addition through the dialogue outside the dialogue
in which we ourselves are the expected interlocutors. And perhaps it is this dialogue outside the
dialogue which is the "longer road" to the travelling of which the Platonic Socrates sometimes
invites his intra-dialogic interlocutors (cf. Rep.
4.435d3; 6.504b1-4, c9-d3), a travelling which,
since it is never performed intra-dialogically,
must be performed extra-dialogically by us along
the lines suggested by the intra-dialogic conversation of which we have been the auditors. But
although these intra-dialogic lines are drawn
clearly, they are not drawn univocally, and hence
they must be studied with an eye as much to their
suggestiveness as to their literal sense.[3] And
this is what we have tried to do in our attempt
to explore the kinds of accounts which one finds
in the Platonic dialogues.

And the result of our exploration was to deline-
ate four types of λόγος in the broad sense:

(1) λόγος in the narrow sense: a descriptive
and/or classificatory and/or diairetic account.
(2) μῦθος: a genetic and/or originary and/or
synagogic account.
(3) ἀκοή: a tale or story, either loosely 'his-

torical' in our sense or fictional.

(4) παραμυθία/παραμύθιον: a consolation, a myth in our sense of an imaginative account of what is outside or beyond one's capacity for rational certitude.

Of these four accounts, none are simply incorrect, although the fourth is false, while the first three may be either true or false. Therefore, in the case of a λόγος or a μῦθος or an ἀκοή, the designation of the kind of account which it is does not tautologically bring along with it any determination as to its truth value. That can only be determined by studying each account itself in its context. However, one can say generally, I believe, that in the Platonic corpus, there are neither any simply true accounts nor any simply false accounts, but only accounts which are more or less true, which means also more or less false. In addition, as accounts, they are all to be treated the same, and the methodology of reading is no different for a μῦθος from what it is for a λόγος.

Finally, although our inquiry began with a survey of the lexicon senses of μῦθος and λόγος, on the basis of our inquiry, we believe that those senses might need revision. In particular, the assumed separation out of the meanings of λόγος and μῦθος into respectively true account and false account may not be as clearcut as it seems. Rather it may stem in many--if not all--cases from a modern and contemporary prejudgment that such a separation out occurred, rather than from a close scrutiny of each term as organically and contextually determined. Therefore, what we have tried to establish with regard to Platonic usage should suggest that a similar attempt at reevaluating the respective meanings of λόγος and μῦθος in all the classical Greek authors, from Homer's use of μῦθος for Λόγος to Aristotle's use of μῦθος for the soul of a tragedy,[4] needs to be undertaken. And in such an undertaking, this work is intended as a first step, as a program for a project, rather than as a completed edifice.

NOTES

[1]Samuel Taylor Coleridge, <u>Biographia literaria</u>, ch. 12.

[2]He does appear once as a spectator: cf. <u>Apol. Socr.</u> 34a1, 38b6. Also cf. above p. 26, note 1.

[3]Cf. St. Thomas, <u>In Aristotelis librum De anima commentarium</u>, Liber I, lectio VIII, section 107: "Wherein it must be noted, that for the most part when /Aristotle/ reproves Plato's opinions, he does not reprove them so much with respect to Plato's intention as rather with respect to the sound /i.e., surface meaning/ of his words. Therefore he does this, because Plato had a bad manner of teaching. For he has said all things figuratively, and he teaches through symbols: intending through the words something other than what those words sound /i.e., mean on the surface/; just as that he has said the soul to be a circle. And therefore lest anyone fall into error on account of these words, Aristotle disputes against him /only/ as much as with respect to what his words sound /i.e., mean on the surface/." (Ubi notandum est, quod plerumque quando reprobat opiniones Platonis, non reprobat eas quantum ad intentionem Platonis, sed quantum ad sonum verborum ejus. Quod ideo facit, quia Plato habuit malum modum docendi. Omnia enim figurate dicit, et per symbola docet: intendens aliud per verba, quam sonent ipsa verba; sicut quod dixit animam esse circulum. Et ideo ne aliquis propter ipsa verba incidat in errorem, Aristoteles disputat contra eum quantum ad id quod verba ejus sonant.)

[4]Aristotle, <u>Poetics</u> 6.1450b1: "Therefore the myth is the ruling-beginning and as it were the soul of the tragedy" (ἀρχὴ μὲν οὖν καὶ οἷον ψυχὴ ὁ μῦθος τῆς τραγῳδίας). The universal contemporary tendency to translate μῦθος in the <u>Poetics</u>

221

by our word 'plot' is very misleading (as is, I
might add, the tendency to translate ἀρχή sometimes by 'principle' instead of consistently
translating it more neutrally as 'ruling-beginning'
or 'origination'). The reason that μῦθος is so
translated in Aristotle must be that his usage of
the term--at least in the Poetics--is so contrary
to our assumptions about its meaning that there
seems no way in English to render it in the usual
way. This, of course, is typical of the translation of μῦθος in many scattered places in both
Plato and Aristotle, but the Poetics is a particularly massive example. However, if our suggested
rendering of the term μῦθος as a genetic or originary account is accurate, the difficulty at least
with regard to meaning dissipates. For Aristotle
means by it something like the unified synoptic
whole (cf. τὸ ἓν καὶ τὸ ὅλον at Poetics 7.1451a1-2
et passim and εὐσύνοπτον at 7.1451a4) which is
the origin of, or out of which are generated, the
disparate speakings and actings of the unfolding
drama. And this is quite consistent with the meaning of μῦθος as we find it in the Platonic corpus.

222

Appendix I

ΜΥΘΟΣ AND ITS DERIVATIVES IN THE PLATONIC CORPUS

This list was compiled on the basis of Ast's Lexicon Platonicum, which is a complete concordance of
the Platonic writings, but which is not exhaustive.
I have supplemented it with des Places' Lexique de
langue philosophique et religieuse de Platon, which
forms tome 14 of the so-called Budé edition of the
Oeuvres complètes of Plato, and which is rather a
dictionary than a concordance, giving only as many
citations as are necessary to illustrate the various meanings of a word, although it occasionally
cites something which is missing from Ast. However,
even the two together are not exhaustive, so I have
had to supplement them by a line by line reading of
the entire Platonic corpus, including the Definiti-
ones and Spuria. I believe, therefore, that the
list is exhaustive.

All references are to the Oxford Classical Text of
the Opera Omnia, ed. J. Burnet, 5 volumes, and
they are listed in each group in the order in
which the OCT presents the works.

(Note: *=cited by Ast alone; **=cited by des Places
alone; ***=cited by both.)

223

μῦθος, ὁ

Theaetetus 156c4. ὁ μῦθος*
           164d9. μῦθος***
Philebus 14a4. μῦθος**
Phaedrus 241e8. ὁ μῦθος
Gorgias 527a5. μῦθος...ὥσπερ γραὸς***
Republic 10.621b8. μῦθος ἐσώθη**
Laws 1.645b1. ὁ μῦθος ἀρετῆς**
    4.712a4. μῦθός τις***
    4.719c1. Παλαιὸς μῦθος***
    6.771c7. μῦθος***
    6.773b4. μῦθος γάμου***
    7.812a2. μῦθος***
    9.872c7-e1. ὁ...μῦθος ἢ λόγος***
Epinomis 975a6. ὁ μῦθος***
Epistles 12.359d5. ὁ παραδεδομένος μῦθος*
Phaedo 110b4. τοῦ μύθου
Theaetetus 164e3. μύθου*
Statesman 268d9. μεγάλου μύθου
      274e1. τοῦ μύθου**
      277b5. θαυμαστὸν ὄγκον...τοῦ μύθου**
Phaedrus 237a9. τοῦ μύθου*
      253c7. τοῦ μύθου
Republic 3.415a2. τοῦ μύθου*
Timaeus 22c7. μύθου***
Laws 1.636d4-5. τοῦ μύθου
    3.682a8. μύθου
    3.683d3. τοῦ μύθου
Statesman 268e4. τῷ μύθῳ*
      277b7. τῷ μύθῳ
Protagoras 361d2. ἐν τῷ μύθῳ
Republic 2.376d9. ὥσπερ ἐν μύθῳ μυθολογοῦντες
    3.390d4. μύθῳ (=Odyssey 20.17)
    8.565d6. τῷ μύθῳ
Timaeus 26c8. ὡς ἐν μύθῳ***
    69b1. τῷ μύθῳ*
Laws 4.713a6. μύθῳ
    8.841c6. ἐν μύθῳ**
    11.927c7-8. τῷ πρὸ τοῦ νόμου μύθῳ***
    12.944a2. μύθῳ***
Epistles 7.344d3. τῷ μύθῳ**

Phaedo 60c2. μῦθον /κατὰ Αἴσωπον/***
      110b1. μῦθον
Sophist 242c8. Μῦθόν τινα*
Statesman 272d5. τὸν μῦθον
Alcibiades I 123a1. κατὰ τὸν Αἰσώπου μῦθον***
Protagoras 320c3. μῦθον λέγων...ἢ λόγῳ διεξελθών***
      320c7. μῦθον
      324d6. οὐκέτι μῦθον...ἀλλὰ λόγον***
      328c3. καὶ μῦθον καὶ λόγον**
Gorgias 523a2. μῦθον...λογον***
Hippias minor 365a2. τὸν μῦθον (=Iliad 9.309)
Republic 2.377c1. καλὸν μῦθον
      3.415c7. τὸν μῦθον
Timaeus 26e4. πλασθέντα μῦθον***
      29d2. τὸν εἰκότα μῦθον***
      68d2. τὸν εἰκότα μῦθον*
Minos 318d11. μῦθον...τραγικόν
Laws 1.636c7. τὸν περὶ Γανυμήδη μῦθον*
    1.636d2-3. τὸν μῦθον...κατὰ τοῦ Διός
    4.713b8-c1. τὸν...μῦθον
    6.752a2. μῦθον ἀκέφαλον***
Epinomis 980a5. κατὰ τὸν ἡμέτερον μῦθον***
Demodocus 383c1. μῦθον
Cratylus 408c8. οἱ μῦθοί τε καὶ τὰ ψεύδη
Republic 1.330d7. οἱ...μῦθοι περὶ τῶν ἐν "Αιδου*
      2.378e5. οἱ μῦθοι
Republic 3.386b8-9. τῶν μύθων
Timaeus 23b5. παίδων...μύθων*
      59c6. τῶν εἰκότων μύθων***
Laws 7.790c3. τῶν περὶ τὰ σώματα μύθων***
    9.865d5. τῶν ἀρχαίων μύθων***
Sophist 242d6. τοῖς μύθοις
Meno 96a1. μύθοισι σαόφροσιν (=Theognis)
Republic 2.377a6. μύθοις πρὸς τὰ παιδία ἢ γυμνασίοις *
      2.377c4. πλάττειν τὰς ψυχὰς...τοῖς μύθοις
      2.377c7. Ἐν τοῖς μείζοσιν...μύθοις
Laws 2.664a6. ᾠδαῖς καὶ μύθοις καὶ λόγοις***
    8.840c1. ἐν μύθοις τε καὶ ἐν ῥήμασιν**
    10.887d2. τοῖς μύθοις*
Phaedo 61b4. ποιεῖν μύθους ἀλλ' οὐ λόγους***
      61b6. μύθους /τοῦ Αἰσώπου/
Statesman 272c7. διελέγοντο πρὸς ἀλλήλους καὶ τὰ
θηρία μύθους*

Republic 1.350e3. ὥσπερ ταῖς γραυσὶν ταῖς τοὺς
μύθους λεγούσαις***
        2.377a4. τοῖς παιδίοις μύθους λέγομεν
        2.377b6. μύθους πλασθέντας
        2.377d5. μύθους...ψευδεῖς
        2.379a4. μύθους
        2.381e3. τοὺς μύθους
        3.391e12. τοὺς τοιούτους μύθους
        3.398b7. λόγους τε καὶ μύθους***
Laws 7.804e4. μύθους παλαιούς*

μυθολόγημα, τό

Phaedrus 229c5. σὺ τοῦτο τὸ μυθολόγημα πείθῃ ἀληθὲς
εἶναι;***
Laws 2.663e5. τὸ μὲν τοῦ Σιδωνίου μυθολόγημα***

μυθικός, -ή, -όν

Phaedrus 265c1. μυθικόν τινα ὕμνον***

μυθώδης, ὁ or ἡ

Republic 7.522a7. μυθώδεις***

μυθολογέω

Phaedo 61e2. διασκοπεῖν τε καὶ μυθολογεῖν***
Phaedrus 276e3. μυθολογοῦντα*
Gorgias 493a5. τις μυθολογῶν κομψὸς ἀνήρ***
        493d3. μυθολογῶ***
Hippias major 286a2. χρῶνται ὥσπερ ταῖς πρεσβύτισιν
οἱ παῖδες πρὸς τὸ ἡδέως μυθολογῆσαι***
Republic 2.359d6. μυθολογοῦσιν***
        2.376d9. ὥσπερ ἐν μύθῳ μυθολογοῦντες***
        2.378c4. μυθολογητέον***
        2.378e3. ὅτι κάλλιστα μεμυθολογημένα***
        2.379a2. δεῖ μυθολογεῖν τοὺς ποιητάς***
        2.380c2. μυθολογοῦντα***
        3.392b6. ᾄδειν τε καὶ μυθολογεῖν***

226

3.415a3. μυθολογοῦντες***
6.501e4. ἡ πολιτεία ἣν μυθολογοῦμεν***
9.588c2. οἷαι μυθολογοῦνται παλαιαὶ γενέσθαι φύσεις*
Timaeus 22b1. μυθολογεῖν, καὶ...γενεαλογεῖν***
Laws 3.682e5. μυθολογεῖτέ τε καὶ διαπεραίνετε***
Epistles 8.352e1. μυθολογοῦντες

μυθολογία, ἡ

Statesman 304d1. διὰ μυθολογίας ἀλλὰ μὴ διὰ δι-
δαχῆς***
Phaedrus 243a4. μυθολογίαν*
Hippias major 298a4. οἱ λόγοι καὶ αἱ μυθολογίαι
ταὐτὸν τοῦτο ἐργάζονται***
Republic 2.382d1. ταῖς μυθολογίαις***
3.394b9-c1. τῆς ποιήσεως τε καὶ μυθολογίας***
Critias 110a3. μυθολογία γὰρ ἀναζήτησις τε τῶν
παλαιῶν***
Laws 3.680d3. τὸ ἀρχαῖον αὐτῶν...διὰ μυθολογίας***
6.752a1. κατὰ τὴν...μυθολογίαν***

μυθοποιός, ὁ

Republic 2.377b11. ἐπιστατητέον τοῖς μυθοποιοῖς*

μυθολόγος, ὁ

Republic 3.392d2. ὑπὸ μυθολόγων ἢ ποιητῶν***
3.398b1. ποιητῇ...καὶ μυθολόγῳ***
Laws 2.664d3. μυθολόγους περὶ τῶν αὐτῶν ἠθῶν***
12.941b5. ὑπό τινων μυθολόγων πλημμελῶν***

μυθολογικός, -ή, -όν

Phaedo 61b5. αὐτὸς οὐκ ἢ μυθολογικός*

227

διαμυθολογέω

Apol.Socr. 39e5. διαμυθολογῆσαι πρὸς ἀλλήλους*
Phaedo 70b6. διαμυθολογῶμεν*
Laws 1.632e4-5. διαμυθολογοῦντες*

παραμυθία, ἡ

Phaedo 70b2. παραμυθίας...καὶ πίστεως***
Sophist 224a4. παραμυθίας /opp. σπουδῆς/***
Euthydemus 290a4. παραμυθία*
Republic 5.450d9. ἡ παραμυθία***
Laws 4.720a1. παραμυθίας...καὶ πειθοῦς***
Axiochus 365a4. πάνυ ἐνδεᾶ παραμυθίας*

παραμύθιον, τό

Phaedrus 240d4. παραμύθιον***
Euthydemus 272b8. παραμύθιον τοῦ μὴ φοβεῖσθαι***
Republic 1.329e5. παραμύθια***
Critias 115b4. παραμύθια***
Laws 1.632e5. παραμύθια***
     4.704d8. παραμύθιον***
     4.705a8. παραμύθιον***
     6.773e5. παραμύθια***
     9.880a7. παραμυθίοις***
     10.885b3. τὸ παραμύθιον***
     11.923c2. παραμύθιά τε καὶ προοίμια***

παραμυθέομαι

Phaedo 83a3. ἡ φιλοσοφία...παραμυθεῖται***
     115d5. παραμυθούμενος***
Sophist 230a2. παραμυθούμενοι***
Statesman 268b3. παραμυθεῖσθαι καὶ...πραΰνειν***
Euthydemus 277d4. μὴ ἡμῖν ἀποδειλιάσειε, παραμυ-
     θούμενος εἶπον***
     288c4. δεώμεθα καὶ παραμυθώμεθα καὶ
προσευχώμεθα***
Protagoras 346b4. παραμυθεῖσθαι***
Ion 540c5. ἀγριαινουσῶν βοῶν παραμυθουμένῳ**

228

<u>Menexenus</u> 237a1. παραμυθούμενος**
     247c5-6. παραμυθεῖσθαι*
<u>Republic</u> 4.442a2. παραμυθουμένη, ἡμεροῦσα***
     5.451b1. παραμυθῇ***
     5.476e1. παραμυθεῖσθαι αὐτὸν καὶ πείθειν
ἠρέμα***
     6.499e2. μὴ φιλονικῶν ἀλλὰ παραμυθούμενος***
<u>Critias</u> 108c7. παραμυθουμένῳ***
<u>Laws</u> 1.625b6. ἀλλήλους παραμυθουμένους***
     2.666a2. αὐτοὺς παραμυθησόμεθα προθύμους εἶναι;***
     9.854a6. διαλεγόμενος ἅμα καὶ παραμυθούμενος**
     10.899d6. παραμυθητέον***
     11.928a1-2. παραμυθούμενός τε καὶ ἀπειλῶν ὁ νόμος**
     12.944b3. παραμυθούμενος***
<u>Epinomis</u> 976a7. παραμυθούμενος**
<u>Epistles</u> 7.329d4. ἐμὲ παραμυθεῖτό τε καὶ...διακε-
λεύετο καὶ ἐδεῖτο...μένειν***
     7.345e4. παραμυθεῖτό τε καὶ ἐδεῖτο μένειν**

     εὐπαραμύθητος, ὁ or ἡ

<u>Laws</u> 10.885b8. εὐπαραμυθήτους***
     10.888c6-7. εὐπαραμύθητοι***

EPISTLES 7.341b7–345c3

341
c
So much then I have to declare about all
persons who have written and who will write,
as many as assert themselves to have envisioned things about which I am serious, having heard /them/ either from me or from
others or as though having found /them/ themselves; it is not for these persons, in accordance with my opinion at any rate, to
understand anything about the business.
Therefore, there is not and never will come
to be any writing of mine at least about
5   these things; for in no way must they, as
other learnings, be uttered, but from much
being-together coming to be in respect to the
business itself and from living-together,
such as light having been touched off from a
d   fire which has leapt up, suddenly it having
come to be in the soul already nurtures itself. And yet I have envisioned so much at
least, that these things having been written
or having been spoken would be spoken best by
me; and that these things having been written
badly would pain me not the least. And if
5   they appeared to me to be both things which
must be written sufficiently and uttered to
the many, what more beautiful than this would
have been enacted by us in our lifetime than
to have written a great benefit for humans
and to have led forth nature into the light
e   for all persons? But I do not regard the taking them in hand which is spoken about them
to be good for humans, unless for some few,
however many are themselves capable of finding out through little showing out, and indeed of the others it would fill the ones

with an incorrect in no way seemly contempt,
5 and /it would fill/ the others with a lofty
and spongy hope, as though they had learned
342 significant things. And still longer things
about these things have come to be in my intellect to speak; for /then/ quickly the
things about which I speak would be more distinct than these things which have been spoken. For there is a certain true speech,
over and against the person who has dared to
write even anything whatever of the suchlike
5 things, /a speech/ which has been uttered by
me many times even before, and therefore it
is likely to be a thing which must be spoken
also now.
    There are to each of the beings three
things, through which things there is a compulsion for exact-knowledge to come to be
present, and it /i.e., exact-knowledge/ is a
fourth--and fifth it is obligatory to posit
b a being itself which indeed both is recogni-
zable and truly is--/and of these things/
one is name, and second is speech, and the
third is look-alike, and fourth is exact-
knowledge. Therefore, you wishing to learn
the thing now being spoken, take it in respect to one, and intellect in this way about
all things. There is something which is spoken to be a circle, for which this itself
5 which now we have voiced is the name. And the
second is its speech, which is composed from
names and verbs; for "the thing holding itself everywhere equal from its extremities to
its middle" would be the speech of that very
thing for which the name is "rounded" and
"circumferent" and "circle." And third is the
c /circle/ which is painted and which is washed
out and which is turned on the lathe and is
perishing, by none of which things the circle
itself, in respect to which all these things
are, is affected, since it is other than
these. And fourth is exact-knowledge and intellect and true opinion in respect to these
5 things; and this in turn must be posited as
all one, since it is not in sounds or in

232

shaped-surfaces of bodies but in souls, by
which it is clear /as/ being other than both
the nature of the circle itself and the three
d things which have been spoken before. And of
these, intellect has approached nearest to
the fifth by cogenericity and by similarity,
but the others hold off more /i.e., are farther away/. Indeed the same is about the
straight as also about circumferent shaped-
surface and about surface-hue, and about good
and beautiful and just, and about both all
5 prepared /i.e., artificial/ body and /body/
which has come to be in accordance with nature, fire and water and all the suchlike
things, and about the living thing all together and habit in souls, and in respect to
makings/doings and affections all together;
for if someone does not grasp the four of
e these in some way somehow at least, never
will he be completely a partaker of exact-
knowledge the fifth. For in addition to these
things, these things take it in hand no less
to clarify the certain which-sort in respect
to each thing than /to clarify/ the being of
343 each, because of the weakness of speeches; on
account of which things no one who has an
intellect will dare ever to put into it /i.e.,
into speech/ the things which have been in-
tellected by him, and /no one who has an intellect will dare ever to put/ these things
into an untransmoving thing, by which indeed
the things which have been written by outlines are affected. And this thing which is
now spoken it is obligatory again in turn to
5 learn. Each circle of those which are written
in enactings or also of those which are
turned on the lathe is full of the contrary
to the fifth--for /each of these circles/
touches the straight everywhere--and the circle itself, we assert, has in itself neither
anything smaller nor bigger of the contrary
nature. And we assert their name to be nothing steadfast in any way, and /we assert/
b nothing to prevent the things which are now

233

called "rounded" from having been called
"straight" and indeed the things /which are
now called/ "straight" /from having been
called/ "rounded," and /we assert/ nothing
will hold less steadfastly /even/ to the
persons transposing /the names/ and calling
/things/ contrarily. And about a speech then
/there is/ the same speech, if it is composed
from names and verbs, /namely the speech as-
5 serting it/ in no way to be sufficiently
steadfastly steadfast; and /there is/ the my-
riad speech in turn about each of the four,
how /each/ is indistinct, but the greatest
thing, the very thing which we bespoke a little before, is that when there are two, both
the being and the certain which-sort, when
the soul seeks to have envisioned not the
c certain which-sort but the what, each of the
four extending out both by speech and in accordance with deeds to the soul the thing
which is not sought, each furnishing the
thing which is spoken and which is shown to
be always easily refuted by sensings, fills
5 all men, so as to speak a word, with all
perplexity and indistinctness. Therefore, in
things in which we are persons who have not
been habituated by a vicious nurture to seek
the true, and /in things in which/ the thing
which has been extended out from the look-
alikes is sufficient, we do not become
laughable to each other, the persons who are
asked by the persons asking, and who are ca-
d pable of both throwing around and refuting
the four things; but in things in which we
compel answering and clarifying the fifth,
of those who are capable of turning /things/
upside down the person wishing /to turn
things upside down/ has mastery, and he makes
the person interpreting /the fifth thing/ in
speeches or written things or answerings to
5 seem to many of those who hear to recognize
nothing of the things which he takes it in
hand to write or to speak, /those who hear/
sometimes failing to recognize how the soul
of the person who has written or who has spo-

234

ken is not refuted, but the nature of each
of the four /is refuted/, since /that na-
ture/ has natured meanly. But the leading-
e   through all these things, the going over upward and downward for each, with difficulty
brings to birth exact-knowledge of a thing
which has natured well in a person who has
natured well; and if he natures badly, as the
aptitude/attitude of the soul of the many
has natured both unto learning and unto
the things which are spoken to be habits, and
/if/ they /i.e., the habits/ are corrupted,
344 not even Lynkeus would make the suchlike persons to see. But, in one speech, neither lear-
ning-well nor memory would ever make the person /who is/ not cogeneric of the business /to
see/--for with respect to the ruling-beginning
it does not come to be in other sorts of
aptitudes/attitudes--so that as many persons
5   as are not natured toward and cogeneric of
both the just things and the other things as
many as are beautiful, but some of whom are
well-learning and memoried of some things and
others of other things, and as many persons
as are cogeneric of them, but are learning-
resistant and unmemoried, of these persons
none ever yet may learn the truth of virtue
and badness unto that which is possible. For
b   with respect to these things there is a compulsion to learn simultaneously the false and
true of the whole beingness, with all diligence and much time, which very thing in the
beginnings I bespoke; and names and speeches
and seeings and sensings, each of them being
5   rubbed with difficulty against each other,
/they all/ being refuted in kindly refutations
and by persons using askings and answerings
without envies, in respect to each thing, prudence and intellect shone out, /intellect/
stretching out unto the most human power. Be-
c   cause of which indeed every man who is serious
about the serious beings is under much obliga-
tion lest he having written ever throws down
/his writings/ unto the envy and perplexity

235

among humans. Indeed, in one speech, from
these things it is obligatory to recognize,
whenever anyone sees someone's writings which
5 have been written either in the laws of a legislator or in any other things with respect
to anything whatever, how these things were
not the most serious things for this person,
if he himself is serious, but they lie some-
where in the most beautiful spot of this person's /spots/; and if these things beingly
having been serious for him were put in wri-
d tings, not "gods," but mortals "themselves
then indeed surely therefore destroyed his
senses."

Indeed the person who has co-followed
this myth and wandering will have envisioned
well, if therefore Dionysius or someone les-
5 ser or greater wrote any of the highest and
first things about nature, how he had, in accordance with my speech, neither heard nor
learned anything healthy of the things of
which he wrote; for similarly /if he had
heard or learned anything healthy of these
things/, he would have reverenced them as I
do, and he would not have dared to throw
them out unto unharmoniousness and improper-
ness. For he did not even write for the sake
of reminders--for it is nothing formidable
e /that/ someone may forget it, if once he
grasps around it by his soul; for it lies
among the briefest of all things /to re-re-
member/--but /he wrote/ for the sake of
shameful ambition, whether as positing it to
be his own or as indeed being a partaker of
an education, of which he was not worthy, he
cherishing the opinion of his partaking of it
345 having come to be. Therefore if from the one
being-together this has come to be to Dionysius, perhaps it would be so, but therefore
in what way it has come to be, the Theban asserts, "Zeus kens;" for, as I spoke, I narrated it only once, but later still not ever
yet. Indeed it is obligatory to internally
5 intellect the thing after this, /namely/ to

whom it is a care to find the thing which has
come to be in respect to them in what way ever
it has come to be, for what cause then we did
not go through it the second and the third and
more times; does Dionysius who has heard only
once thus both believe himself to have envi-
b sioned and has he envisioned sufficiently,
either he himself having found it or also having learned it before from others, or /does
he believe/ the things which have been spoken
/by me/ to be mean, or thirdly /does he believe them to be/ not in accordance with himself but greater /than he/, and /does he believe himself/ beingly not to be capable of
living /while/ taking care of both prudence
and virtue. For if /he believes them to be/
5 mean, he battles with many witnesses speaking
the contrary things, who would be altogether
much more authoritative judges about the suchlike things than Dionysius; and if /he believes himself/ to have found or to have
learned /them/, and therefore /believes them/
to be worthy in regard to the education of a
free soul, how would he, since he is not a
c wondrous human, ever have dishonored the leader and authority of these things so reckless-
ly? And how he dishonored, I would declare.

BIBLIOGRAPHY

(OCT=Oxford Classical Text; LCL=Loeb Classical Library; B=Bude; T=Teubner)

Aesopus, Fables, texte établi et tr. par Émile
    Chambry (Paris, 1927)./"Notice," pp. xxi-xxv.7
Alfarabi, Philosophy of Plato and Aristotle, tr.
    Muhsin Mahdi (Glencoe, Ill., 1962).
Anastaplo, George, "Human being and citizen: a be-
    ginning to the study of Plato's Apology of
    Socrates," in Ancients and moderns (see be-
    low), pp. pp. 16-49.
Ancients and moderns: essays on the tradition of
    political philosophy in honor of Leo Strauss,
    ed. Joseph Cropsey (New York, 1964).
Aristophanes, Aristophanes, with English transla-
    tion by Benjamin Bickley Rogers (London, LCL,
    1930-), 3 vols.
Aristophanes, Clouds, ed. with intro. and commen-
    tary by K.J. Dover (Oxford, 1968).
Aristoteles, De anima, ed. W.D. Ross (Oxford, OCT,
    1956).
Aristoteles, De animalibus historia, in Aristotelis
    opera, ed. I. Bekker (Oxford, 1837), vol. 4,
    Historia animalium.
Aristoteles, De arte poetica, ed. W. Christ (Leip-
    zig, T, 1882).
Aristoteles, De generatione animalium, ed. H.J.D.
    Lulofs (Oxford, OCT, 1965).
Aristoteles, Aristotle's Metaphysics, a revised
    text with intro. and commentary by W.D. Ross
    (Oxford, 1924), 2 vols.
Ast, Friedrich, Lexicon Platonicum (Leipzig, 1835),
    3 vols. in 2.
Bacon, Francis, Selected writings of Francis Bacon
    (New York, Modern Library, 1955).

Benardete, Seth, "XPH and ΔEI in Plato and others," Glotta, 43 (1965), pp. 285-298.

Benardete, Seth, "Eidos and diaeresis in Plato's Statesman," Philologus, 107 (1963), pp. 193-226.

Benardete, Seth, "On Plato's Timaeus and Timaeus' science fiction," Interpretation; a journal of political philosophy, 2, no. 1 (Summer 1971), pp. 21-63.

Benardete, Seth, "The right, the true, and the beautiful," Glotta, 41 (1963), pp. 54-62.

Blake, William, The complete writings of William Blake with all the variant readings, ed. Geoffrey Keynes (New York, 1957).

Bluck, R.S., "The second Platonic epistle," Phronesis, 5 (1960), pp. 140-151.

Boeder, Heribert, "Der fruehgriechische Wortgebrauch von Logos und Aletheia," Archiv fuer begriffsgeschichte, 4 (1959), pp. 82-112.

Brann, Eva, "The music of the Republic," ΑΓΩΝ, 1, no. 1 (April 1967), pp. i-vi, 1-117.

Brochard, V., "Les mythes dans la philosophie de Platon," L'année philosophique, 11 (1900), pp. 1-13. /Passim, but esp. p. 4./

Buck, Carl D., "Words of speaking and saying in the Indo-European languages," American journal of philology, 36, nos. 1 & 2, pp. 1-18, 125-154.

Buffiere, Félix, Les mythes d'Homère et la pensée grecque (Paris, 1956)./Pp. 1-3, 15, 32-44./

Cohen, Percy S., "Theories of myth," Man, n.s. 4 (1969), pp. 337-353./Passim./

Coleridge, Samuel Taylor, Selected poetry and prose of Coleridge, ed. Donald Stauffer (New York, 1951).

Couturat, L., De platonicis mythis (Paris, 1896).

Denniston, J.D., The Greek particles (Oxford, 1970).

de Santillana, Giorgio, Hamlet's mill; an essay on myth and the frame of time, by Giorgio de Santillana and Hertha von Dechend (Boston, 1969). /Pp. 48-51./

Descartes, René, The philosophical works of Descartes, tr. E.S. Haldane and G.R.T. Ross (Cambridge, Eng., 1968), 2 vols.

des Places, Édouard, Lexique de la langue philo-
    sophique et religieuse de Platon (Paris, B,
    1964), in Oeuvres complètes (see below),
    tome XIV, pts. 1 & 2.
Dickinson, Emily, The poems of Emily Dickinson,
    including variant readings critically com-
    pared with all known manuscripts, ed. Thomas
    H. Johnson (Cambridge, Mass., 1955), 3 vols.
Diels, Hermann, ed., Die fragmente der Vorsokrati-
    ker...5. aufl. herausgegeben von Walther
    Kranz (Berlin, 1934-1937).
Diogenes Laertius, Lives of the eminent philoso-
    phers, with English tr. by R.D. Hicks (Cam-
    bridge, Mass., LCL, 1950), 2 vols.
Dorter, Kenneth, "Imagery and philosophy in
    Plato's Phaedrus," Journal of the history of
    philosophy, 9 (July 1971), pp. 279-288.
Edelstein, Ludwig, "The function of the myth in
    Plato's philosophy," Journal of the history
    of ideas, 10 (Oct. 1949), pp. 463-481.
Else, Gerald F., Aristotle's Poetics: the argument
    (Cambridge, Mass., 1957).
Euclidis, Elementa, text of I.L. Heiberg, ed. E.S.
    Stamatis (Leipzig, T, 1969), volume 1.
Euclidis, The thirteen books of Euclid's Elements,
    tr. with intro. and commentary by Sir Thomas
    Heath, 2d ed. rev. (New York, 1956).
Euripides, Fabulae, ed. Gilbert Murray (Oxford,
    OCT, 1902).
Fournier, H., Les verbs "dire" en Grec ancien
    (Paris, 1946).
Friedlaender, Paul, Plato: an introduction, tr.
    Hans Meyerhoff (New York, 1958).
Frutiger, Perceval, Les mythes de Platon; étude
    philosophique et littéraire (Paris, 1930).
    /Passim./
Gaffney, Susan K., "Dialectic, the myths of Plato,
    metaphor and the transcendent in the world,"
    American Catholic Philosophical Association.
    Proceedings, 45 (1971), pp. 77-85.
Geddes, James, An essay on the composition and
    manner of writing of the antients, parti-
    cularly Plato, Glasgow, 1748 (New York,
    1970 facsimile reprint).

Goldschmidt, Victor, Essai sur le "Cratyle": con-
    tribution à l'histoire de la pensée de Platon
    (Paris, 1940).
Goldschmidt, Victor, Le paradigme dans la dialec-
    tique platonicienne (Paris, 1947). /Pp. 97-
    103./
Graves, Robert, The Greek myths (Baltimore, 1955),
    2 vols.
Grene, David, Greek political theory: the image of
    man in Thucydides and Plato /originally pub-
    lished as Man in his pride/ (Chicago, 1965).
Grimm, Jakob Ludwig Karl, Grimm's fairy tales. Compl.
    ed. Tr. Margaret Hunt, rev. James Stern. With
    212 illustrations by Josef Scharl (New York,
    Pantheon, 1944).
Guthrie, W.K.C., History of Greek philosophy (Cam-
    bridge, Eng., 1962-).
Hegel, Georg Wilhelm Friedrich, The philosophy of
    history, with prefaces by Charles Hegel and
    the tr. J. Sibree. Rev. ed. (New York, 1956).
Heidegger, Martin, Being and time, tr. John Macquar-
    rie and Edward Robinson (New York, 1962).
Heidegger, Martin, Discourse on thinking, tr. John
    M. Anderson and E. Hans Freund (New York, 1966).
Herodotus, Historiae, ed. C. Hude (Oxford, OCT,
    1927).
Hesiodus, Carmina, ed. A. Rzach (Leipzig, T, 1913).
Hesiodus, Hesiod, the Homeric hymns and Homerica,
    with English tr. by Hugh G. Evelyn-White
    (Cambridge, Mass., LCL, 1936).
Hirsch, E.D., Validity in interpretation (New
    Haven, 1967).
Homerus, Ilias, ed. W. Dindorf (Leipzig, T, 1855).
Homerus, Odyssea, ed. T.W. Allen, in Opera (Oxford,
    OCT, 1917), vols. 3 & 4.
Hyland, Drew A., "Why Plato wrote dialogues," Phi-
    losophy and rhetoric, 1, no. 1 (Jan. 1968),
    pp. 38-50.
Jonas, Hans, The phenomenon of life (New York,
    1966).
Kafka, Franz, The penal colony: stories and short
    pieces, tr. Willa and Edwin Muir (New York,
    1961).
Kierkegaard, Søren, The concept of irony, tr. Lee

   M. Capel (New York, 1965).

Kirk, G.S., Myth: its meaning and functions in ancient and other cultures (Berkeley, 1970). /Passim, but esp. chs. I, V, & VI./

Kirk, G.S., The nature of Greek myths (Woodstock, N.Y., 1975)./Passim, but esp. Part I, ch. 1./

Klein, Jacob, "Aristotle, an introduction," in Ancients and moderns (see above), pp. 50-69.

Klein, Jacob, A commentary on Plato's Meno (Chapel Hill, 1965).

Klein, Jacob, Greek mathematical thought and the origin of algebra, tr. Eva Brann (Cambridge, Mass., 1968).

Klein, Jacob, Plato's trilogy (Chicago, 1977).

Koyré, Alexandre, Discovering Plato, tr. Leonora Cohen Rosenfield (New York, 1960).

Leibniz, Gottfried Wilhelm, Freiherr von, Discours de métaphysique et correspondance avec Arnauld, intro., texte, et comm. par Georges Le Roy, deuxième éd. (Paris, 1966).

Liddell, Henry George, A Greek-English lexicon, comp. by Henry George Liddell and Robert Scott. A new /i.e., 9th/ ed. rev. and augm. by Sir Henry Stuart Jones with Roderick McKenzie (Oxford, 1968).

Louis, Pierre, Les metaphores de Platon (Paris, 1945).

Lysias, Selected speeches, ed. C.D. Adams (Norman, Okla., 1970).

Machiavelli, Niccolò, The chief works and others, tr. Allan Gilbert (Durham, N.C., 1965), 3 vols.

McClain, Ernest, "Plato's musical cosmology," Main currents in modern thought, 30, no. 1 (1974), pp. 34-42.

Mara, Gerald, Political wisdom: politics and philosophy in Plato's Statesman and Republic (Unpublished Ph.D.Dissertation, Bryn Mawr College, 1974).

Martin, Henri, Études sur le Timée de Platon (Paris, 1841), 2 vols. in 1.

Marx, Werner, The meaning of Aristotle's ontology (The Hague, 1954).

Melville, Herman, Moby Dick, ed. Harrison Hayford and Hershel Parker (New York, Norton Critical

Ed., 1967).

Merlan, Philip, "Form and content in Plato's philosophy," Journal of the history of ideas, 8,
no. 4 (Oct. 1947), pp. 406-430.

Milton, John, Milton's Lycidas; the tradition and
the poem, ed. C.A. Patrides (New York, 1961).

Mulhern, John J., "Treatises, dialogues, and interpretation," Monist, 53 (1969), pp. 631-
641.

Nettleship, Richard Lewis, Lectures on the Republic of Plato (New York, 1968).

Nietzsche, Friedrich Wilhelm, Beyond good and evil,
tr. Walter Kaufmann (New York, 1966).

Parmenides, Parmenides: a text with tr., commentary, and critical essays by Leonardo Tarán
(Princeton, 1965).

Pépin, Jean, Mythe et allegorie (Aubier, 1958).
/Pp. 33-34, 41-42, 43-44, 46-50, and passim./

Pieper, Josef, Enthusiasm and divine madness, tr.
Richard and Clara Winston (New York, 1964).

Pindarus, Pindari Carmina cum fragmentis, ed. C.M.
Bowra (Oxford, OCT, 1935).

Plato, Opera omnia, ed. John Burnet (Oxford, OCT,
1967), 5 vols.

Plato, Plato, with English tr. (Cambridge, Mass.,
LCL, 1914-1964), 12 vols.

Plato Oeuvres complètes (Paris, B, 1920-1964), 14
vols.

Plato, The works of Plato. A new and literal version chiefly from the text of Stallbaum by
George Burges (London, 1854-1865), 6 vols.

Plato, The Epinomis of Plato, tr. with intro. and
notes by J. Harward (Oxford, 1928).

Plato, Plato's Epistles, tr. with critical essays
and notes by Glenn R. Morrow (Indianapolis,
1962).

Plato, Plato's Euthyphro, Apology of Socrates, and
Crito, ed. with notes by John Burnet (Oxford,
1970).

Plato, Gorgias, a revised text with intro. and commentary by E.R. Dodds (Oxford, 1959).

Plato, Plato and Parmenides: Parmenides' Way of
Truth and Plato's Parmenides, tr. with intro.
and commentary by Francis MacDonald Cornford
(Indianapolis, n.d.).

Plato, Plato's Phaedo, ed. with intro. and notes
    by John Burnet (Oxford, 1972).
Plato, Phédon, tr. Léon Robin (Paris, B, 1926),
    in Oeuvres complètes (see above), tome IV,
    pt. 1.
Plato, Plato's Phaedo, tr. with intro., notes and
    appendices by R.S. Bluck (New York, 1955).
Plato, Plato's Phaedo, tr. with intro. and commen-
    tary by R. Hackforth (Cambridge, Eng., 1972).
Plato, The Phaedrus of Plato, with English notes
    and dissertations by W.H. Thompson (New York,
    1973).
Plato, Phèdre, tr. Léon Robin (Paris, B, 1933), in
    Oeuvres complètes (see above), tome IV, pt. 3.
Plato, Plato's Phaedrus, tr. with intro. and com-
    mentary by R. Hackforth (Indianapolis, 1952).
Plato, Phaedrus, and, the Seventh and Eighth Let-
    ters, tr. Walter Hamilton (Harmondsworth,
    Eng., 1973).
Plato, Plato's examination of pleasure (The Phi-
    lebus), tr. with intro. and commentary by
    R. Hackforth (Indianapolis, 1945).
Plato, The Republic of Plato, ed. with critical
    notes, commentary, and appendices by James
    Adam (Cambridge, Eng., 1926), 2 vols.
Plato, The Republic of Plato, tr. with notes and
    an interpretive essay by Allan Bloom (New
    York, 1968).
Plato, The Symposium of Plato, ed. with intro. and
    commentary by R.G. Bury, 2d ed., (Cambridge,
    Eng., 1973).
Plato, Plato's theory of knowledge: the Theaetetus
    and the Sophist of Plato, tr. with a running
    commentary by Francis MacDonald Cornford
    (London, 1967).
Plato, ΠΛΑΤΩΝΟΣ ΤΙΜΑΙΟΣ: the Timaeus of Plato, ed.
    with intro. and notes by R.D. Archer-Hind
    (London, 1888).
Plato, Plato's cosmology: the Timaeus of Plato, tr.
    with commentary by Francis MacDonald Cornford
    (Indianapolis, n.d.).
Riddell, James, A digest of Platonic idioms, in
    Plato, The Apology of Plato, with a revised
    text and English notes (Oxford, 1877).

245

Riezler, Kurt, Man, mutable and immutable (Chicago, 1950)./Pp. 313-315, 316-317./

Robin, Léon, Études sur la signification et la place de la physique dans la philosophie de Platon (Paris, 1919).

Robin, Léon, Platon (Paris, 1968).

Rose, H.J., Handbook of Greek mythology (New York, 1959).

Rosen, Stanley, "The non-lover in Plato's Phaedrus," Man and world, 2, no. 3 (August 1969), pp. 423-437.

Rosen, Stanley, Plato's Symposium (New Haven, 1968).

Sallis, John, Being and Logos: the way of Platonic dialogue (Pittsburgh, 1975).

Schaerer, René, La question platonicienne (Neuchatel, 1938).

Schuhl, Pierre-Maxime, Essai sur la formation de la pensée grecque: introduction historique à une étude de la philosophie platonicienne (Paris, 1934).

Schuhl, Pierre-Maxime, La fabulation platonicienne (Paris, 1968)./Pp. 10, 15-19, 20, 24-25, 34, 44-45, 71, 108, 115./

Shakespeare, William, All's well that ends well, ed. G.K. Hunter (London, Arden Ed., 1967).

Shakespeare, William, King Lear, a new variorum edition, ed. Horace Howard Furness (New York, 1963).

Shakespeare, William, Othello, a new variorum edition, ed. Horace Howard Furness (New York, 1963).

Shorey, Paul, The unity of Plato's thought (Chicago, 1960).

Shorey, Paul, What Plato said (Chicago, 1933).

Sinaiko, Herman L., Love, knowledge, and discourse in Plato (Chicago, 1965).

Smyth, Herbert Weir, Greek grammar (Cambridge, Mass., 1973).

Stewart, J.A., The myths of Plato (Carbondale, Ill., 1960). /Passim./

Stormer, Gerald D., "Plato's theory of myth," Personalist, 55, no. 3 (Summer 1974), pp. 216-223.

Strauss, Leo, The argument and the action of
    Plato's Laws (Chicago, 1975).
Strauss, Leo, City and man (Chicago, 1964).
Strauss, Leo, ed., History of political philo-
    sophy, edd. Leo Strauss and Joseph Cropsey,
    2d ed. (Chicago, 1972).
Strauss, Leo, Liberalism, ancient and modern (New
    York, 1968).
Strauss, Leo, Natural right and history (Chicago,
    1953).
Strauss, Leo, Persecution and the art of writing
    (Glencoe, Ill., 1952).
Strauss, Leo, The political philosophy of Hobbes,
    tr. Elsa M. Sinclair (Chicago, 1963).
Strauss, Leo, Thoughts on Machiavelli (Glencoe,
    Ill., 1958).
Strauss, Leo, What is political philosophy? and
    other studies (Glencoe, Ill., 1959).
Swift, Jonathan, The writings of Jonathan Swift,
    edd. Robert A. Greenberg and William B.
    Piper (New York, Norton Critical Ed., 1973).
Tarán, Leonardo, Academica: Plato, Philip of Opus,
    and the pseudo-Platonic Epinomis (Philadel-
    phia, 1975).
Tarrant, Dorothy, "Colloquialisms, semi-proverbs
    and word-play in Plato," Classical quarterly,
    40 (1946), pp. 101-117.
Tarrant, Dorothy, "More colloquialisms, semi-pro-
    verbs and word-play in Plato," Classical
    quarterly, n.s. 8 (1958), pp. 158-160.
Tarrant, Dorothy, "Plato as dramatist," Journal of
    Hellenic studies, 75 (1955), pp. 82-89.
Taylor, Alfred Edward, A commentary on Plato's
    Timaeus (Oxford, 1928).
Thomas Aquinas, Saint, In Aristotelis librum De
    anima commentarium. Editio secunda cura ac
    studio P.F. Angeli M. Pirotta (Taurini,
    Italia, 1936).
Thompson, D'Arcy Wentworth, Science and the clas-
    sics (London, 1940).
Thucydides, Historiae, ed. H.S. Jones (Oxford,
    OCT, 1942), 2 vols.
Tolstoy, Leo, War and peace, tr. Louise and Aylmer
    Maude (New York, Norton Critical Ed., 1966).

Verdenius, W.J., "Notes on Plato's Phaedrus,"
    Mnemosyne, s. 4, 8 (1955), pp. 265-289.
Vernant, Jean-Pierre, Mythe et pensée chéz les
    Grecs (Paris, 1971), 2 vols. /Passim./
Vlastos, Gregory, Plato's universe (Seattle, 1975).
Voegelin, Eric, Order and history, vol. 3, Plato
    and Aristotle (Baton Rouge, 1957).
Vries, Gerrit Jacob de, A commentary on the Phae-
    drus of Plato (Amsterdam, 1969).
Westcott, Brooke F., "The myths of Plato," Contem-
    porary review, 2 (1866), pp. 199-211, 469-481.
Writers at work: the Paris Review interviews, ed.
    Malcolm Cowley (New York, 1959).
Xenophon, Opera omnia, ed. E.C. Marchant (Oxford,
    OCT, 1901-1920), 5 vols.
Zaner, Richard, The way of phenomenology (New York,
    1970).
Zaslavsky, Robert, "A hitherto unremarked pun in
    the Phaedrus," Apeiron, 15, no. 2 (1981).
Zaslavsky, Robert, "The Platonic Godfather: a note
    on the Protagoras myth," Journal of value in-
    quiry, 15 (1981).
Zuercher, Josef, Lexicon Academicum (Paderborn,
    1954).

INDEX VERBORUM GRAECORUM

(Note: adverbial, comparative, and superlative
forms are indexed under the positive adjectival
form.)

Εὔφημος, ὁ   190, 204

Ζεύς, ὁ   123, 178,
    188
ζήτησις, ἡ   107
ζήτημα, τό   52
ζητητής, ὁ   192
ζῶ   102, 119,
    120, 190, 204
ζῷον, τό   51, 61,
    105, 121, 144, 164, 182,
    187, 188

ἡδονή, ἡ   63, 105,
    126, 179
ἡμέρα, ἡ   28, 73
ἥμερος, -ον   105
Ἥρ (ἦρ=ἔαρ)   160, 190
Ἥρα, ἡ   178
Ἡράκλειτος, ὁ   124, 182
ἠρέμα   104, 215
ἡσυχία, ἡ   147

θαυμάσιος, -α, -ον   111, 132
θαυμαστός, -ή, -όν   52, 131
θεῖος, -α, -ον   27, 70,
    105, 109, 111, 112, 113,
    117, 118, 119, 125, 127,
    215
θεογονία, ἡ   151, 184
θεολογία, ἡ   151, 183,
    184
θεός, ὁ   109, 118,
    122, 123, 124, 126, 127,
    128, 132, 133, 134, 174,
    177, 178, 191
Θερσίτης, ὁ   194
Θηβαῖος, -α, -ον   112
θηρίον, τό   187, 188
θνήσκω   53, 158,
    190, 204
θυμός, ὁ   169, 170,
    187

ἰδέα, ἡ   104, 113,
    129, 130, 136, 155, 179
ἴδιος, -α, -ον   136
ἰδιώτης, ὁ   61
ἰδιωτικός, -η, -ον   61
Ἱμεραῖος, ὁ   73
ἵμερος, ὁ   73
Ἱπποκένταυρος, ὁ   27
ἰσόθεος, -ον   61
ἴσος, -η, -ον   50, 191,
    203, 204, 216
Ἰταλία, ἡ   175
Ἰταλικός, -ή, -όν   204

κακός, -ή, -όν   87, 101,
    112, 117, 129, 130, 193,
    203, 215
Καλλικλῆς, ὁ   202, 204
κάλλος, τό   120
καλός, -ή, -όν   17, 19,
    23, 101, 102, 103, 106,
    109, 111, 115, 117, 120,
    124, 135, 136, 154, 180,
    188, 205, 216
κατάψυξις, ἡ   32
καυστός, -ή, -όν   49
Κέβης, ὁ   216
κέντρον, τό   50
κινέω   74, 122
κίνησις, ἡ   147, 206
κλῆρος, ὁ   193
Κλωθώ, ἡ   191, 192
κνῆσις, ἡ   127
κόσμος, ὁ   61, 103,
    119, 121, 143, 146
Κρατύλος, ὁ   51
Κρόνος, ὁ   178
κύκλος, ὁ   50

Λάχεσις, ἡ   191
λέγω   17, 18,
    23, 26, 52, 70, 90, 100,
    101, 104, 108, 109, 110,

255

256

INDEX LOCORUM ANTIQUORUM

(Note: an unprefixed page number signifies a mere citation of the work or part of it; when a passage has been given in the text, the prefixes are E for English and G for Greek; projected but unwritten works are in brackets.)

Plato

Alcibiades I	108, 196, 225
Apology of Socrates	26, 49, 52, 64, 65, 95, 101–102, 105, 106, 115, 180, 206, 221, 228 (23c4–5) E63, G105; (30e4–5) E65, G106; (33c4) E63, G105; (34d4–5) E95, G137
Axiochus (fr. *Spuria*)	228
Charmides	7, 108, 134 (155d3–4) EG108
Cratylus	51–52, 75, 76–77, 81–82, 96, 107, 110–111, 115, 117, 118, 119, 120, 123, 125, 139, 147, 158, 182, 191, 203, 255 (396b7–c3) E110–111, G111; (399c1–6) EG111; (399d10–e3) E76, G119; (400a5–b7) E76–77, G119–120; (401b1–e1) E81–82, G123–124; (402a8–10) E147, G182; (403b5–6) G203; (403e4) E203; (406a3–5) EG107; (408d2–3) E96, G139; (420b7–9) E75, G119; (421a7–b1) E51–52, G52; (438e2–3) EG51
Critias	18, 97, 115, 146, 147, 149, 172, 173, 175, 181, 214, 227, 228, 229 (110a3–6) EG181

Phaedo

13, 17, 18, 26, 47, 49, 52, 53, 63,
67, 69, 70, 89, 105, 109, 112, 113,
114, 115, 132, 133, 170, 188, 195,
196, 199, 200, 202, 205, 206, 210,
212, 214, 216, 224, 225, 226, 227,
228, 236
(60b1-c7) E89, G132; (60d1) G132;
(61a3-4) G109; (61b6) G132;
(62a8) E236; (64d2-7) E63, G105;
(85c7-d4) E70, G112; (89a9-c4) E212-
213, G216; (99c9-d1) G70;
(107b4-10) E199, G205;
(110a8-b4) E199-200, G205;
(110b6) E200, G205

Phaedrus

13, 17, 24, 27, 38, 49, 50, 51, 53,
55, 56, 57, 58, 59, 60, 61, 62, 63,
64, 65, 66, 67, 69, 71, 72, 74, 75,
76, 77, 78, 80, 81, 83, 84, 85, 86,
87, 88, 90, 91, 92, 93, 95, 96, 97,
98, 99, 100, 101, 102, 103, 104, 105,
106, 107, 108, 109, 110, 111, 113,
114, 116, 117, 118, 119, 120, 121,
122, 123, 124, 125, 126, 127, 129,
130, 133, 134, 135, 136, 137, 138,
139, 158, 163, 164, 182, 183, 224,
226, 227, 228
(227c7-d2) E58, G100; (228c1-2) G108;
(229d5-e4) E24, G27; (229d7) E64,
G105; (229e1-2) E64, G105;
(229e5-6) G64; (230a5-6) E64, G105;
(230c2-3) G107; (237a7) G107;
(242a7-b4) E111, G111-112;
(243a2-7) EG116; (243b2-3) E72, G114;
(244a1) G116; (244a5-6) EG117;
(245c5) E76, G119; (245d2-3) G120;
(245d8-e1) G121; (245e2-3) E78;
(245e6-246a2) E81, G122;
(246a4-6) E71, G113; (247a1-2) G123;
(247a6-7) EG124; (247a8-b1) EG81;
(247c3) EG81; (247c3-6) E71, G113;
(247c7) E69, G110; (249b5-c4) E84,
G126; (249c6-d3) EG125; (250e4-
251a1) EG126; (255c1) EG120;
(255c2-7) EG120; (258b10-c5) E60,

G102; (258d1-5) E59, G101;
(258d7) E61, G103; (259a3) G106;
(259c2) G65; (259c4-5) G64;
(259c6) E66, G107; (259c7) G107;
(259d1-2) G107; (259d2-3) E66, G107;
(259d4) G107; (259d4-5) G107 & G109;
(259d7) G109; (259e5) G106;
(261a8) G136; (261a8-9) EG136;
(264b7) E38, G51; (264c2-5) E38,G51;
(265a9-b5) E85, G127;
(265c8-d1) EG127; (265d3-7) E85-86,
G129; (265e1-266b1) E86-87, G130;
(266b3-c1) E90, G133;
(266b7-c1) G106; (270c1-2) EG124;
(270c10-d1) G106; (270e2-5) EG134;
(271a4-b5) E92-93, G136;
(271a6) EG135; (272b5-6) E93, G137;
(273d4) G136; (273d5-6) E92, G136;
(273d8-e4) E92, G136; (274a1-2) E93,
G137; (274b6-7) EG135; (275b3-4) E55,
G97; (275e3) E95, G138;
(276a5-6) E95, G138; (276e1-3) EG183;
(278a8-b2) EG101

Philebus   18, 51, 61, 90-91, 94, 102, 122, 124,
131, 132, 133, 135, 137, 224
(14d8-e4) E91, G133; (15d4-8) E90-91,
G133; (18c7-d2) E94, G137;
(64b6-8) E61, G103

/Philosopher/   115
Protagoras   14, 28, 138, 198, 199, 200, 204, 205,
214, 224, 225, 228
(320c2-4) EG205; (328c3-4) E199,G205;
(329a3-4) EG137; (347e1-348a6) EG138

Republic   6, 13, 17, 18, 21, 22, 23, 26, 49,
50, 52, 53, 62, 63, 69, 70, 71, 90,
93, 101, 103, 104, 105, 106, 109,
110, 111, 112, 115, 117, 121, 122,
123, 124, 125, 127, 129, 136, 137,
141, 142, 143, 144, 146, 147, 149,
150, 151, 152, 153, 154, 155, 156,
157, 159, 160-161, 162, 163, 164,
165, 166, 167, 168, 169, 170, 171,
172, 173, 174, 175, 176, 181, 182,
183, 184, 185, 186, 188, 189, 190,
191, 192, 193, 194, 195, 202, 203,

208, 210, 211-212, 214, 215, 219,
224, 225, 226, 227, 228, 229
(1.336b5) E155, G188;
(2.358c6) G184; (369d11) EG117;
(372d4) EG117; (376d9-10) EG183;
(382b9-c1) EG184;
(3.392d2-3) E163, G192; (393a3) E21,
G26; (393a6-b2) E21-22, G26;
(393c1-4) E22, G26; (393c11-d2) E23,
G26; (394b3-6) E23, G26;
(411d7-e1) E155, G188;
(5.476d8-e7) E211, G215;
(6.450d3-4) G215; (450d10) G215;
(500d4-9) EG215; (500d10-e5) EG215;
(501e4) EG183; (506d8-507a4) E70-71,
G112; (508d4-6) EG123;
(509b6-10) EG121; (509d1-4) EG110;
(511b7) E150, G184;
(7.516c1) G110; (517b5) G110;
(532d6-e3) E103-104, G104;
(533c7-d4) E62, G104-105;
(8.548b8-c1) E69, G109;
(565d4-e1) E156, G188;
(566a2-5) E156, G188; (568d4-6) E156,
G188; (569a8-b1) E156, G188;
(10.596d1) E203; (607b5-6) G186;
(614a1) E157; (614a7-8) G189;
(614b2-4) E158-159, G190; (614c1)G190;
(614c3-d1) E160-161, G190;
(616b1) EG189; (616c7-d2) E163, G191;
(617b7-c5) E163, G191-192;
(618b6-c6) E165, G192; (618e3-4)G190;
(619b7-8) E166, G192; (619c6-d1)E166,
G192-193; (619d5-7) E167, G193;
(619d7-e5) E168, G193; (620a2-3)E169,
G193; (620c2-3) E170, G193-194;
621c4-d2) EG191

Rival-lovers	108
Sophist	18, 19, 50, 53, 90, 97, 115, 129, 175, 214, 225, 228
	(216a1) G115
Spuria	223, 225, 228
Statesman	14, 51, 53, 88, 89, 90, 97, 115, 118, 129, 131, 132, 207, 214, 224, 225,

Others

INDEX NOMINUM

269

INDEX RERUM

(Note: this is as much a key word index as a
subject index, and it is meant to serve as both.)

273

277

281

212, 232

logic 8, 173

logography 38, 61, 163

logos 1, 4, 13, 15, 17, 98, 184

longing 73, 113

look 24, 35, 37, 50, 64, 66, 74, 84, 85, 86, 87, 92, 103, 104, 127, 145, 149, 155, 210, 211

look-alike 35, 36, 37, 38, 40, 41, 43, 84, 184, 206, 232, 234

loop 81, 113

lot 151, 157, 159, 164, 166, 167, 168

love 46, 67, 74, 98, 114, 117, 126, 127, 154, 168, 169, 171, 210

love of honor 46, 168, 169, 171

lover 58, 68, 73, 84, 90, 120, 126, 127, 174

low 45, 56, 57, 73, 75, 125

luck 75, 127, 133, 167, 206

madness 99, 118

male 88

man 8-9, 28, 46, 49, 59, 63, 68, 73, 89, 97, 102, 125, 134, 138, 142, 148, 151, 155, 158, 159, 160, 168, 169, 171, 176, 183, 185, 188, 196, 197, 202, 218, 234, 235

manifold 62, 86, 87, 139, 153

manner 45, 56, 61, 86, 103, 111, 114, 115, 157, 186, 191, 221

many 6-7, 33, 34, 41, 42, 45, 58, 83, 84, 89, 90, 91, 94, 125, 134, 138, 149, 156, 158, 161, 163, 167, 169, 186, 211, 215, 231, 232, 234, 235

marriage 14, 207, 208

masks 27

mastery 93, 101, 234

mathematics 28, 36, 143

maturity 49

mean 41, 48, 108, 128, 235, 237

memory 42, 46, 62, 83, 88, 94, 113, 131, 168, 235

metamorphosis 64, 65, 105, 154, 170

metaphysics 8

method 7, 8, 19, 22, 24, 35, 53, 62, 65, 66, 85, 86, 87, 88, 90, 91, 118, 134, 179, 220

midair 81, 111

middle 36, 38, 50, 187, 232

mimetic 45

mind 5-6, 9, 34, 45, 125, 133, 149, 197, 198, 217, 218

misanthropy 168, 170

misogyny 170

misology 155

mob 24, 202

model 24, 143, 158

moderation 73, 74,

284

noetic 94
noises 62
non-lover 58, 73, 74, 100
nourishing 72
nuptial number 143
nurture 31, 40, 65, 156, 231, 234

oak 95
object 32, 38, 69
old 58, 90, 124, 205
oligarchy 100
onomatogenetic 77, 111
onomatology 83, 110, 158
ontogenetic 25
operative 84, 126
opinion 1, 36, 41, 43, 45, 75, 119, 142, 207, 211, 212, 221, 231, 236
oracle 189
oratory 60
order 19, 77, 85, 93, 99, 119, 149, 151, 166, 197, 198
origins 7, 15, 25, 28, 55, 64, 116, 149, 150, 181, 189, 197, 203, 207, 208, 219, 222
oscillation 200
ourania 111
ousiology 80, 82
outline 29, 157, 166, 183, 233
overturn 40, 41
oyster 125

paean 58
pain 13, 32, 89, 90, 199, 207, 231

painting 95, 215, 232
palinode 56, 57, 64, 69, 71, 72, 75, 80, 85, 88, 92, 99, 103, 107, 113, 116, 117, 126, 127, 137, 158, 182
pan-mimic 203
pantheon 93, 178
paper 95
paradigm 15, 26, 34, 35, 36, 45, 89, 155–156, 215
paramyth 17, 201, 209, 210, 211, 212, 213, 214
paronomasia 160
partaking 46, 47, 63, 64, 82, 166, 233, 236
participle 158
partitive 80, 152, 153
past 30, 61, 164
patchwork 16
pathos 14
patricide 162
pay 71, 158
peace 147
peak 75
pedagogy 86
people 25
perfect xi, 23, 65, 89, 91, 92, 93, 95, 125, 132, 134, 135, 142, 149, 151, 155, 164, 183, 185, 203, 209
periodic 14
perishing 15, 156, 232
perpetuation 65, 206
perplexity 36, 39, 43, 44, 162, 165, 234, 235

291